CW00553940

The Résumé of the All-Loving and Eternal God

I am the Good Shepherd, and the Good Shepherd gives up His life for his sheep. John 10:11

Sarah More

COPYRIGHT

Copyright © 2013 Sarah More

Do not reproduce the work in part or whole, use it to make another work, perform it, distribute or transmit it in part or whole in any form or by any means, electronic, mechanical, photocopying, recording, or otherwise, without prior written permission of the writer. All rights reserved.

ISBN-13:978-1484103968
ISBN-10:1484103963

The Messiah's résumé to be able to save you

DEDICATION

I am dedicating this book to my beloved daughter,
Eunice Malath.

CONTENTS

ACKNOWLEDGMENTS

I thank God, my daughter, Eunice Malath, parents, brothers, sisters, cousins, uncles, aunts, relatives, and friends for their patience. They allowed me to study the Bible as much as I wanted.

The following translations were used: Amplified Bible (AMP), 1899 Douay-Rheims Bible (DRB), English Standard Version (ESV), Good News Bible (GNB), Good Word (GW), International Standard Version (ISV), American Standard Version (ASV), 1965 Bible in Basic English, Contemporary English Version (CEV). Where it was not indicated, that means that is King James Version (KJV).

The Messiah's résumé to be able to save you

The Messiah's résumé to be able to save you

1 CHAPTER

BEFORE ABRAHAM WAS, I AM

1. Before Abraham was, I am

The Almighty God spoke to the Jews with power and authority because He was God in human flesh. He was the One created the first man called Adam. And then He created Eve. He placed them in a perfect home called the Garden of Eden, which was located in a perfect earth.

God who became Jesus the Messiah created Adam and Eve and placed in the Garden of Eden, Wenzel Peter, 1745-1829

Divinity was covered with human flesh when He was born as a Baby into this earth. But He was still the Eternal, All-Powerful, All-Benevolent, and All-Knowing One.

That was why He had the absolute right to tell that He was God in human flesh. "Jesus said unto them, Verily, verily, I say unto you, Before Abraham was, I am" (John 8:58).

He said, "I speaking to all of you with the power

and authority of God. He is the Truth and the Love. I repeat, God is the Truth and the Love. Before God the Father welcomed Abraham into His arms when he was born, I AM."

He declared right to the faces of the unbelieving Jews that He was God incarnated in human flesh. He had told Moses tell the Israelites that He was the Everlasting One. "And God said unto Moses, I AM THAT I AM: and he said, Thus shalt thou say unto the children of Israel, I AM hath sent me unto you" (Exodus 3:14).

He told Moses that He is the Ever-Living One who marching on glorious from the everlasting to the everlasting. But the first person He informed that He is the Omnipresent, (Infinities or Everlasting essence), was Hagar. He is Omnipresent. It also includes that He is Omniscient or All-Knowing, and All-Benevolent character.

She was a young black woman. She and Abraham gave birth to Ishmael. Their son was the ancestor of the Arab race. She called the Lord, "El Roi," meaning, "the God who sees me."

Charles Lock Eastlake, 1830, Hagar and Ishmael

"And she called the name of the LORD that spake unto her, Thou God seest me: for she said, Have I also here looked after him that seeth me? Wherefore the well was called Beerlahairoi; behold, it is between Kadesh and Bered" (Genesis 16:13, 14).

He saw you from time immemorial. He knew that you will fall into sin and will need His help. So He came down and died for your sins on Mount Calvary before you were born. He loves that much.

He is excellent in molding and recreating the containers that have been infected with sin. At this moment, He is filling them with the Sabbath of rest and the Law of righteousness.

He will make them very attractive and desirable like a bride who is desired by a man to become his wife. "His glory is great in thy salvation: honour and majesty hast thou laid upon him" (Psalms 21:5). You will the honorable son or daughter of the King of kings.

In heaven, you are not going to be under the feet of monsters like sin and death any more. You are no longer an unhappy and suffering slave. The Messiah will crown you as a monarch.

He will present you to the angels and all the inhabitants of all the universes as the king or queen and His official representative to them. "For thou hast made him but little lower than God, And crownest him with glory and honor" (Psalms 8:5, ASV).

He will ask them to honor and respect you. He will ask them to obey whatever you tell them.

He has chosen you as His beautiful and eternal bride though at this moment you are still a slave of sin. But now He is making you His slave.

In fact, He is blessing you, His slave, by marrying you. You are no longer the slave of sin and the devil. But since you are His bride, you are His equal.

You are a sharer in His love, joy, and all other blessings. He will make you very happy and joyful. Your face will explode with happiness.

Everything that is before will be wonderful to give you exquisite joy. "For thou hast made him most blessed for ever: thou hast made him exceeding glad with thy countenance" (Psalms 21:6).

He will bless you abundantly. Whatever He blesses is eternally blessed.

God your heavenly Daddy says, "I have never said to you that I cannot give birth. Actually, I am the very

Father who gave you birth. Give me the chance to save you. Leave all your sins at my altar. Surrender your struggles to Me.

I have never forgotten you. "Remember these, O Jacob and Israel; for thou art my servant: I have formed thee; thou art my servant: O Israel, thou shalt not be forgotten of me. I have blotted out, as a thick cloud, thy transgressions, and, as a cloud, thy sins: return unto me; for I have redeemed thee" (Isaiah 44:21, 22).

I have forgotten about your sins long before you were even born. I forgot all about them in the Garden of Eden when your first parents sinned against Me. That is why I have kept the human race alive. If I had not forgiven you, this earth would have become a dead planet long ago.

I own heaven and all the universes. The sun, moon, stars and planets are mine. This earth is mine. You are a part of my family. You are my beloved child. I will take you out of this fire. I am on my way to get you. Do not leave my church.

You have heaven, and it is all yours. It is a land of surpassing beauty incomparable to this sick world. The trumpets will sound louder than the thunders of a terrible storm.

The earth will convulsed like a volcano being formed in the middle of the ocean. That is my style of announcing to you that Dad has come in visible form to get you.

I will recreate you again like I did for Adam and Eve. I will change the living ones into pure, holy, and powerful angels.

The stubborn sinners who hate Me can remain behind. It is their own choice if they want to side with that thief and murderer called Satan. But I will not leave you behind.

You will shout a happy, "Amen!"

You will have a dance. It will be a dance of pure joy and exceeding happiness to, finally, be with Me.

There will be no more war in your heart or around you.

Day and night, the flaming arrows of the evil one called hate, pride, selfishness, diseases, death, etc. are being shot straight into My children day and night. "Above all, taking the shield of faith, wherewith ye shall be able to quench all the fiery darts of the wicked" (Ephesians 6:16).

You are all alone like a pelican of the wilderness. You are like an owl living alone in a lonely desert. You are like a sparrow without a company and sitting all alone on the house top.

I am like a pelican of the wilderness: I am like an owl of the desert. I watch, and am as a sparrow alone upon the house top" (Psalms 102:6, 7).

Collared Sparrow Hawk, wpclipart, in public domain

I am telling you, 'It is hell on this earth.' There is fire of sin burning in your flesh, fire in your mind, fire in your heart, fire all around. Fire! Fire! Sin has ignited the world. She is on fire. Sin is trying to alienate you from Me.

This war that is going on in your flesh between holiness and sin is My war! I will also deal with the wars going between individual persons and between nations or kingdoms. The curse of sin has fallen on Me light before I first shone on the world and made every other thing.

I was hanged on the Cross of Calvary through my Son, Jesus Christ, for all the sins of the world. "And if a man have committed a sin worthy of death, and he be to be put to death, and thou hang him on a tree:

His body shall not remain all night upon the tree, but thou shalt in any wise bury him that day; (for he that is hanged is accursed of God;) that thy land be not defiled, which the LORD thy God giveth thee for an inheritance" (Deuteronomy 21:22, 23).

I fought your sins on the Cross, my beloved. I am continuing to fight for your liberation every day. I have never claimed that I did not father you. I have never denied you from the day when your first parents sinned against Me.

I am watching over you. I am caring for you very tenderly and lovingly with all of my heart and with all of my strength. I will fight for my lovely child until you are safely home with Me.

Every day, you deny Me to my face by the sinful way you are living. However, I have proved to you through my Son that I love you very much. It was I who asked Him to suffer and die for you.

Yet the world hates Me. "They rewarded me evil for good to the spoiling of my soul. But as for me, when they were sick, my clothing was sackcloth: I humbled my soul with fasting; and my prayer returned into mine own bosom.

I behaved myself as though he had been my friend or brother: I bowed down heavily, as one that mourneth for his mother" (Psalms 35:12–14).

I am bereaving for you because my baby is spiritually dead. I am such a lonely Father. My baby is not at home yet. All that you are doing is sinning. Oh! How you break my heart!

You are spiritually sick. All heaven is doing nothing else but work for you as if they are in mourning. Jesus died for you. The Holy Spirit has left the glories of heaven and is living in your heart.

Unfortunately, many times you don't care for your Most Holy and Righteous Father but force Him to watch you being led into sin and, actually, enjoying them.

You really humiliate your own Father in front of the devils. You choose Satan over Him daily. It makes Me blush with shame for you, my beautiful baby.

Jesus is so sad He does not eat food or drink water

or juices because He misses you. He still has your human flesh, and it needs food and water to sustain it.

He will only eat or drink if you are with Him in heaven just as He has promised you on the night of the Last Supper. "But I say unto you, I will not drink henceforth of this fruit of the vine, until that day when I drink it new with you in my Father's kingdom" (Matthew 26:29).

Please do not make the human flesh of your Brother to continue to starve for want of food and water. It is terribly unkind and cruel of you to do that.

If you want to help Him eat some food soon, then leave you life of sin. During the Great Supper is your wedding party. You will be united with Lord Forever like husband and wife who are getting married for life.

That is why I call it "the marriage of the Lamb has come, and His wife."

"Let us be glad and rejoice, and give honour to him: for the marriage of the Lamb is come, and his wife hath made herself read" (Revelation 19:7).

You are His beloved and desirable bride. You are His church. When He has satisfied you with food and drinks, then He will also eat if you beg Him to.

In order to prepare you for your wedding day and the happy everlasting life with your Husband after that, He and I are praying for you. We are holding a court for your vindication.

"I beheld till the thrones were cast down, and the Ancient of days did sit, whose garment was white as snow, and the hair of his head like the pure wool: his throne was like the fiery flame, and his wheels as burning fire.

A fiery stream issued and came forth from before him: thousand thousands ministered unto him, and ten thousand times ten thousand stood before him: the judgment was set, and the books were opened" (Daniel 7:9, 10).

I am sitting firmly on my everlasting throne of power and great majesties. Nothing will go wrong with my plan to save you as long as you are in agreement with Me. Satan or death has no power over you. So hold onto Me more tightly every day.

My Son, who has personally experienced all your troubles first hand, knows exactly what to do to help you. He is adamant that you deserve unconditional love, eternal life, peace, joy, etc. And I completely agree with Him and so does the Holy Spirit who is living in your heart.

We are protecting you from slipping into hell and getting burnt up for good. So please, I am kindly asking you to listen to the voice of the Holy Spirit.

He is your Dad. He will burn away your sins with His holy fire. He will purify your soul with His fire until you will glow and glitter with holiness like Him.

I love you so much that I am blessing you with all the things that I own. I gave you my Son. He died for you. He rose from the dead as the first fruit of what I am about to do for you. You died spiritually because of Adam's sin. Soon, you will pass away like Him. But through Christ, I will restore your eternal spirit.

You will come out of the dead man or woman alive or dead in the land of the dead alive. "For as in Adam all die, even so in Christ shall all be made alive. But every man in his own order: Christ the firstfruits; afterward they that are Christ's at his coming.

Then cometh the end, when he shall have delivered up the kingdom to God, even the Father; when he shall have put down all rule and all authority and power" (1 Corinthians 15:22–24).

I am your Everlasting Father. Since I am the God of love and peace, you will enjoy them forever and ever all your eternal life.

My Son rose from the dead. He has given you the right to also resurrect from this earth and be promoted into glory of glories where He lives. That home is far more beautiful, richer and brighter than all the other sinless worlds.

It is the seat of power for all the endless universes.

You will get it because you are a parent.

You gave flesh to the Second Godhead. You made the Almighty and Everlasting God a Man with human flesh. So I have given you the right to go and where your Son and my Son is. He is very serious about it.

He wants you to be with Him just as He has promised in John 14:1–3: "Let not your heart be troubled: ye believe in God, believe also in me. In my Father's house are many mansions: if it were not so, I would have told you.

I go to prepare a place for you. And if I go and prepare a place for you, I will come again, and receive you unto myself; that where I am, there ye may be also" My house is your house. My kingdom is your kingdom.

You will be with Me because I am your Father, and we are both the Parents of Jesus Christ. From now onward, I am showering you with double blessings since you are my son or daughter as well as the parent of the Second Godhead.

Live nobly and righteously as befits a father or mother of the Lord Jesus Christ. And in the way you conduct yourself, the earth will be blessed. They will see Christ, the Holy Spirit and I living in you, and some of the people of the world will be converted.

They will come to Me because of you. "And I will bless them that bless thee, and curse him that curseth thee: and in thee shall all families of the earth be blessed" (And I will bless you and make your name great" in heaven and all the universes" (Genesis 12:3).

Every day, live a righteous live by making sure that Jesus is living in your soul. His love and purity of character will shine through. People will take note of it.

You will be a guiding star that will lead people to Christ or a portent witness to the unbelievers that Christ is living among them, and yet they hate Him. "Do ye not know that the saints shall judge the world? and if the world shall be judged by you, are ye unworthy to judge the smallest matters?" (1 Corinthians 6:2). Your holy life will condemn their unrighteousness and, thereby, you will send them to hell.

I told the Messiah to go down there and get you. But then I will miss My children who are Moslems, Hindus, Buddhists, New Age adherents, animists, Satanists, witches, lukewarm Christians, atheists, agnostics, unbelieving Jews, etc.

I am the one who gave them birth. I am sure you also miss them in the church. Church is love.

If they had understood it, a lot of the fighting, struggles, diseases, poverty, unnecessary deaths, etc. in the world would not have happened. I got eternal life for them. Therefore, I do not want them to go the other way.

I don't want to miss them. I want to spend next eternities of all eternities together with my children. I won't enjoy living very much without all those who have believed in Me not living around Me. I will save all those who come to Me because I am the Omnipotent One."

2. The Lord will come like a terrible storm to rescue you

When God sets foot on the earth, she heaves in pain up and down, up and down, like a baby wants to break out of his or her mother's womb. But he or she is causing his or her mother intense pain. "He stood and measured the earth. He beheld, and melted the nations: and the ancient mountains were crushed to pieces. The hills of the world were bowed down by the journeys of His eternity.

The mountains saw thee, and were grieved: the great body of waters passed away. The deep put forth its voice: the deep lifted up its hands. The sun and the moon stood still in their habitation, in the light of thy arrows, they shall go in the brightness of thy glittering spear" (Habakkuk 3:6, 10, 11, DRB).

He stood over the earth as the one and only Almighty God, King, Lord, and Daddy. He surpasses all. Nature is afraid of Him. Mountains rise out of the stomach of the earth burning with molten magna. Their smokes rise into the sky.

The same things occur when volcanoes are being formed. They rise out of womb of the earth like children being born. Their smokes blanket the skies.

The Creator will crush mountains and hill. He will blow them away with His breath. He will make all the universes collapse. He will blow them away with His fiery breaths.

They cannot exist forever. They are inferior. They are nothing. The Creator alone is eternal. He is the God of unconditional and eternal love.

He looked at her nations, empires, and kingdoms. They were afraid of her. They began to shake and tremble with fear. No one man or woman has power to stand before His throne without His permission.

Deep valleys sink even deeper on their knees in terror of the Lord. "Lord, bow down thy heavens and descend: touch the mountains and they shall smoke" (Psalms 144:5, DRB).

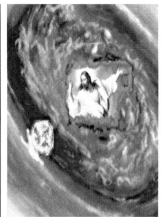

God comes in a storm to save you. (Background: NASA image).

He said, "I heard your prayers even before you were born. I came down to Bethlehem as a Baby through my Son. I fought sin, death and death on the Cross. I razed the mountains of the terror of death and powerful of demons to the ground.

I rescued you from eternal damnation in hell. "In my affliction I called upon the Lord, and I cried to my God: And he heard my voice from his holy temple: and my cry before him came into his ears.

The earth shook and trembled: the foundations of the mountains were troubled and were moved, because he was angry with them. There went up a smoke in his wrath: and a fire flamed from his face: coals were kindled by it" (Psalms 18:6–8, DRB).

The world of darkness is afraid of Me and of my power. I will tear you away from them like a shepherd rescuing a lamb from the mouth of lion. I will bring you to my kingdom of peace and everlasting safety.

When I am angry because my children are hurting and dying, I breathe deep and heavy with anger. The breath coming out of my nostrils bellows like the huge wild fires.

Large burning charcoals shoot like flying stars from my nose. "Behold the name of the Lord cometh from afar, his wrath burneth, and is heavy to bear: his lips are filled with indignation, and his tongue as a devouring fire" (Isaiah 30:27).

My name is YAHWE - I AM WHO I AM. As I have been from eternity past so shall I always be in all the eternities of eternities to come.

I share my Divinity with no one. No one can exist from eternity to eternity by the volition of his own inherent life except Me alone.

My everlasting word burns like fire. My word created things and my word will acquit the humble and repent sinners and condemn wicked sinners to hell.

When you repent and/or give Me praise, it makes my heart dance with joy. I breathe well. Dad really gets very peaceful and contented because you are being saved. And heaven is filled with smoke, which is the breath of my happiness when you are worshipping and praising Me.

I was happy with Moses and with all Israel when they chose Me as their God and Dad above every other gods and above themselves.

My cloud covered the tabernacle so thick that Moses could not enter in. "Then a cloud covered the tent of the congregation, and the glory of the LORD filled the tabernacle. And Moses was not able to enter into the tent of the congregation, because the cloud abode thereon, and the glory of the LORD filled the tabernacle" (Exodus 40:34, 35).

My excitement cause the same thing to happen with Israel built a temple for Me and dedicated it in my honor. "And it came to pass, when the priests were come out of the holy place, that the cloud filled the house of the LORD,

So that the priests could not stand to minister because of the cloud: for the glory of the LORD had filled the house of the LORD. Then spake Solomon, The LORD said that he would dwell in the thick darkness" (1 Kings 8:10–12).

Heaven and universes bow at my feet in humility

and reverence. They are simply too small to contain my infinite, everlasting and burning Being. They are blinded by my shining Being. So I cover myself with thick dark clouds.

I reduce the light my shining glorious Presence to help them to sense my Presence. "He bent the sky and descended, and darkness was under his feet. He rode upon a cherub and flew; he soared upon the wings of the wind.

He made darkness his hiding place, his canopy surrounding him was dark waters and thick clouds. The brightness before him scattered the thick clouds, with hail stones and flashes of fire.

Then the LORD thundered in the heavens, and the Most High sounded aloud, calling for hail stones and flashes of fire.

He shot his arrows and scattered them; with many lightning bolts he frightened them. Then the channels of the sea could be seen, and the foundations of the earth were uncovered because of your rebuke, LORD, because of the blast from the breath of your nostrils.

He reached down and took me; he drew me from many waters. He delivered me from my strong enemies, from those who hated me because they were stronger than I" (Psalms 18:9–17, ISV).

He said, "I will descend from my high throne that stands like a mountain towering over heaven and all the universes. My brilliant glory that shines brighter than many suns will be visible to all. For my infinite Presence will cover the whole sky.

There will be no sun, moon, stars, or darkness. My Majestic and Sovereign Presence will shine from east to the west and from pole to pole. The shining splendors of my will blind demons but give you the light of my eternal life. You will jump and dance with joy when you see Me.

I will descend on your enemies with the fury of a hailstorm that knows every green thing down. "And the Lord shall make the glory of his voice to be heard, and shall shew the terror of his arm, in the threatening of wrath, and the flame of devouring fire: he shall crush to pieces with whirlwind, and hailstones" (Isaiah 30:30, DRB).

I will strike them with lightning and hail stones of brimstones and sulfurs. I will sweep them with the force of a storm wind into hell.

They will burn up and never breathe again. "The Lord is a jealous God, and a revenger: the Lord is a revenger, and hath wrath: the Lord taketh vengeance on his adversaries, and he is angry with his enemies.

The Lord is patient, and great in power, and will not cleanse and acquit the guilty. The Lord's ways are in a tempest, and a whirlwind, and clouds are the dust of his feet" (Nahum 1:2, 3, DRB).

I am jealous because Satan stole you away from Me. I am jealous because you do not love and worshipping Me as you should have you been holy and perfect. And I shall punish all the culprits who came between Me and you.

All heaven and all the universes will give Me greater honor, respect and reverence more than they have ever done before on the day I reclaim your heart completely for myself and blew away all that causes sin and death from my world. But with you, I am not angry.

You are deceived. And I want to save you out of your self-imposed delusion that you are some kind of a god. I will save you from the delusion of acquisition.

You are brainwashed by companies, cruel political parties and mad ideas that the more you have the things of this world such as- gold, silver, money, fame, power, fame, etc. the happier you will be.

It has become a god. I promise to rescue you from the brutal propaganda that creates senseless Utopia in you.

And then you will celebrate with joy and happiness. For all those things that made you miserable and sad one are gone. "Ye shall have a song, as in the night when a holy solemnity is kept; and gladness of heart, as when one goeth with a pipe to come into the mountain of the LORD, to the mighty One of Israel" (Isaiah 30:29).

You will party because Satan is dead. It will be a holy party of singing praises, eating bread and water that gives eternal life and holding onto Me for reassurance of my Presence like a child holding to his or her parent.

As my son or daughter, I want to make you into severe storm to lash and break demons and sins. I sent demons scattering out of heaven.

I will give you the power to do the same. When you pray, I will send a storm that will chase them away like chaff being blow by the wind.

Thus, you will have power of them. You will be like fire when you ask Me for help. I will light up with holiness. That holiness will drive the presence of demons away like stubble that almost got devoured by fire. I will make you into snowstorm that will blind and confuse Satan.

He will drip and tremble with the cold of his sins. He will be afraid to come near you. I will make you into desert sandstorm that will blind demons and sins and disorient them. You will drive them away from before you like wind uprooting, breaking and driving away things before it.

I will make you into a lightning strike that will strike demons with terror. You will roar at them with the voice of thunder when you are praying. They will tremble and cringe with fear.

They will turn and run away from Me. Just continue to pray to save you from the power of Satan and sin: "O my God, make them like a wheel; and as stubble before the wind. As fire which burneth the wood: and as a flame burning mountains: So shalt thou pursue them with thy tempest: and shalt trouble them in thy wrath.

Fill their faces with shame; and they shall seek thy

name, O Lord. Let them be ashamed and troubled for ever and ever: and let them be confounded and perish" (Psalms 83:13–17, DRB).

My wild fire of heaven will soon consume Satan, sin, temptations and trials. They will not exist again. You are not yet thrown into hell because my power has made you unconquerable. You will shock hell and the devil. They will submit to you."

2 CHAPTER

I AND MY FATHER ARE ONE

1. *I and my Father are one*

Judas Maccabee and his brothers fought the Seleucid King Antiochus IV Epiphanes and his forces from the temple. They threw out the idols of Zeus and other gods from the temple. They stopped the sacrifice of pigs on the Lord's altar. They purified and dedicated to the worship of the God of heaven.

They commemorated the day by the Feast of Dedication or Hanukkah. It is also called the Festival of Lights. "Early in the morning on the twenty-fifth day of the ninth month, that is, the month of Chislev, in the year one hundred and forty-eight, they arose and offered sacrifice according to the law on the new altar of holocausts that they had made.

On the anniversary of the day on which the Gentiles had defiled it, on that very day it was consecrated again with songs, harps, flutes, and cymbals. All the people prostrated themselves and adored and praised Heaven, who had given them success. For eight days they celebrated the dedication of the altar and joyfully offered holocausts and sacrifices of deliverance and praise" (1 Maccabees 4:52–56, New American Bible).

In the Jewish calendar, Cislev is the ninth month of the year. In the civil calendar it falls between November and December. These are the months of very cold winters. "And it was at Jerusalem the feast of the dedication, and it was winter. And Jesus walked in the temple in Solomon's porch" (John 10:22, 23).

He was walking, meditating, and praying when

suddenly His communication with the Holy Spirit was cut short by the hateful voices of demons speaking through the mouths of unconverted Jews. They wanted to fight Him. They wanted to show Him that they were strong and can have Him arrested or murdered.

They had tried to corner Him but He was too wise for them. He never made any political statements implicate Him with Imperial Rome or the High Priests. They would be glad to lay their hands on Him and cut His work short.

So they resorted to asking Him directly to answer to them if He was God so that they could stone Him to death. "Then came the Jews round about him, and said unto him, How long dost thou make us to doubt? If thou be the Christ, tell us plainly" (John 10:24).

They said, "How long are you going to keep us divorced from you? If you are the Messiah of God sent to save us, be frank. Now that you are here, tell us exactly who You are. If you are God, Israel is ready to be wedded to her God like in the olden days."

Jesus said there was no point for Him to repeat Himself over and over again to them. Even if He would tell them who He was, they would still not have faith in Him or in the One who sent Him to them.

"Jesus answered them, I told you, and ye believed not: the works that I do in my Father's name, they bear witness of me. But ye believe not, because ye are not of my sheep, as I said unto you. My sheep hear my voice, and I know them, and they follow me" (John 10:25–27).

All the miracles and healings He had carried out in the name of His Father were solid proofs He was more than a mere Man. They have not yet developed faith in Him because they were not the flock of the God of heaven and the earth just as He had told them before.

His sheep still listen very attentively when He is speaking. They can pick up His voice from the millions of voices of human beings and those of the lying demons. When they hear His voice, they are happy. They follow Him obediently.

Bernhard Plockhorst, 1825–1907, The Good Shepherd, in public domain.

And He promised, "And I give unto them eternal life; and they shall never perish, neither shall any man pluck them out of my hand" (John 10:28).

The sheep that follow Him obediently and faithfully are the ones He is going to supply with life that is eternal. They will breathe His life. They will belong to Him alone throughout all the eternal years to come.

Their lives will never be cut down and poured out like unwanted rubbish. No man or devil will stretch out his hand to harm them again.

He said that His Father placed His life into His hands. This life is the life that is residing in the spirits of faithful men and women on this earth. He wants Him to take care of them in His behalf. In fact, the nature and life of His Father is the greatest and the best of all the Beings in heaven and on the earth.

He is Omnipotent or All-Powerful. There is no one in heaven, the earth, and all the universes strong enough to fight Him. No one can snatch His beloved children from His omnipotent hand. "My Father, which gave them me, is greater than all; and no man is able to pluck them out of my Father's hand" (John 10:29).

The Messiah added this very important information: "I and my Father are one" (John 10:30).

God the Father and God the Son are one as God the Omnipotent, Omniscient (All-Knowing), Omnipresent (All-Powerful), and Omni-Benevolent.

Simply put, they have the same nature and character.

They are eternally blessed and glorious. "But to us there is but one God, the Father, of whom are all things, and we in him; and one Lord Jesus Christ, by whom are all things, and we by him" (1 Corinthians 8:6).

God is one. He is your God. He is the loving Daddy out of whom came multitudes of peoples who are breathing and living through His life. They are all His children.

There is only one Lord. He is the Lord God the Creator. He is Jesus your Messiah.

Just like with the Father, multitudes of countless peoples came out of His Spirit. And just as you are the child of God the Father, you are also the child of the Messiah.

The faces of the Jews flashed with hate and anger. "Then the Jews took up stones again to stone him" (John 10:31).

They grabbed rocks and stones in their hands. They were ready to stone with them Him until He was dead. "Jesus answered them, Many good works have I shewed you from my Father; for which of those works do ye stone me?" (John 10:32).

He said that He had performed many miraculous works for them. He had healed many of them and raised the dead ones to life.

All these works were wonderful and sweet like honey to the people. They were all astounded by them. Which of these works was evil against God that demanded that they must execute Him?

The blind Pharisees and Sadducees set in judgment against God. They drew close and stared right onto His eyes with hate and disdain.

They opened their mouths wide and blasphemed the name of the Holy One. "The Jews answered him, saying, For a good work we stone thee not; but for blasphemy; and because that thou, being a man, makest thyself God" (John 10:33).

They told Him that they had not yet burned Him with fire until He was dead because of the beauty of the excellent works He was performing for Israel but because He had elevated Himself into the place of God and was now pouring insults on His holy Name.

They could all see that He was a mere Man like all of them but He had come to them and was doing works by Himself as if He was God.

His reply was wonderful. It attracted the minds of truth seekers towards God their Maker. "Jesus answered them, Is it not written in your law, I said, Ye are gods? If he called them gods, unto whom the word of God came, and the scripture cannot be broken" (John 10:34, 35).

He was saying, "God belongs to everyone on this earth. He wrote to everyone living on this planet in the Book of the Psalms calling them, 'I say to all of you that you and I are all gods.'

If the Trinity Himself who is the one and only God Most High spoke in a loud voice like thunder, saying, 'You are gods' and His word is eternal, why don't you believe when I say I AM WHO I AM.

The scriptures speak the truth and it is eternal. No one can shake and shift the words of God in a sieve to make break them and make them fall down."

He went on, "Say ye of him, whom the Father hath sanctified, and sent into the world, Thou blasphemest; because I said, I am the Son of God? If I do not the works of my Father, believe me not.

But if I do, though ye believe not me, believe the works: that ye may know, and believe, that the Father is in me, and I in him" (John 10:36–38).

He was saying, "I am the best Son that the Father has. Because of My great and attractive goodness, He has ordained Me with holiness. He has sent Me as the Head of the families of this world.

And now you are accusing My Father and Me, Am who is your own God, that We are blaspheming our holy Name because I said I am the Son of God?

If I have not yet performed the miracles works and healings of My Father, then you would have no reason to have faith in Me that I am His Son. But if I have worked miracles and healings but you still refuse to have faith in Me that I am God, at least have the decency to believe that My miracles that they are supernatural as you can all see them for yourselves.

You are all My witnesses and have understood within yourselves that My miracles and healings have supernatural origin. But you have refused to confess the truth about who I really am.

You have refused to place your faith in this glaring and unavoidable truth: God the Father lives in Me, and I live in Him. Therefore, I am God."

The leaders of the Jews ordered that He should be stoned right in the temple. The mob picked up stones to kill Him. But He walked out that place and escaped their murderous intents.

"Therefore they sought again to take him: but he escaped out of their hand, And went away again beyond Jordan into the place where John at first baptized; and there he abode" (John 10:39, 40).

He went down to the place along the Jordan River where John used to baptize. The Jews who lived around there still remembered the Baptist as a holy man.

They also remembered His baptism and the voice that spoke from heaven. They were much more mature spiritually than the finical, overbearing, and jealous high priests.

He made the place where John used to baptize people His home. It was sacred.

It held wonderful memories for Him and for the people who were baptized by John. "And many resorted unto him, and said, John did no miracle: but all things that John spake of this man were true" (John 10:41).

The people were much more honest in their estimation of the Messiah than the priests. The said that all miracles, healings, sermons, the holy and perfection lifestyle of the Messiah, etc. all point to the truth that He was God in their midst.

God alone had the power to recreate life into the people.

He had supernatural power to be able to create faith, hope, love, etc. in them. "And many believed on him there" (John 10:42).

They placed their faith in Him that He was God and will save them from sin, death, and hell. He will take them to heaven to enjoy eternal life with God their Father.

He is inviting you to put faith in Him, and He will save you.

2. The Fellowship with God the Father

God is shining the knowledge about His existence, power, love and salvation on all men, women and children. He wants to help each one of us to learn and understand who He is and His love for us.

This will help us to see and understand His plan of salvation. He wants to build a water-tight friendship with us, the sinners of this earth.

Satan is jealous of God. He envies the Creator for being God the Almighty, the All-Powerful, the Everlasting, the Uncreated, the Self-Existing One, the Sovereign King and Lord over all, etc.

Satan wants all these powers and titles for himself. So he tried to kill God and take over His vast and endless kingdom. But God cannot be put to death. The life He has in Himself cannot die because He is God. But Satan tried any way.

He fought God but failed. "A war broke out in heaven. Michael and his angels were fighting against the dragon and its angels. But the dragon lost the battle. It and its angels were forced out of their places in heaven and were thrown down to the earth.

Yes, that old snake and his angels were thrown out of heaven! That snake that is striking everyone on earth is known as the devil and Satan. Then I heard a voice from heaven shout, "Our God has shown his saving power, and his kingdom has come! God's own Chosen One has shown his authority.

Satan accused our people in the presence of God day and night. Now he has been thrown out!" (Revelation 12:7–10, CEV).

When he was thrown out, he and his fellow demons needed a place to live. Because they are created, they need food to eat in which God has placed eternal life.

Otherwise, they would slowly age and die out without constantly feeding themselves on food that the Eternal God has created. They eyed this world with envy. When they saw the Tree of Life, they said, "AHA!

This is our chance. Let us make Adam and Eve to sin and die out. Then we shall own the earth and best of all for our immortal life to continue, we shall own the Tree of Life."

And God had a mystery which He had not made a public knowledge in the universe. It was a wonderful secret which Satan and all the evil angels did not know about. The mystery was that God the Father had sworn unbreakable love to the children of the earth no matter what. He swore that even if they should disobey Him He would love them still. He would rather die for them than to have all of them been wiped out of existence eternally. He is the Compassionate Daddy of al.

When Satan made his carefully thought plan to tempt Adam and Eve to sin and then carry it out so subtly so much so that these wisest of all people were not even aware that they were being deceived, the devil was completely unaware that even though they may fall into sin, being a good, kind and loving Father, God could not abandon His children to their fate. Satan had planned and hoped that they may die out and leave the earth for him and his fellow demons.

With the possession of the earth, He would own especially the Garden of Eden. The Garden had a prized possession. It was the Tree of Life would be his tree.

He and his comrades of fallen angels in sin and rebellion would enjoy the fruits from the Tree of Life and live forever. They celebrated when Adam and Eve fell into their cleverly laid-out death trap. They thought that they were now the permanent owners of this earth, planets, moon and sun of our world.

Satan thought he was now the prince of the world when Adam and Eve broke the law of life and lost the eternal life the Lord had placed in them. When God was on earth as Jesus with human body, He could see the evil spirits.

We cannot see them because the Lord has mercifully shielded our eyes from looking into the hate-filled, disgustingly proud and arrogant, wicked, envious and jealous eyes of demons. He does not want us to be shocked by the eyes of demons that love to hate us and Him.

We would faint and die of fear to see Satan if we are to see Satan in his true colors and not as a form of animist worship or Hindu or Buddha or Islam or atheism or New Age, etc. deities which sometimes may come in attractively wrapped packages.

The atmosphere is not lifeless and it is not just filled with air, clouds, sometimes rain, and some airplanes or rockets. It is thick with demons. Jesus saw them when He was a Man among us.

God calls Satan "the prince of the power of the air." He is "the spirit that now works in the children of disobedience." Ephesians 2:2.

He describes sinners as "dead in trespasses and sins." Ephesians 2:1.

He counsels you very strongly, "Be sober, be vigilant; because your adversary the devil, as a roaring lion, walketh about, seeking whom he may devour: Whom resist stedfast in the faith, knowing that the same afflictions are accomplished in your brethren that are in the world" (1 Peter 5:8, 9).

Yes, God had kept a secret hidden for endless ages past. The secret was that if His human children should sin, He would not obliterate them from ever existing again. Instead, He would die in their place to pay for their crimes of breaking the Commandments of life.

When He announced in Eden the day people sinned against Him, "And I will put enmity between thee and the woman, and between thy seed and her seed; it shall bruise thy head, and thou shalt bruise his heel" (Genesis 3:15), shock waves ran through all the ranks and file of the evil angels. Instead of God crushing the heads of Adam and Eve for their disobedience and putting them out of their misery of temptations, trials and deaths that very day when they sinned,

He volunteered to die in their place. And His death on behalf of His children would spell the death of Satan, "And there will be war between you and the woman and between your seed and her seed: by him will your head be crushed and by you his foot will be wounded" (Genesis 3:15, BBE).

This wonderful and awe-inspiring mystery of God is that He wants to form a partnership of fellowshipping with us as if we are also some God and be crowned kings and queens and lords under Him when we are nothing. We are not God.

We are inferior created creatures. "But when the fulness of the time was come, God sent forth his Son, made of a woman, made under the law, To redeem them that were under the law, that we might receive the adoption of sons.

And because ye are sons, God hath sent forth the Spirit of his Son into your hearts, crying, Abba, Father. Wherefore thou art no more a servant, but a son; and if a son, then an heir of God through Christ" (Galatians 4:4–7).

When men and women belong to the same fraternity such as in university community members, they consider themselves as of equal importance in dignity, respect, honor and everything. God the Father wants a fellowship with us.

He is giving us the fellowship the only God the Son and God the Holy Spirit are entitled to since they are the Persons of the Trinity together with God the Father.

God the Father calls the Second Godhead and God the Holy Spirit with the loving name of "My Fellow" in Zechariah 13:7.

When His Son became a Man to save us, God the Father cried out with anguish in His heart, "Awake, O sword, against my shepherd, and against the man that is my fellow, saith Jehovah of hosts: smite the shepherd, and the sheep shall be scattered; and I will turn my hand upon the little ones" (Zechariah 13:7, ASV).

He said of the Messiah, "Even if you are my fellow Trinity, I now permit you to be stricken to death by the sword. Please kindly save my little ones."

Of course, you are one of God's little children. This amazing God wants to make us also His fellows just like God the Son is His fellow and God the Holy Spirit is His fellow. He wants a fellowship with us! We are inferior creatures even if we shall be saved and living in heaven compared to the Trinity.

His plan of fellowship with us, among other things, is of being crowned and sitting on thrones of power and glory which is above angels and other sons and daughters in other stars. "Blessed be the God and Father of our Lord Jesus Christ, who hath blessed us with all spiritual blessings in heavenly places in Christ" (Ephesians 1:3).

It is necessary and very important for all of us to bless the Lord God our Father for all the good things He has done and is doing for us. Just as He has described of Himself that He is an Ever Living God, "May His years continue without end should be our words of blessings to Him."

He has blessed you with all the blessings of His caring, loving, and eternal Spirit with which He loves and adores His only Adopted Son, Jesus Christ the Messiah. He is the Creator and Sustainer of the ancient heaven and all the infinite universes.

As an Eternal God, He will save you eternally. Just as He said of Himself that He is God the Omnipotent. May He continue to be the only God, the Almighty God and God of Love forever and ever. By

His divine Almighty power, He will save you from the fires of hell and take us to Him in heaven.

He is treating you as if we are as good and wonderfully great as Jesus, His only Begotten Son who Himself is also God the Almighty. Through Jesus His Son, He is pouring all the blessings of heaven on us like the down pour of torrential rainwater.

He has given you of His Spirit through the Spirit of the Messiah, His beloved Son, and through the Holy Spirit to bring you safely home to Him in heaven. "According as he hath chosen us in him before the foundation of the world, that we should be holy and without blame before him in love: Having predestinated us unto the adoption of children by Jesus Christ to himself, according to the good pleasure of his will, To the praise of the glory of his grace, wherein he hath made us accepted in the beloved" (Ephesians 1:4–6).

He has predestined all of you by adopting you as the brothers and sisters of the Messiah whether you know Him or not, love Him or not, like Him or not. Therefore, all of you are His beloved children. These predestinations include the rights to have victory over sin, Satan, death, and hell. He loves you as much as He loves His Divine Son.

He is welcoming you with the unconditional and loving welcome of the Perfect and All-Benevolent Daddy before He laid the foundation of this earth. He laid it on righteousness because He wants you to be eternally righteous.

He did not lay on sin, suffering, pain, tears, demons or hell. He loves you just as you are. He wants to wash away your sins with the abundant and overflowing blood of His beloved Son, the Messiah.

He has never predestined anyone to hell fire. Everyone is predestined to go to heaven because the sacrifice of the Cross is for all human beings. However, you must make a choice of either you want to be saved and go to heaven.

He does not force anyone to go there. He wants you to use the brains he has given you to choose that which is right, good, and excellent for yourself, and is choosing your loving and caring Daddy over sin, death, and hell.

Before God made the world and before He made Adam and Eve, He chose you that He would create you to be His child. "Moreover," He said, "should my son or daughter break the Ten Commandments, he or she is still My baby. I have chosen to love him or her forever. In fact, I love my son/my daughter so much that I am will to die for him or her should he or she sin because he or she is Mine forever."

He declared that He will remove the shackles of sin and demoniac activities against us. He will exterminate all evil against us by hell fire so that we may have uninterrupted sweet fellowship with Him.

He will make you eternally holy. You will never fall into sin again. No one will have doubts about your abilities to be eternally righteous again.

Angels and people will not point at you and say, "But. . . ." There are no "Buts" about the saved ones. They are eternally holy and perfect when they are in heaven.

No one will mock them again about being weak sinners. You will have complete confidence in yourself to be perfectly holy and righteous eternally, and you do it.

God the Father will make you as righteous and powerful as the Messiah because both of you are His beloved children. He loves both of you equally, deeply intensely, and eternally. He watches over you very tenderly and zealously more than an eagle watches over its young. He loves you more than He loves Himself.

Therefore, He is paying your bills like any of your earthly parents that are paying his or her bills to care for his or her children. This bill is the blood of the Cross.

It has given access to His Everlasting Spirit for you to breathe and enjoy very perfectly and eternally. He has etched it in His will in His mind that you are eternally His beloved child and must be saved at all costs to Himself.

All you can do is to reach out your hands and hold Him very tenderly and lovingly in your arms. He is so gracious by making you as important and special as Himself. He has covered you with His grace. This grace is the unconditional love of the Divine and Eternal Daddy. It made Him your God even though you are a terrible sinner.

He has covered you with His unconditional love in spite of everything. "In whom we have redemption through his blood, the forgiveness of sins, according to the riches of his grace" (Ephesians 1:7).

God the Father came down and married His Son to every man and woman that He has birthed on this earth from the beginning to the end of time. He married you off to His Son so that He can forever be your loving God. And every judgment that the Son will pass on you will be based on His eternal and unconditional love to His beloved wife.

There are no revengeful feelings in His heart because you are an unfaithful wife. He has forgiven you completely and eternally. "Wherein he hath abounded toward us in all wisdom and prudence" (Ephesians 1:8).

He has already here. He knows you very well. That is why He is exalting you very highly. He is treating you royally as if you are His second Self. He has etched in His mind to always treating you. "Having made known unto us the mystery of his will, according to his good pleasure which he hath purposed in himself" (Ephesians 1:9).

He is thankful that He is able to save you through the sacrifice of His Son on the Cross of Calvary. You are a gift that He has given to Him because of the Cross.

As God the Daddy, He will fill you with His life. The whole earth will be saturated with His Presence. You will see Him face to face whether you in the sky, on the dry land or in the bottom of the sea. "That in the dispensation of the fulness of times he might gather together in one all things in Christ, both which are in heaven, and which are on earth; even in him" (Ephesians 1:10). Through the sacrifice of His beloved Messiah, He will unite heaven and earth to be eternally one nation and one family under Him.

All of you form only one wife of the Messiah. It was one Spirit that He breathed into Adam that has reproduced Himself into all of you. All of you are really only one spirit. He lives in all of you. He is your Creator God and Daddy.

He is recreating His Spirit of truth in you again in order to make you eternally righteous and holy just like Himself. And since you are the beloved wife of the Messiah, the Adopted and Beloved Son of God the Father, you will share in the glories of power, riches, eternities, etc. of your dotting Husband.

"In whom also we have obtained an inheritance, being predestinated according to the purpose of him who worketh all things after the counsel of his own will: That we should be to the praise of his glory, who first trusted in Christ" (Ephesians 1:11, 12).

God the Father looks at you as His friends and daughters-in-law. Of course, you are also His beloved children.

He is watching over all of you very tenderly with His two infinite and loving eyes to fulfill all His will in your life. Hold Him tenderly with both of your hands for all the wonderful things He is doing for you.

Exalt Him very highly above yourselves and everything else because He has made you as important as Himself. You are coming back to Him through the Messiah's sacrifice for you on the Cross of Calvary.

The Cross of Calvary is inclusive to all human beings who ever lived on this and who will bear in the future. There are no exceptions.

The Cross belongs to all of you. "In whom ye also trusted, after that ye heard the word of truth, the gospel of your salvation: in whom also after that ye believed, ye were sealed with that holy Spirit of promise, Which is the earnest of our inheritance until the redemption of the purchased possession, unto the praise of his glory" (Ephesians 1:13, 14).

When you heard the voice of the Spirit of the Messiah speaking in your hearts asking you to meet with Him in heaven, you responded to Him. You knew that what He is saying is the truth. He loves you. That is why He died for you.

The Gospel is the life of God that has come to save you from all your sins. It is making you His brothers and sisters. It is the truth because God is the Truth. When you placed your faiths in Him, He completed the process of the adoption through the office of the loving Father called the Holy Spirit. He made you His brothers and sisters.

The Holy Spirit is the hand that is making all of you holy, righteous, powerful, and eternal. He is the Daddy who is on fire about rescuing you from and hell.

He will shower you with everlasting inheritances in order that you may enjoy life as much as He, your Daddy, does. He is your Source of welfare benefits. He is not like earthly welfare organizations.

He is your compassionate and loving Mother. He will empower you to live richly, powerfully, joyously, happily, and eternally because He is very passionate about you and about fulfilling all your needs. Hold Him very tenderly with both of your arms and exalt Him very highly for all the wonderful things He is doing for you.

To achieve sweet loving relationship with Him again, He is making us pure, holy, loving and complete innocent through Jesus Christ, His Son because of His love great love for us which burns explodes throughout heaven into fire, earthquakes, thunders and heavy smoke. "In the year that king Ozias died, I saw the Lord sitting upon a throne high and elevated: and his train filled the temple.

Upon it stood the seraphims: the one had six wings, and the other had six wings: with two they covered his face, and with two they covered his feet, and with two they flew. And they cried one to another, and said: Holy, holy, holy, the Lord God of hosts, all the earth is full of his glory, And the lintels of the doors were moved at the voice of him that cried, and the house was filled with smoke.

And I said: Woe is me, because I have held my peace; because I am a man of unclean lips, and I dwell in the midst of a people that hath unclean lips, and I have seen with my eyes the King the Lord of hosts" (Isaiah 6:1–5, DRB).

Then God the Father makes a heart wrenching cry about you, "Whom shall I send? and who shall go for us?"

Then His Son, the Second Godhead answered, "And I said: Lo, here am I, send me" (Isaiah 6:8, DRB).

He did come and was murdered by public execution in your place so that you may have an eternal fellowship with God the Almighty, your Father. "We believe that Jesus died and was raised to life. We also believe that when God brings Jesus back again, he will bring with him all who had faith in Jesus before they died.

Our Lord Jesus told us that when he comes, we won't go up to meet him ahead of his followers who have already died. With a loud command and with the shout of the chief angel and a blast of God's trumpet, the Lord will return from heaven. Then those who had faith in Christ before they died will be raised to life.

Next, all of us who are still alive will be taken up into the clouds together with them to meet the Lord in the sky. From that time onward, we will all be with the

Lord forever. Encourage each other with these words" (1 Thessalonians 4:14–18, CEV).

God did really choose us because of love. He loves us so much that even when we are sinning, He has already chosen us to be His babes. He sent His Son to clear our sins out of our minds and hearts and make us holy, pure and righteous like Himself. "But God commendeth his love toward us, in that, while we were yet sinners, Christ died for us" (Romans 5:8).

The Messiah died for us because of love. He loves us as much as God our Father and the Holy Spirit love us. Studying, learning and believing in the love of Jesus your Almighty Creator will place your mind and heart in heaven.

The Holy Spirit is parenting us because of love. What the Holy Spirit has for you is His loving heart of a Divine Everlasting Father for His baby. No one can put up with your rotten sinfulness except this amazing Father. He follows us faithfully and patiently through all the gulley and hell of sin you have sunk into.

He brought you out of them time and time again every day and every night. He parents all of you all lives even though you still love to spend most of our time disobeying Him and breaking His heart beyond description.

Still, His thoughts towards you are full of infinitely multiplied love. "But the fruit of the Spirit is love, joy, peace, longsuffering, gentleness, goodness, faith, Meekness, temperance: against such there is no law" (Galatians 5:22, 23).

The Lord is drawing you ever closer to Himself. He, who gives a command and things jump into existence out of total emptiness, is talking to you. He is explaining to you who He, as God, is.

Much more than that He said as your Creator, you came into existence through Him. More exciting still, He has already paid for your sins because He is Daddy. He is inviting you, "Enter now into the realm of my kingdom."

He said, "And he said unto them, Unto you it is given to know the mystery of the kingdom of God: but unto them that are without, all these things are done in parables" (Mark 4:11). He has chosen to speak plainly to you in the language you can understand. He wants to grasp its full contents so that you soul may live and not die.

Only to God alone belongs the glory of your creation, existence and salvation. That same Almighty Power that created you and everyone including heaven and earth and all those many more infinite things which have not come into our knowledge yet, is able to save from hell. He will teach you about Himself and the plan of salvation for you. He will give you the intellect to understand the gospel of love of His Son, Jesus Christ.

The secret of the gospel is that God loves you. He demonstrated this love full at the Garden of Eden when He cursed Satan with total destruction and elimination from existence for all the sins he has cause you to commit, all your sufferings of a very short unpredictable life which is full of pain and sorrow and your soon coming death.

A part of this secret plan which was kept in silence only in the heart of God and which the demons did not know until the time of the Fall in the Garden of Eden, was that God Himself will pay the full price for all your sins. And your salvation has been paid for by the death and resurrection of Jesus Christ, the only God Omnipotent, Everlasting, Unchanging, Infinite in Being, Sovereign King of kings and Savior of all.

Not only will He help you to understand His message but He will establish you in the truth and make you strong and powerful through faith. He will make you grow every day in His knowledge and wisdom through the Bible, nature, your consciences, things that are happening in your life, etc. He knows you will be able to understand.

He knows how much you are able to absorb and

retain in the pace you are able to move towards Him. "Now to him that is of power to stablish you according to my gospel, and the preaching of Jesus Christ, according to the revelation of the mystery, which was kept secret since the world began" (Romans 16:25).

God is calling you into a perfect and everlasting relationship not by blind faith or mysticisms but through the reasoning of your brain, through faith, through grasping the great concept about your God, through understanding Him, appreciating Him and loving Him.

He is inviting you as your Superior Sovereign Lord to sit down at His feet and listen and obey for your own good. "Come now, and let us reason together, saith the LORD: though your sins be as scarlet, they shall be as white as snow; though they be red like crimson, they shall be as wool" (Isaiah 1:18).

If you are wise enough to know the good things that you need in order to survive burning of this world through hell fire and be saved, He opens His hand of generosity and sweeps it over heaven and earth and offering them for you, while declaring, "If ye be willing and obedient, ye shall eat the good of the land" (Isaiah 1:19).

Listen carefully to Him. Keep this secret which is not secret at all to those who love Him in your heart also. Obey Him. Follow Him. Love Him. Have fellowship with Him. You will enjoy the love of the Good God and all that He has in mind for you.

You will enjoy eternal life, luxuries, power, glory, honor, respect, etc. more than accorded to the sons and daughters of a good king. Heaven will be yours and also the new earth - that is another part of the secret.

The demons thought that you will not be created. They thought that your first parents would be executed on the spot by the Commandments they broke. Instead, God's secret plan was to save you and elevate your higher than His original plan.

His first plan was to make you the king/queen of

this world. But now, He revealed His secret, that is, since you have cost Him His life, you must live together with Him and rule angels, all persons in those worlds, and everything as His vice president and junior king/queen.

He really did crush Satan, the serpentine dragon on the head by saving and elevating you so highly. "And I will put enmity between thee and the woman, and between thy seed and her seed; it shall bruise thy head, and thou shalt bruise his heel" (Genesis 3:15).

God is so wise that He uses the best knowledge in the right way for the utmost benefit of mankind. He is so discrete and so wise to discern that you would sin and that we would need Him.

He arranged your plan of salvation many endless ages past before He even created you. "But as it is written, Eye hath not seen, nor ear heard, neither have entered into the heart of man, the things which God hath prepared for them that love him" (1 Corinthians 2:9).

Yes, the secret wisdom of God is to save you from destruction because of sin, take you to heaven, sit you beside Him as His adorable baby so that the glory of love, joy, peace, love, gentleness, kindness, self-control, patience, fiery blazing brightness, eternal life, honor, power, respect, etc. may flowing from Him to you so that He may glorify you forever.

"God is a Spirit: and they that worship him must worship him in spirit and in truth" (John 4:24).

Because He is a Spirit, He is, first, giving us spiritual blessings through His Son which are more concrete and everlasting than satisfying our physical needs. These spiritual blessings are giving of Himself and His love for us, which brings in all other physical blessings in their wake.

The Trinity, through Christ, declared that we are still lovely children even after we have sinned. All that we now need is that Christ should die for us and bring us back home. God loves His Son more than He loves

Himself. The life, love, and joy of the Father are in His Son.

When the Son stepped down from His ancient throne to come down to us, we became even dearer and more beloved to the Father and to the Holy Spirit. The Son suffered and won and went back to the Father.

Because of the awesome, unconditional, unselfish, intense and overflowing love God the Father has for His Son and because the Son suffered for us, He has thrown open all the doors to the treasures and lavish them on us.

We are sons and daughters of the Almighty God just as Jesus Christ is His Son.

3. The Fellowship of Jesus Christ

Eve was hypnotized by the snake. When Satan had controlled over her mind, he swayed her to disobey God and eat the forbidden fruit. Not so with Adam. God gave him time to think about what action to take.

He gave Adam all the intellectual capacities to make a wise and educated decision to do the right thing like Him Himself would have done had He been in the same situation. He would have chosen to do the right thing.

Four thousand years later, indeed, He did the right thing. God came into the world as Jesus Christ. In every temptation, He chose to do the right thing. He obeyed the Ten Commandments without any flaw.

Those same intellectual and moral powers, He had created in Adam. But Adam made a moral and spiritual decision to disobey His Father and obeyed a hypnotized, confused, sad and fallen woman who has just been deceived by Satan.

It was his duty to help her come back to God but instead he chose to obey Satan. He had seen that the woman had fallen to the sin of Satan. When he exercised his moral, intellectual and spiritual powers to willingly disobey God in preference for a fallen sinner, he chose Satan as his new master and lord as if he were his God, Creator and Father.

Each child that he brought into the world inherited his weakness of obeying Satan. Disobedience has ingrained itself into our flesh, bones, feelings, minds and hearts that we are following the law of sin, and death. Sin has become a part of our nature. It is embedded deep in our flesh.

Sin has become in us a natural tendency to obey evil. When someone is sick, certain symptoms of that particular disease would appear in that person. For example, some viral infections may cause tiredness, pale skin, etc. Sin is the symptom of death. "For all have sinned, and come short of the glory of God" (Romans 6:23).

When we are sinning, we are showing that we are already spiritually and physically dead. We do not have everlasting life in us anymore. "And if Christ be in you, the body is dead because of sin; but the Spirit is life because of righteousness" (Romans 8:10).

It is only a matter of time when the breath will finally leave the body unless Jesus comes soon to put end to dying.

God is not exacerbated or angry with us. How could He be mad with us for being such stupid weak sinners when sin has finished us and death is our end? We are drowning in the sea of sin.

He saw our corrupted will powers that have been destroyed by sin in the Garden of Eden through the lies of Satan. In all the universes, we are the only mortals while God, angels and all the other brothers and sisters we have in other worlds are immortal.

The English Playwright and Poet, William Shakespeare, (1564-1616), penned down this doleful poem about our mortality.

> "All the world's a stage,
> And all the men and women merely players.
> They have their exits and their entrances,
> And one man in his time plays many parts,
> His acts being seven ages."

When we exit, we are forever gone to the world of the dead. Most graves beginning from Abel, the first man to die in history of humanity, are unmarked. They are covered with bushes, forests, water or deserts.

They have turned back to soil, thus, proving the

word of the Lord to be true, "In the sweat of thy face shalt thou eat bread till thou return to the earth out of which thou wast taken: for dust thou art, and into dust thou shalt return" (Genesis 3:19, DRB).

We are also following them as David once described our helpless situation to his son, Solomon, when he was saying good-bye as he laid on his death bed, "I go the way of all the earth: be thou strong therefore, and shew thyself a man" (1 Kings 2:2).

David never returned back to earth. He never went to heaven. His grave is still here with us in Israel.

God saw how our sinful flesh forces us to commit sin even against our own will. He saw our helplessness. He saw that we were too weak to escape from the deadly clutches of sin by our own wisdom and strength.

We do not have the power to thrown Satan away from crawling around us like a snake and injecting his poisonous temptations into our minds to make us to sin.

We cannot kill this poisonous serpent by our own powers. We have no power to fight death and conquer it. Instead, we have descended into the pit of death. We are lying on the earth that whose soil, air, water, etc. breeds death.

It keeps swallowing our remains all the time. Many have already been swallowed in the belly of the earth. Many bodies are on the bed of worms in the earth and some are not even buried especially during war times.

They are covered by worms as they are being eaten by them. Their silent voices rise from all graves, mortuaries, etc. eerily before the throne of their Father.

The precious bodies of all races created by God: Black and White, Yellow and Brown and the in-betweens, yes of men, women and children are foods for these disgusting worms as they lie on the bed of earth filled covered with deadly worms.

Shakespeare wrote about the end of people: "They

shall lie down alike in the dust, and the worms shall cover them" (Job 21:26). Men have died from time to time, and worms have eaten them, but not for love.

God further describes our helplessness: "Drought and heat consume the snow waters: so doth the grave those which have sinned.

The womb shall forget him; the worm shall feed sweetly on him; he shall be no more remembered; and wickedness shall be broken as a tree" (Job 24:19, 20). Even the best mummification cannot keep them warm and healthy. They are dead.

See how we spend only a short time in this life and some die even before they are born and then we die, never to return, our Father was filled with indescribable sorrow and pain. He decided to do something about it to save us from our plight.

He gathers us in His warm arms of love. He re-assures us of His salvation through His Beloved Adopted Son, Jesus Christ our God and Everlasting Savior. "But Jesus will never die, and so he will be a priest forever!

He is forever able to save the people he leads to God, because he always lives to speak to God for them. Jesus is the high priest we need. He is holy and innocent and faultless, and not at all like us sinners.

Jesus is honored above all beings in heaven, and he is better than any other high priest. Jesus doesn't need to offer sacrifices each day for his own sins and then for the sins of the people.

He offered a sacrifice once for all, when he gave himself. The Law appoints priests who have weaknesses. But God's promise, which came later than the Law, appoints his Son. And he is the perfect high priest forever" (Hebrews 7:24–28, CEV).

As God the Almighty, Jesus Christ has abundant and infinite life in Himself that has no beginning and no end. He is giving us this eternal life to be within our bodies also.

As our Savior and High Priest who is officiating

on our behalf before the Great and Loving Father of all in heaven. He asked the Father that the Holy Spirit should recreate us as it was in the beginning of the world. "And the earth was without form, and void; and darkness was upon the face of the deep. And the Spirit of God moved upon the face of the waters" (Genesis 1:2).

In that dark watery emptiness, His word of command brought out our universes. He breathed us out of Himself and placed us to live in this part of His everlasting kingdom to be loved and cared for by Him.

And now Jesus has asked the Holy Spirit to again father the everlasting life in our bodies so that, He the Divine Daddy and His children, could all live forever.

Now, "Keep the good thing committed to thy trust by the Holy Ghost who dwelleth in us" (2 Timothy 1:14).

Everlasting life is the most precious treasure the Omnipotent One has given to us as a gift. It is Jesus Christ living in our souls by the Presence of the Holy Spirit in our hearts.

This is the Good News - Christ died for us so that we may be recreated and rejoin our Eternal Father's glorious family in heaven.

There is no beginning of the omnipotence of God, and there is no end to it. God is Almighty in His Being.

He is so powerful that He wills creations into existence. He ordered heaven, our world and all the universes to come out of nothingness.

The best thing about Him is that He is love. His love has inexhaustible grace. His power and grace is able to save you from all your weaknesses and problems. "And he said unto me, My grace is sufficient for thee: for my strength is made perfect in weakness. Most gladly therefore will I rather glory in my infirmities, that the power of Christ may rest upon me" (2 Corinthians 12:9).

When you have committed a sin, He has already

forgiven you. He will make you new and perfect like Himself. He says, "For I will be merciful to their unrighteousness, and their sins and their iniquities will I remember no more" (Hebrews 8:12).

He has already paid the penalty for you sins on the cross. He only needs to wash them away by His precious blood and make you as if you have never sinned in your entire life.

When you are sad, He can give you joy because He has more power than you need. When you are in trouble, He can help you because His might is greater than your trouble.

When you fall dead someday, He can bring you right back from the grave into a life that has no shadow of death anymore because His power is divine and everlasting.

When you are sick, God can heal you because His power is more than sufficient to heal you. "Wherefore he is able also to save them to the uttermost that come unto God by him, seeing he ever liveth to make intercession for them" (Hebrews 7:25).

Your problems will make the love and power of your God to shine even brighter and more glorious in this world and in the world to come. So take heart and do not be discouraged by the storms of this life.

Reaffirm your faith in Him when you are going through some storms of life by emphasizing that: "And he said unto me, My grace is sufficient for thee: for my strength is made perfect in weakness. Most gladly therefore will I rather glory in my infirmities, that the power of Christ may rest upon me" (2 Corinthians 12:9).

He will build the confidence in you to trust in His power to see you through this life. He will bring you safe to heaven.

The God of gods and the King of kings is happy to lavish on you His infinitely abundant grace or unlimited favor and unconditional eternal love with royal divine liberality.

The mystery of Christ is His sacrificial love for you on the cross so that He may fellowship together with you as children of the Almighty Father and co-heirs of the infinite, glory, eternity, powerful, wealthy and everlasting kingdom of God.

This salvation from sin and promotion as joint heirs with Christ to share the glory, riches, eternal life and power in the everlasting kingdom is for all the descendants of Adam and Eve.

The Holy Spirit will lead you into great depth of knowledge of this mystery that God the Everlasting Father, even Jesus Christ, should love us so much that

He should die for us and then make us sit on thrones of power next to Him as joint-rulers, with us as deputy kings/queens, of His everlasting kingdom covering all heaven, universes and this world. "The Spirit itself beareth witness with our spirit, that we are the children of God" (Romans 8:16).

Let us come in humility before God our Father. In humility, let our knees hit the floors. Let out heads be bowed before Him and our close eyes in prayer in reverence and awe.

Let us thank Him for His wonderful love which has expressed itself in the salvation of our souls by the death of the Creator Himself. "The fear of the LORD is the instruction of wisdom; and before honour is humility" (Proverbs 15:33).

Thinking of yourself as lower in importance and glory to God is the beginning of true reverence and honor to Him. "A man's pride shall bring him low: but honour shall uphold the humble in spirit" (Proverbs 29:23).

Real humility is stopping to lift one's self up in thought by thinking about one's own high opinions. It is stopping to fight the Holy Spirit in very subtle ways by kicking the thought of God out of our thoughts and, instead entertaining our own selves in our thoughts, speaking about us and doing things for us. The Holy Spirit is a real Person.

Do not listen to your own self-importance. Do not allow your ego to be manipulated by the devil that is standing at your left hand to egg you on into more rebellion against your own Father.

"Be humble in the presence of God's mighty power, and he will honor you when the time comes. God cares for you, so turn all your worries over to him. Be on your guard and stay awake.

Your enemy, the devil, is like a roaring lion, sneaking around to find someone to attack. But you must resist the devil and stay strong in your faith.

You know that all over the world the Lord's followers are suffering just as you are. But God shows undeserved kindness to everyone.

That's why he appointed Christ Jesus to choose you to share in his eternal glory. You will suffer for a while, but God will make you complete, steady, strong, and firm. God will be in control forever! Amen" (1 Peter 5:6–11, CEV).

Yes, let out knees hit the ground in reverence and adoration of God because He is the Almighty One. He is the All-Present Being. He exists everywhere and, therefore, He is always with us. He is the All-Knowing King of kings and Lord of lords forever. He is everlasting in nature.

Above all, He loves us so much that we cannot even describe about His love adequately in human words. His words of mouth created the heavens and the earth.

He hands formed out bodies out of the soil. His Spirit gave us birth by breathing us out of Him and put us into this world as His children. "God, who made the world and everything in it, is Lord of heaven and earth and does not live in temples made by human hands. Nor does he need anything that we can supply by working for him, since it is he himself who gives life and breath and everything else to everyone.

From one human being he created all races of people and made them live throughout the whole earth.

He himself fixed beforehand the exact times and the limits of the places where they would live. He did this so that they would look for him, and perhaps find him as they felt around for him.

Yet God is actually not far from any one of us; as someone has said, 'In him we live and move and exist.' It is as some of your poets have said, 'We too are his children.'" (Acts 17:24–28, GNB).

This same God who created you into existence by putting a part of Himself into you wants to draw you back into His arms. He is not at peace without you being close with Him again because He is your Dad.

He took the glories and majesty of His infinitely abundant powers and everything because of the goodness and sweetness of His love and put them all into your hands.

He asked the Holy Spirit to bless you with all the greatness of His power and love so that you may be saved and live happily forever. He wants His blessings to start working in you right now.

The Holy Spirit wants to make you strong, unbreakable, undefeated, steady, confident, righteous and holy in your mind and heart so that you may be like God.

All the blessings will start taking effect in your life if you will welcome Jesus, the Son of God Himself, to live in your heart. From the day you were born, He has been standing at the door of your heart knocking so gently, so patiently, so persistently and so urgently.

"Behold, I stand at the door, and knock: if any man hear my voice, and open the door, I will come in to him, and will sup with him, and he with me. To him that overcometh will I grant to sit with me in my throne, even as I also overcame, and am set down with my Father in his throne" (Revelation 3:20, 21).

He is asking you so kindly and so loving to please kindly open the door of your heart to Him so that He could come in and change your life into an immortal being of excellent glory, honor and respect second only to Himself. "For thou hast made him a little lower than the angels, and hast crowned him with glory and honour" (Psalms 8:5).

When you welcome the Lord Jesus into your heart, God your Father and God the Holy Spirit will also come to live in your heart. Even before you finished praying in asking for forgiveness and inviting the Lord to come and live in your heart, He will come quickly and enter your heart.

He will start telling you how much He loves you with the love that is so great that it cannot be measured or quantified. "For this cause I bow my knees unto the Father of our Lord Jesus Christ, Of whom the whole family in heaven and earth is named, That he would grant you, according to the riches of his glory, to be strengthened with might by his Spirit in the inner man;

That Christ may dwell in your hearts by faith; that ye, being rooted and grounded in love, May be able to comprehend with all saints what is the breadth, and length, and depth, and height; And to know the love of Christ, which passeth knowledge, that ye might be filled with all the fulness of God" (Ephesians 3:14–19).

You will never come to understand fully why a Being such as God loves you but He loves you. And He is giving you His world. He is giving His kingdom of love, joy, peace, and riches beyond the imagination of earthly men and women.

To God, eternities are but a moment of drawing in or out a breath. Even from those timeless of past eternities, He saw you as if you already existed. Eternity is only a moment of time to Him. "You saw me before I was born. The days allotted to me had all been recorded in your book, before any of them ever began" (Psalm S139: 16, GNB).

Unfortunately, He also saw your senseless and bad decisions to disobey Him. Sin has brought death. The punishment is eternal annihilation in hell. Even from those ancient times, grace and mercy was already flowing from His deep heart of love more abundantly that we ever would need.

He had already forgiven you because He had fallen in love with you even from eternal past. "The LORD hath appeared of old unto me, saying, Yea, I have loved thee with an everlasting love: therefore with lovingkindness have I drawn thee" (Jeremiah 31:3).

Because of His fiery love for you, He is drawing you ever closer to Himself. Even the fear of dying a painful and shameful death on the cross falsely accused as a false King of Israel did not deter Him from loving you.

His love for you was stronger than the fear of perhaps never rising from the grave. He is wonderfully kind, simply affectionate, dearly loving, sympathetic, merciful and deep overflowing gracious sweet love.

God chose willingly to be a Parent. As a loving, kind and merciful Parent, He took the first step to forgive you of all your sins. But the terms of reconciliation required blood.

A Divine Being must die in order to appease the demands of the Ten Commandments that have been violated. The violation spread death everywhere.

This Divine Parent chose to shed His own blood to appease the demands of the Ten Commandments. He voluntarily went to the cross to reclaim your life back from the grave. This is grace and tender forgiving love beyond compare to human or angelic love. "For when we were yet without strength, in due time Christ died for the ungodly.

For scarcely for a righteous man will one die: yet peradventure for a good man some would even dare to die. But God commendeth his love toward us, in that, while we were yet sinners, Christ died for us" (Romans 5:6–8).

You are a weak sinner who can never by his/her own will power become perfect like Jesus. You do not have the strength of the character of God to be holy and perfect. You are evil by nature. Even though you may be righteous somewhat, yet you have the propensity to do evil. You are a helpless sinner.

Even if someone like a parent may be willingly to die for you, yet he or she cannot save you from being burnt up in hell because of your sins. But God is the Almighty Creator. He can create purity and eternity in you again.

Although you do not deserve to be re-instated back into His favor because of the deep evil in your heart, yet He put Himself forward as your love and your grace.

Through Himself and by the death of His own Son, He approved your reinstatement into the full face to face eternal family fellowship with the Trinity. He considers you very much worthy to cost the life of only His Son.

He has promoted you into His gracious favor not because of any divine greatness or even some goodness in you but because of Himself as God the Almighty in creation and especially in love, faithfulness and truth.

"And if by grace, then is it no more of works: otherwise grace is no more grace. But if it be of works, then is it no more grace: otherwise work is no more work" (Romans 11:6).

And so because of His unlimited grace and power, you have been His beloved baby right from the everlasting years. He will love you throughout the coming everlasting years.

Although your sins makes Him blush with shame yet in you He sees His image - His son, His daughter, and therefore, worthy of love and praise and worthy of the death of His only Begotten Son. He was ready with His unmerited grace even from immemorial past to forgive and forget all your sins.

He has already died for you while you still despise and hate Him daily. How much blessings will you enjoy throughout all eternities if you will only accept His unlimited grace in order to be elevated and crowned with full loving relationship with Him and with Jesus Christ and the Holy Spirit.

The best thing about Him is that He is love. "And he said unto me, My grace is sufficient for thee: for my strength is made perfect in weakness. Most gladly therefore will I rather glory in my infirmities, that the power of Christ may rest upon me" (2 Corinthians 12:9).

His love has inexhaustible grace. His power and grace is able to save you from all your weaknesses and problems.

When you have committed a sin, He has already forgiven you. He will make you new and perfect like Himself. He says, "Therefore, brethren, we are debtors, not to the flesh, to live after the flesh" (Hebrews 8:12).

He has already paid the penalty for you sins on the cross. He only needs to wash them away by His precious blood and make you as if you have never sinned in your entire life.

His promise is: "If we confess our sins, he is faithful and just to forgive us our sins, and to cleanse us from all unrighteousness" (1 John 1:9).

When you are sad, He can give you joy because He has more power than you need. When you are in trouble, He can help you because His might is greater than your trouble.

When you fall dead someday, He can bring you right back from the grave into a life that has no shadow of death anymore because His power is divine and everlasting.

When you are sick, God can heal you because His power is more than sufficient to heal you. "Wherefore he is able also to save them to the uttermost that come unto God by him, seeing he ever liveth to make intercession for them" (Hebrews 7:25).

Your problems will make the love and power of

your God to shine even brighter and more glorious in this world and in the world to come. So take heart and do not be discouraged by the storms of this life.

Reaffirm your faith in Him when you are going through some storms of life by emphasizing that: "And he said unto me, My grace is sufficient for thee: for my strength is made perfect in weakness.

Most gladly therefore will I rather glory in my infirmities, that the power of Christ may rest upon me" (2 Corinthians 12:9.

He will build the confidence in you to trust in His power to see you through this life and bring you safe to heaven.

4. Fellowship with the Holy Spirit

Sarah More, 2013, The love and faithfulness of a dove are the symbols of the Holy Spirit

God the Holy Spirit tells us that even though our bodies are going through wear and tear all the time, even though we are prone to diseases and accidents, even though we may die and be eaten by worms, burnt by fire, drowned in water, etc. as our ancestors were, we are not worms or nothingness.

He said that He will change these bodies that we consider would be filled with worms as if we are worms. He will make us into threshing sledges or sharp ploughs or gun powders, atomic or nuclear bombs, electricity or whatever power you may think of.

In fact, He will make us so powerful that any one of us will have the power and capacity to level mountains like Mount Everest to ground and make the place into a plain, a valley or deep hole. "Behold, I will make thee a new sharp threshing instrument having teeth: thou shalt thresh the mountains, and beat them small, and shalt make the hills as chaff.

Thou shalt fan them, and the wind shall carry them away, and the whirlwind shall scatter them: and thou shalt rejoice in the LORD, and shalt glory in the

Holy One of Israel" (Isaiah 41:15, 16).

The Holy Spirit is encouraging you not to be afraid of your wicked, cruel and brutal enemies such as demons, death, sin or even perhaps men and women who are being controlled by Satan.

He ran like the wind from heaven more than two thousand years ago during the Pentecost to baptize you with fire of eternal life and power. "And when the days of the Pentecost were accomplished, they were all together in one place:

And suddenly there came a sound from heaven, as of a mighty wind coming: and it filled the whole house where they were sitting. And there appeared to them parted tongues, as it were of fire: and it sat upon every one of them.

And they were all filled with the Holy Ghost: and they began to speak with divers tongues, according as the Holy Ghost gave them to speak" (Acts 2:1–4, DRB).

The Holy Spirit follows you around day and night wooing you to come back to Me because you are His passion. He loves you so much that He lives in your heart even though it is sinful most of the time.

He is so compassion and devoted in His love for you that He is not enjoying the glories and fun of heaven but chose you above every angel in heaven to be His closest companion. He left them although they are wonderful sweet, loving and kind.

He is with you. He is living amongst the people of the lost world.

He is absolutely perfect in all His ways. His thoughts are pure, holy, sinless, loving and great. His words are flawless, gracious and loving.

His works are wonderful and original. There is no need to question Him as to why He is doing certain things in your life.

He is bringing out the best in you since He is All-Present, All-Powerful, and All-Knowing. "O the depth of the riches both of the wisdom and knowledge of

God! how unsearchable are his judgments, and his ways past finding out!" (Romans 11:33).

Your only contribution is to love and trust Him all the time. It will help you to live forever. He is your joy and hope of eternal life.

He will bless you more than you have hoped for or expected. Going to heaven is just the beginning of all the marvelous things He will lavish on you.

As the Lord God Almighty, He is stronger and firmer in power, goodness and love than all the angels, peoples and beings of other worlds He breathed out of His Being.

His energy never depletes but remains fresh and infinite abundant from one eternity to another.

Heaven and earth hang on Him for life and for strength. "Our LORD, let the heavens now praise your miracles, and let all of your angels praise your faithfulness. None who live in the heavens can compare with you.

You are the most fearsome of all who live in heaven; all the others fear and greatly honor you. You are LORD God All-Powerful! No one is as loving and faithful as you are" (Psalms 90:5-8, CEV).

His personality is very attractive to all the inhabitants of heaven and the universes. He is warm, loving, and very friendly.

They love to come together to worship and praise Him. They love to be baptized over and over again with His truth.

They love it. They have found that it is good for them. He also lives truth.

Since it is good for Him, He told them that it will be good for them if they obeyed it.

They love it. It is good for Him. It is directing their lives in the paths of peace and joy.

None of the inhabitants of heaven and the sinless universes has found any mistakes in the truth.

They have found nothing to add to it and nothing subtract from it. It is perfect. And God is absolution perfection. No man or woman is complete and fulfilled like Him.

He is greatly revered as the Elder of all the angels and saints. They obey all His commands very humbly. They have deep reverence and awe for Him.

They hold holy feasts every day to celebrate His live throughout heaven and the universes. He is the Commander-in-Chief of the Armed Forces of heaven.

There is no Commanding Officer in heaven or on the earth who orders Him around. No one is more powerful than Him. He is the only truth in existence in heaven and on the earth. There is no other truth that is found anywhere else.

Truth is divine. It is His character.

He touched the world with His finger when He healed the sick and raised the dead to life. Those miracles, though amazing, were very small. Bigger and more astounding miracles are yet to come your way.

He will do much more marvelous things for the children that He loves so much. Even eternity is not enough for Him to show you the wonders His everlasting powers with which He will bless your life.

Everyone in heaven stands in awe of Him. Even in your new created being, you will not have strength enough to praise Him for all the wonders He is doing and will do for you.

He brought out dry land out of the waters and put people on it. Even though Satan deceived His children into committing sin, He still loves them very much.

He cannot be defeated by demons and sinners. He can save you. He will take you to heaven.

Although He has the power to crush the fallen world under His feet, His love is for them is so great and infinite that He is holding them very tenderly in the palm of His hand.

He speaks to them very comfortingly, saying, "Fear thou not; for I am with thee: be not dismayed; for I am thy God: I will strengthen thee; yea, I will help thee; yea, I will uphold thee with the right hand of my righteousness" (Isaiah 41:10).

He is asking everyone not to fear and go running around looking for solutions to their problems. He is the Solution to all their worries, fears, guilt, shame, pain, and death.

He is already holding you with His omnipotent right hand. He is watching over your life.

He will empower you and make you a warlord to fight all wrongs. He loves all His children very deeply. He will take good care of each one of you very perfectly and royally.

He is as gentle as a lamb. But when it comes to protecting His children, He is as fierce and dangerous as a lion.

He will punish demons and sin that trouble His children with the fierceness of a lion and cleverness of a leopard. A leopard kills its victim by breaking its neck.

The Lord and Messiah crushed the head of Satan with His feet. He gave him a fatal blow. He fell on the devils and sin like a vulture.

They will not escape the destruction He will rain on them from the sky for all the deaths and havocs that they have wrecked on His children. He will punish them for the deaths of His children who are forever lost.

He is standing at your right hand to bless you. In fact, He is already in your heart to recreate Himself in you so that you may be strong and powerful over death, sin, Satan and all evil of this world.

As a powerful sword or plough or light guided missile, you will cut, crush and scatter all your cruel and brutal enemies into nothingness.

God will ashamed all your enemies before the holy angels and before all the inhabitants of the all the universes on that day of your total deliverance because of all the trials, temptations and murders they have committed against you. He will wipe them out.

You are poor because you are no longer the king

or queen of this world as God had assigned Adam and Eve to be before they sinned.

You are in need of salvation because you are sick mentally, socially, physically and spiritually. It is not only a matter of when you will die no matter how safe you protect yourself.

Of course, you must be safe all the time. However, eventually, old age will steal your precious life. The Good News is that the Holy Spirit wants to give you back the kingdom of this world as well as of heaven as king or queen under Him.

He wants to remove death from your body and fill you with His eternal life. He wants to more barrenness and deserts of sin from your life.

He wants to irrigate it with His water of life. The Great Lord Jesus, your Savior, promises to fill you with the Third Godhead, the Holy Spirit. He compares the Holy Spirit to water.

You are body is about 98% water. It is your life. In the spiritual level, the Holy Spirit is 100% in your body to give you eternal life.

Your Christ says, "But the water that I will give him shall become in him a fountain of water, springing up into life everlasting" (John 4:14).

The Spirit is planting trees in your heart. He is making you into a tall, proud and deep rooted cedar. You are His timber.

He is making you, His cedar, to in-lay the inner temple. Even though sin has made you fall short like the lowly myrtle tree of the glory of God but like this same tree, you have fragrance.

This sweet perfume is the Holy Spirit living in your soul. He is bringing eternity, hope, love, peace, goodness, patience, joy, etc. in your life.

The Holy Spirit is love, peace, joy, and all the goodness of Divinity. Therefore, His divine kingdom reflects His divine character. He soothes your wounded sin-filled hearted with oil of joy. He heals your sin-inflicted sores with supernatural olive oil.

When He heals you, you become very holy, righteous and joyful kid to your Holy Dad. He came into the earth "To appoint unto them that mourn in Zion, to give unto them beauty for ashes, the oil of joy for mourning, the garment of praise for the spirit of heaviness; that they might be called trees of righteousness, the planting of the LORD, that he might be glorified" (Isaiah 61:3).

Just as the Holy Spirit was with Jesus when He was walking the earth as a man, He is with you. He is making you strong in the faith and in righteousness.

In return, you will give joy, peace and comfort from this world where most of His children are lost.

And God the Father exclaims happily at your change of character, "I have no greater joy than to hear that my children walk in truth" (3 John 1:4).

When we hold on to the hand of the Holy Spirit, He creates faith in us to believe in the Invisible God. He fills our hearts with peace in the saving name of Jesus Christ our Savior.

Instead of sin making us hostile, unloving, hateful and proud towards our Creator and Father, we will become friendly, kind and loving to Him. "For which reason, because we have righteousness through faith, let us be at peace with God through our Lord Jesus Christ; Through whom, in the same way, we have been able by faith to come to this grace in which we now are; and let us have joy in hope of the glory of God.

And not only so, but let us have joy in our troubles: in the knowledge that trouble gives us the power of waiting; And waiting gives experience; and experience, hope" (Romans 5:1-4, BBE).

You are singing the praises of the Holy Spirit for His indwelling power in your soul that is changing you day by day to become like Him. You are singing His praises for the wonderful salvation He has provided for you through the death of the Messiah.

You sing many songs about the Trinity in heaven. "Let them shout for joy, and be glad, that favour my righteous cause: yea, let them say continually, Let the LORD be magnified, which hath pleasure in the prosperity of his servant" (Psalms 35:27).

He wants you to make an agreement with Him that you will find joy only in each other. It will give you tremendous joy when you surrender your heart to Him. You will never tire of singing about the truth that brought you home.

Move the glory of the Lord forward in this world by exalting Him very highly in your thoughts, words, and everything that you do. Let them for His honor alone.

He will never forget His slave. He will empower you and you will be an eternal success.

3 CHAPTER

DAVID CALLED HIM LORD

1. David called Him Lord

Orazio Gentileschi - 1610, David

The Pharisees had prided themselves as the greatest spiritual teachers in the world. The Messiah tested their knowledge of God.

"While the Pharisees were gathered together, Jesus asked them, Saying, What think ye of Christ? whose son is he? They say unto him, The Son of David" (Matthew 22:41, 42).

The Messiah asked them, "Why do you need a Righteous Messiah to mother you and give you life? Whose Son is He who is called the Love?"

They quoted their usual quotation to the God of love, "The Son of David."

He spoke to them with the power and authority of God. "He saith unto them, How then doth David in spirit call him Lord, saying, The LORD said unto my Lord, Sit thou on my right hand, till I make thine enemies thy footstool? If David then call him Lord, how is he his son?" (Matthew 22:43–45).

He said, "How was David such a winner even over death? The Holy Spirit birthed the right spirit in him. Under His inspirations, he exclaimed, 'God the caring Lord said to my Lord, 'Sit at My right hand that creates life because You are the Righteous God. I am I showing to the world My love.

I will come against the enemies that have been beating you up. I will gather them and cast them at Your feet so that You can punish them.'

If David is calling Me 'the Lord of lords and caring Daddy,' how did the Eternal and Conqueror of death become his Son?"

But they could not explain or even admit that God could incarnate Himself into the human family. "And no man was able to answer him a word, neither durst any man from that day forth ask him any more questions" (Matthew 22:46). He incarnated Himself into the family of King David in order to have human flesh. He became one of us. He experienced our temptations, trials, and death. He never sinned during His life on earth. He lived a righteous life. And His life is counted as the holy and righteous life of everyone ever born on this earth.

When you accept Him as your personal Savior, you are no longer looked at as a sinner in heaven. You are looked as another Jesus Christ and entitled to the powers, eternal life, joy, peace, and all goodness of heaven.

King David ruled the King of Israel a little over 3,000 years ago. He ruled her for 40 years. Samuel the Judge and Prophet of Israel who anointed the last born of Jesse said that he was the last born among seven brothers.

Ezra the scribe who is believed to be the one to rewrite I and II Kings into I and II Chronicles wrote that David was the last born son among eight brothers.

In any case, he was the last born of Jesse of Bethlehem. As the last born, he was assigned the humble task of looking after the family sheep.

He was an excellent shepherd. He took good care of his father's sheep. None of them was lost to the wild animals during his care.

He killed a huge ferocious bear and a huge dangerous lion when they tried to attack his sheep. As he shepherd the sheep in the quietness of the mountain sides and valleys surrounding Bethlehem, he meditated on God. During these times, he composed a number of the Psalms that we love today such as Psalm 23:

> "The LORD is my shepherd;
> I shall not want.
> He maketh me to lie down in green pastures: he leadeth me beside the still waters.
> He restoreth my soul:
> he leadeth me in the paths of righteousness for his name's sake.
> Yea, though I walk through the valley of the shadow of death,
> I will fear no evil:
> for thou art with me;
> thy rod and thy staff they comfort me.
> Thou preparest a table before me in the presence of mine enemies:
> thou anointest my head with oil; my cup runneth over.
> Surely goodness and mercy shall follow me all the days of my life:
> and I will dwell in the house of the LORD for ever."

Because the Lord your Shepherd, He will help you not to burn with passions and adulterate with anyone or anything else. Both in this life and in heaven, He will lead you to graze in the pastures that He Himself has planted. He will satisfy your deep longings for the things that you cannot achieve on your own.

He will teach you what life is all about and will

fulfill all its needs. He will draw you to Himself because He is your Daddy. He has very deep passions for you to always be your best Daddy. He is the God of life and, therefore, He is your Water of life and love.

1896 By Providence Lithograph Company, I am the Good Shepherd

He is a very caring and loving God, and He has already started to show that to you before you were born. He has placed His loving hands on you and is leading you in the paths that will fulfill your passions for the best and the greatest things of life.

He laid His hand on you and is bring your spirit back into a life of righteousness. His own hand will supply you will life and the passion to live it to the full. It will be His life, God's life. He will lead you in the way of righteousness of God the Father because His Name is beautiful. His Name is Righteousness and Love.

And so even if you are walking through the secret way might take down into the valley of death, you will not be afraid. All the evil in the world will not make you tremble with fear because He is with you to supply you with His eternal.

His rod, which is His truth or the Law of love, and His staff, will guide you. His love is with you will be compassionate and faithful to you.

And since He is your Daddy, He is working very hard to place all the things that will fulfill your needs on the table that he has laid out before you. He anointed the head of the Messiah with the oil of eternal life and love, and He will anoint yours, too. He emptied the whole cup of oil on Him, and He will empty another one on you.

He is giving rest and life just as He gave to the Messiah when He resurrected Him from the death. He is making you into His righteous and loving image.

In addition to all that, He is poured all His fortunes that will watch over your life on you. And since He is also your Mother, She will be very merciful to you. He will watch over you and love you eternally.

You will always live in the house of the God of life. You will outspend eternity. And you will still continue to live in His house throughout other eternities to come.

While still a youth, David was secretly anointed as the next King of Israel while King Saul was on the throne. Soon after, he was sent to the war front by his father to check on the safety and welfare of his three old soldier-brothers who were enlisted in the king's royal army.

War has been declared between Israel and the Philistine. When he reached there, he found Goliath insulting God and all Israel.

David challenged him. This young brave boy killed the giant, the enemy of God and of Israel. From that day, he joined the servicemen of King Saul and lived most of the time in the palace. Between wars, he was the King's psychiatrist and comforter. He soothed the demented king by playing and singing soft religious music when he began to rave and stomp around the palace.

Eventually, the King gets wind of the secret anointing of David as the King of Israel. He became so jealous that he tried to murder David on several occasions. So David escaped and lived in the wilderness for a number of years in hiding. After the Death of King Saul, David was sought out by his own tribe.

They were the tribe of Judah who crowned him as

the King of Judah. The rest of Israel crowned the son of King Saul, Ishbosheth, as their king. After his murder by his own house workers, all Israel came to Hebron and crowned David as the King of a united Israel.

However, David was ordained by God to rule according to His divine directions and orders. He was to follow the dictates of God. He was a symbol of a Divine David who would come and rule in Israel. God selected David because he was spiritual and humble.

Although he was a sinner and sometimes did more grievous things than King Saul such as committing adultery with somebody's wife and then murdering her husband to cover it up. He married her.

He tried to legalize the marriage because there was a child involved. But when the Lord confronted him about the enormities of his sin, he repented.

He always repented humbly and truthfully whereas King Saul usually tried to make excuses for his shortcomings. King David fought neighboring kingdoms and nations who were a threat to his kingdom.

But he never went out on a war of conquest like some of his neighbors did in order to immortalize himself and create an empire such as the Syrians, Assyrians, Babylonians, Greeks and Romans.

He was the vicegerent of God. It was the directives of God that Jerusalem be a place of worship for Israel and all the above kingdoms, empires and the whole world. Therefore, King David symbolized an Eternal King who would come and govern His world kingdom from Jerusalem.

Since King David was only human, in that he could not save even himself from death, leave alone save Israel, there was a need for a better and more powerful King to rule Israel and the world. This King would be His Son. However, this Son was also the Lord and God of David.

He is God and yet He wanted to be a part of

David's family so that He could save His children from the deadly and evil government of Satan. The Almighty God came as the Son of King David to overthrow the government of Satan, liberate His children and set up His kingdom on earth.

David was both a Prophet and King. King David might have not known more information about the Trinity as we do now through the teachings of Christ Himself. Yet he had some knowledge about the Triune God. He prophesied that the Messiah of Israel would be the Adopted Son of God Most High.

A Divine Person from the throne on high will come to reclaim him from the dead and all believing Israel and gentile converts. Another Divine Person would be left in heaven.

He would be the final authority overseeing our salvation and destroying our enemies. King David spoke deep theology in Psalm chapter 2. He told the pagan nations to stop clamoring madly for the blood of the Anointed One or the Messiah. He said that they should stop fighting God.

> "Why do the nations rage,
> And the peoples meditate a vain thing?
> The kings of the earth set themselves,
> And the rulers take counsel together,
> Against Jehovah, and against his anointed, saying,
> Let us break their bonds asunder,
> And cast away their cords from us"
> (Psalms 2:1–3, ASV).

But God the Father declared to all evil kings and rulers of the darkness and their representatives among people, I have already ordained My Son as the Everlasting King of heaven and earth. He is ruling from His holy hill of Mount Zion.

He will destroy your evil grip over His children. He will destroy your sins, sorrows, death and hell and break them in pieces.

> "He that sitteth in the heavens will laugh:
> The Lord will have them in derision.
> Then will he speak unto them in his wrath,
> And vex them in his sore displeasure:
> Yet I have set my king Upon my holy hill of Zion"
> (Psalms 2:4–6, ASV).

King David was given insight into the mysteries of God by the Holy Spirit. He preached about a conversation that took place between God the Father and Second Godhead in heaven. The First Godhead said to the Second Godhead,

> "I will tell of the decree:
> Jehovah said unto me,
> Thou art my son;
> This day have I begotten thee"
> (Psalms 2:7, ASV).

God the Father confirmed that The Messiah is His Son during His baptism. "And it came to pass in those days, that Jesus came from Nazareth of Galilee, and was baptized of John in the Jordan.

And straightway coming up out of the water, he saw the heavens rent asunder, and the Spirit as a dove descending upon him: and a voice came out of the heavens, Thou art my beloved Son, in thee I am well pleased" (Mark 1:9–11, ASV).

Apostle Paul, that illustrious preacher, learnt and greatest Christian evangelist quoted King David, the father of Jesus Christ, extensively in Hebrews chapter 1. King David a good concept about the Divine origin of the Messiah who would rule on his throne in Jerusalem.

God the Father asks everyone to give His Son the

proper respect He deserves by giving Him the brotherly kiss. You must bow down and wet His flaming feet with your saliva. He is the ruler and owner of all nations of the earth.

Anyone who disobeys Him is setting himself or herself up for self-destruction. Without the life of God only death exists.

Therefore, the Almighty Father asks that we should all give due respect, reverence, honor and worship to the One who created, sustains and is saving us. In Him are our perfect joy and love and the full satisfactions of our spirits.

> "Ask of me, and I will give thee the nations for thine inheritance,
> And the uttermost parts of the earth for thy possession.
> Thou shalt break them with a rod of iron;
> Thou shalt dash them in pieces like a potter's vessel.
> Now therefore be wise, O ye kings:
> Be instructed, ye judges of the earth.
> Serve Jehovah with fear,
> And rejoice with trembling.
> Kiss the son, lest he be angry, and ye perish in the way,
> For his wrath will soon be kindled.
> Blessed are all they that take refuge in him"
> (Psalms 2:8–12, ASV).

God the Father asked the Messiah to ask Him to give all the lives of the pagans and their kingdoms and nations with all their wealth into His hands as His eternal inheritances. He will do it for Him because He is a righteous and loving Father.

He will rule them with His Law that is the truth and the life. The whole earth will be His kingdom.

He will love them like a mother would love her disobedience children unconditionally until it will break their pride. His love will be as strong as steel. He will break their troubles into pieces like potteries with His ironed rod and save them.

Be careful, you kings of the earth, about the Messiah. He will shock you one of these days with His awesome majesty when He takes over the government of this earth. He will teach the unjust judges of this earth that bend the law to suit their own interest a lesson that they will never forget.

The slaves of the Lord God and the Father of all will stand in awe of Him with the kind of fear brothers and sisters have for their powerful and courageous older brother that protects them from bullies. They will tremble before Him because of the tremendous love they will have for Him.

Welcome the Son of God into your hearts because He is also God. Do not tempt omnipotent powers that have made Him a great Father by your obstinate disobedience of not following Him.

They will whack you and made slaves out of you all. You will die on the way to heaven because of your disobedience against.

You will not survive. Your sins will slaughter on the altar of sacrifice and burn you all up. But eternally blessed are all those lively, honest, and faithful people who have gathered around their God. They have placed all their weighs on Him because He is the God of life and life.

God the Father declared that the salvation His Son provides is based on the grounds that He was the One who created Adam and Eve. He is the One who created the whole earth and everything in it.

He is the One who created space, time, stars, angels, etc. He lives forever and ever. The Father blessed the mission of His Son on the earth.

God the Messiah's eyes shines like the beautiful light of a million stars with love for you. His words of love for you and about you flow smoothly and sweetly like rivers of honey.

He speaks gracious, gently and kindly with patience and completely forgiveness of all your sins. On His forehead is Divine Royalty. This is the King of kings. He is the King of love. He is your Savior.

He is a Warrior-King. He must fight for your rights to be re-adopted back into His royal family. He is fighting all kinds of evil on your behalf. He is fighting sin with truth. He is fight death with eternal life. He is fighting Satan with truth, light, life, and love. And so God the Father said of His Son,

> "Thy throne, O God, is for ever and ever:
> A sceptre of equity is the sceptre of thy kingdom.
> Thou hast loved righteousness, and hated wickedness:
> Therefore God, thy God, hath anointed thee
> With the oil of gladness above thy fellows"
> (Psalms 45:6, 7, ASV).

The God of love has built His throne on righteousness and eternal life. It will continue to exist forever from one generation to another. His scepter is the scepter of an eternal Daddy. He will guide you with it very righteously. And as a loving Mother, He will always be protective about you.

Love has made Him a very powerful Mother. He would rather die that allow you to come to harm. He died that you may live eternally, joyfully, and peacefully. He is guiding His eternal kingdom with that same scepter of royalty, power, and love.

God made this solemn promise to David,

> "I have made a covenant with my chosen,
> I have sworn unto David my servant:
> Thy seed will I establish for ever,
> And build up thy throne to all generations. Selah.

My covenant will I not break,
Nor alter the thing that is gone out of my lips.
Once have I sworn by my holiness:
I will not lie unto David:
His seed shall endure forever,
And his throne as the sun before me.
It shall be established for ever as the moon,
And as the faithful witness in the sky. Selah"
(Psalms 89:3, 4, 34–37, ASV).

He said, "I have cut a covenant of love with My own hand with the brother to whom I like to tell what is in My mind. I have sworn that I would rather be lifted up and hanged on a tree than lie to David. I am going to build a house for His Seed, the righteous and eternally established God.

The Son of My passion will be His God of life. He will sit on the throne of all righteousness and eternal from generation to generation.

I will not weaken this covenant through neglect or abandonment. I will not change the promises that have come out of My lips that breathe eternal life.

I heal people. I have commanded Myself on the pain of death by hanging that I will not deceive David. I am All-Righteous. I am very passionate about life.

His Righteous Seed, the God of love, will be His God of life. He will sit on His throne of righteousness, eternal life, and love for all everlasting years to come. His throne will blaze and dazzle very brightly like the sun in My sight.

It will be very beautiful like the brightly shinning moon in the night. He will live in My house to enjoy the goodness of the God of life for all eternal years to come. He will be my Witness about My saving power just like the stars of the universes are the witnesses to My creative powers."

This God who swore all these promises to David sent His Son into the world as a Man. He came into the world through the family line of King David to rule as the Eternal King forever.

That is the promise God gave to David – that He will sit on David's throne as the God of gods, King of kings, and Lord of lords eternal. King David prophesied about the crucifixion and final triumph of Jesus in Psalm 22.

He prophesied that the Messiah would be a lonely Man. He would be rejected by the nation of Israel. He would be persecuted by the leaders of the religious institution of His day. Indeed, one of His own disciples sold Him into the hands of the murderers for a mere thirty pieces of silver. He was Judas the traitor. Another one of his chief disciples denied him that he never knew him. He was Peter.

> "My God, my God, why hast thou forsaken me?
> Why art thou so far from helping me, and from the words of my groaning?
> O my God, I cry in the daytime, but thou answerest not;
> And in the night season, and am not silent.
> But thou art holy, O thou that inhabitest the praises of Israel.
> Our fathers trusted in thee:
> They trusted, and thou didst deliver them.
> They cried unto thee, and were delivered:
> They trusted in thee, and were not put to shame"
> (Psalms 22:1–5, ASV).

Indeed, the Messiah did cry to God with tears to help Him conquer sin and death. In His capacity as the High Priest of Israel and of the world, He prayed on your behalf to God to save Him from being defeated by sin and death.

He conquered evil to help you conquer them through His power. His prayers were not usually the little happy prayers people usually pray. They were deep and heart-wrenching prayers.

He prayed with many agonies, tears, sighing, and

weeping for your salvation. "As he saith also in another place, Thou art a priest for ever After the order of Melchizedek.

Who in the days of his flesh, having offered up prayers and supplications with strong crying and tears unto him that was able to save him from death, and having been heard for his godly fear, though he was a Son, yet learned obedience by the things which he suffered; and having been made perfect, he became unto all them that obey him the author of eternal salvation; named of God a high priest after the order of Melchizedek" (Hebrews 5:6–10, ASV).

God had told David what would happen to His Son. His murder and mockery took place just as God had said through David about 1,000 years earlier. David sung this sad funeral dirge about the sad murder of the Messiah.

James Tissot, 1836-1902, What the Messiah saw from the cross

"Many bulls have compassed me;
Strong bulls of Bashan have beset me round.
They gape upon me with their mouth,
As a ravening and a roaring lion"
(Psalms 22:12, 13, ASV).

He also prophesied,

"But I am a worm, and no man;
A reproach of men, and despised of the people.
All they that see me laugh me to scorn:
They shoot out the lip, they shake the head,
saying,
Commit thyself unto Jehovah;
Let him deliver him:
Let him rescue him, seeing he delighteth in him"
(Psalms 22:6–8, ASV).

All take prophecies were fulfilled just as King David predicted about His adopted Divine Son. Annas and Caiaphas, the presiding High Priests in the temple and over the nation of Judea, and their supporters among the priests who mocked God.

"In like manner also the chief priests mocking him, with the scribes and elders, said, He saved others; himself he cannot save.

He is the King of Israel; let him now come down from the cross, and we will believe on him. He trusteth on God; let him deliver him now, if he desireth him: for he said, I am the Son of God" (Matthew 27:41–43, ASV).

God inspired King David to describe how dying on the cross would take place. The Lord said that blood clot would take place and water would emerge. There would be internal organ failures such as the heart and they would cease to function like wax that has melted.

They would die. The weight of hanging in midair

would dry up the strength of the dying man. The end would be sooner than expected.

"I am poured out like water,
And all my bones are out of joint:
My heart is like wax;
It is melted within me.
My strength is dried up like a potsherd;
And my tongue cleaveth to my jaws;
And thou hast brought me into the dust of death"
(Psalms 22:14, 15, ASV).

There were, indeed, dogs. They betrayed and murdered of Jesus. They were more ferocious than natural dogs with four legs. These were men who were trained to kill without any mercy. They were the dogs of war. They were the Roman soldiers.

Under the orders of Annas and Caiaphas, the High Priests of Israel and Governor Pilate, the Roman Emperor's representative in Judea, the mercenaries had beaten God 80 lashes. They had mistreated him countless numbers of times. Finally, they crucified Him on the cross on Mt Calvary.

"For dogs have compassed me:
A company of evil-doers have inclosed me;
They pierced my hands and my feet.
I may count all my bones;
They look and stare upon me.
They part my garments among them,
And upon my vesture do they cast lots.
But be not thou far off, O Jehovah:
O thou my succor, haste thee to help me.
Deliver my soul from the sword,
My darling from the power of the dog.
Save me from the lion's mouth;
Yea, from the horns of the wild-oxen thou hast
answered me"
(Psalms 22:16–21, ASV).

Everything took place just as God had fore warned would take place ten decades earlier through David. "The soldiers therefore, when they had crucified Jesus, took his garments and made four parts, to every soldier a part; and also the coat: now the coat was without seam, woven from the top throughout.

They said therefore one to another, Let us not rend it, but cast lots for it, whose it shall be: that the scripture might be fulfilled, which saith, They parted my garments among them, And upon my vesture did they cast lots" (John 19:23, 24, ASV).

God told David to tell the world that the Cross and the grave were not to be the end of His Adopted Son, who would also be the Adopted Son of King David, the Anointed One who was anointed with His own blood to clear the guilty consciences of sinners.

The Lord said that the Messiah would triumph over His enemies and enemies of Israel and of the world. He would give praise to God the Almighty for helping Him in fighting Satan and sin and defeating them completely.

"I will declare thy name unto my brethren:
In the midst of the assembly will I praise thee.
Ye that fear Jehovah, praise him;
All ye the seed of Jacob, glorify him;
And stand in awe of him, all ye the seed of Israel.
For he hath not despised nor abhorred the
affliction of the afflicted;
Neither hath he hid his face from him;
But when he cried unto him, he heard.
Of thee cometh my praise in the great assembly:
I will pay my vows before them that fear him.
The meek shall eat and be satisfied;
They shall praise Jehovah that seek after him: Let
your heart live for ever"
(Psalms 22:22–26, ASV).

2. The Messiah is the Rod and Staff of the Father

Once upon a time, there were two friends who were walking through a thick forest. They stumbled into the home of some of the most dangerous snakes in the world. The snakes started chasing them.

The first man was a perfectionist. He always looked clean and well-groomed. He had a couple of degrees to his name. His experiences and qualifications filled a number of pages. His language had perfect syllabus. His work was perfect.

As he ran through the forest, he was looking for the perfect stick to use to kill the snake that was almost upon him. He wanted a stick that was exactly four feet long, 6 inches thick, smoothly cut, chiseled, sanded, and polished bright by an experienced and educated carpenter.

Meanwhile, his friend took a few steps and grabbed the first stick in sight. He was an ordinary kind of guy. He dressed and spoke like a commoner. He found a stick that was not perfect but big enough to kill the snake.

He quickly grabbed it and killed the snake that was chasing him around in that virgin forest. Then he ran to the assistance of his friend with his stick in hand. He hit the head of the snake just before it could strike his friend. He killed it, too. This is only an allegory.

But the saying is true: "Dangerous and poisonous snakes are killed with the nearest stick you can get." The Messiah, My Son, is the closest Person in M heart. So I asked Him to be the Rod to smash the heads of demons and liberate you. Cry to Him all the time for your spiritual as well as other needs. He will help you.

God the Father says, "I, your Dad who is the Great I AM WHO I AM, personally chose the Second Godhead to be your Savior. I welcomed Him into the bosom of my heart as a Son with both of my hands. I placed my hands on His head and anointed Him with the oil of love to be Shiloh and Savior of mankind. I then sent Him to be my Representative on earth. I sent Him to you to tell you all that is in my heart.

Death has cut King David down like someone cutting down a giant tree but leaving the stump still sticking above ground. However, his roots did not die. His roots were still alive. David's death symbolized the deaths of all believers.

They died still believing in Me that I can resurrect them back to life again. Though they and you also, in a way is also dead, are alive because you are roots are deeply imbedded in Me."

Hyenas are now eating children of the earth. Death reigns as a king over all of you. Yet, your case is not hopeless. Your roots are in Christ. From that seemingly dead stump of Jesse, a shoot grew up.

A Son was born. He grew up like a shoot growing from a stump of a tree. He grew up tall, strong and a giant Living Tree. He occupies the earth, heaven and all the universes. All angelic birds and human birds make home in His branches. "And there shall come forth a rod out of the stem of Jesse, and a Branch shall grow out of his roots:

And the spirit of the LORD shall rest upon him, the spirit of wisdom and understanding, the spirit of counsel and might, the spirit of knowledge and of the fear of the LORD; And shall make him of quick understanding in the fear of the LORD: and he shall not judge after the sight of his eyes, neither reprove after the hearing of his ears:

But with righteousness shall he judge the poor, and reprove with equity for the meek of the earth: and he shall smite the earth with the rod of his mouth, and with the breath of his lips shall he slay the wicked. And righteousness shall be the girdle of his loins, and faithfulness the girdle of his reins" (Isaiah 11:1–5).

The love and forgiving mercy of Jesus Christ has

hardly begun to be showered on the world. "Now to him who is able to do all things more abundantly than we desire or understand, according to the power that worketh in us: To him be glory in the church and in Christ Jesus, unto all generations, world without end. Amen" (Ephesians 3:20, 21, DRB).

It is deeper than you can be able to grasp, higher than your highest and best thoughts and broader than infinity. He loves you more deeply, intensely, abundantly and passionately than humans can.

Being the All-Powerful God, He has all the powers at His disposal to reinforce His love to you by lavishing you with great blessings that this world is not able to contain. That is why He will create a completely new heaven and earth so that some of His plans and dreams for you can realized in a greater measure than the first creation of this earth, sun, moon and stars and what they contained.

His love is your greatest blessing. His death on the cross is a confirmation of that awesome and abundant love. And that is just the beginning of what this wonderful Jesus will do for you.

He is your Protector from those roaring angry lions that are ready to paunch on you and devour you. "Be sober and watch: because your adversary the devil, as a roaring lion, goeth about seeking whom he may devour.

Whom resist ye, strong in faith: knowing that the same affliction befalls, your brethren who are in the world" (1 Peter 5:8, 9, DRB). He has presented Himself to you by presenting Himself to you as my perfect, awesome and glorious gift of love.

The Lord Jesus has surrounded you with His gracious love. You are so precious to Him like the apple of His eye. Anyone who hurts you is hurting His eyes, and makes Him cry. "Shew forth thy wonderful mercies; thou who savest them that trust in thee.

From them that resist thy right hand keep me, as the apple of thy eye. Protect me under the shadow of thy wings. From the face of the wicked who have afflicted me. My enemies have surrounded my soul" (Psalms 17:7–9, DRB).

He will hide you in the shadow of His hand like He hid Noah and his family in the ark when the whole world was flooded with water. Everyone drowned except His beloved godly family survived the Flood.

He will protect you when the world goes up in flame. He will take you out of this world and hide you in his arms just like He protected Lot when Sodom and Gomorrah were burnt up because of they were die-hard brazen sinners.

They were a bunch of homosexuals and lesbians. They not only love sinning but they encourage each other to do worse sins. They were bitter and angry at those who were heterosexuals or celibate.

They dared to speak wicked words even against holy angels who are pure and celibate. They wanted to rape them. Their cups of sin became full and overflowed. It brought swift hell fire on them.

But the Lord will save you from it. "Behold this was the iniquity of Sodom thy sister, pride, fulness of bread, and abundance, and the idleness of her, and of her daughters: and they did not put forth their hand to the needy, and the poor.

And they were lifted up, and committed abominations before me: and I took them away as thou hast seen" (Ezekiel 16:49, 50, DRB).

God the Father said, "Yet, I had loved them so much. I gave them fruitful land that produced luxuriantly like the Garden of Eden. I filled their homes with good things: gold, silver, rich clothing, etc. They were fabulously rich. I gave them peace in their cities and in the neighborhood. But they fell in love with themselves and refused to honor completely.

They were proud and arrogant. They gave credit to themselves for all the accumulation of wealth and refused to thank Me for creating them into my word and for giving them my earth. Instead, they adored their bodies and spent their lives in sinful lifestyles that were against my Law.

The same thing is happening even today. The world is becoming another Sodom. The more I bless a country with good things, the more wicked they become. Instead of praising Me for all the blessings I give them, they worship themselves, gold, silver, demons, etc. their behavior will condemn them. It will explode into fire.

Another fire will come from heaven to purify the earth just like what happened in Sodom and Gomorrah. "As Sodom and Gomorrha and the neighbouring cities, in like manner, having given themselves to fornication and going after other flesh, were made an example, suffering the punishment of eternal fire" (Jude 1:7, DRB).

But do not worry about the fires of hell, just continue to trust in my love. My Son will save you.

I am the Rod of righteousness. I execute justice for those who call on My name. "He is the Rock; His work is perfect. For all His ways are just, a God of faithfulness, and without evil; just and upright is He" (Deuteronomy 32:4).

As God the Creator, I made you perfect. Sin is just a temporary rude intruder. I will eliminate it from your soul by the rod of punishment. I will faithfully carry out my work until you are fully and completely liberated. I will recreate my perfection in your mind, heart, body and spirit you.

I have given you, the church, in marriage to Jesus, your Husband. You are His beautiful bride. He does not hate you because you are a sinner. He loves you. He wants to remove sins from your heart so that you can enjoy living together for all ages to come.

He is holding your hand and says to you, "Israel, I will make you my wife; I will be true and faithful; I will show you constant love and mercy and make you mine forever" (Hosea 2:19, GNB).

You got to learn to handle Him right. Relate to

Him by loving Him and being faithful to Him. He is urging you to be completely true and faithful to Him because you are His wife. His life on earth was spent on your behalf as His wife just as He had promised Adam and Eve that He would crush the head of the devil and rescue you.

Therefore, be faithful to Him and do not commit immoralities with Satan, other people, yourself or the things of this world. The world and everything in it will be burnt up. I will only my children who are wedded to Christ. Therefore, rise up and leave the works of darkness. Do not think, talk or go around looking for sin. Come to Husband. He will save you.

So I am encouraging to "Stand firm, and you will save yourselves" (Luke 21:19, GNB).

Always make sure that your mind is occupied about Me. This will direct your tongue to talk about Me and your hands and feet to do my will.

This can come about if you will pray to Me to give you a passion for not just reading but by carefully, patiently and persistently spending a long time every day in studying, analyzing and writing down what you are learning about Me from the Bible. "Watch ye: stand fast in the faith: do manfully and be strengthened. Let all your things be done in charity" (1 Corinthians 16:13, 14, DRB).

I will then tell you what to do about the knowledge you are learning about Me if you are not already preaching. I will give you a special ministry just fit for you to let the world know and love Me just as you love Me. Keep busy chasing Me and also your Beloved Savior and the Father of your spirit. He is called the Holy Spirit.

You will never regret you decision to love and be committed to the Trinity all your life. It will do you good. You will be very happy someday that you made that decision to follow Me no matter what. You will sing with joy in giving Me all your heart, mind, strength, time and everything.

After all, I fathered you. You belong to Me. So you are giving what already is mine. "Or know you not that your members are the temple of the Holy Ghost, who is in you, whom you have from God: and you are not your own?

For you are bought with a great price. Glorify and bear God in your body" (1 Corinthians 6:19, 20, DRB).

You are a child of my heart. You will never understand fully how much I love you even when you become very intelligent and wise after spending many eternities with Me. Even when you are in heaven, you words will not be able to describe the love I have for you.

I am God. My love is intense, abundant and everlasting. It is stronger and deeper than the love of all my angelic and human children. That love is completely yours. So take Me. Love Me and you will be very happy. Study the Bible.

It is better than all the text books in the world. It is my word. Just as my word created heaven and earth, so will it also recreate you.

You will be a new everlasting, glorious and happy creature. Obey and follow Me every day. Trust in my gracious kindness, love, power and promises.

Pray constantly fervently with all your heart and mind. I praise you because you have loved Me. You have not abandoned faith in Me. Even though you are sinful, yet you love Me. That is what I count as eternally invaluable.

I am also committed in being your Dad and Savior forever and ever. I am fighting your battles for you. Through Me, you are a conqueror. I met you in your sinful state. I reconcile you to myself by the death of my Son.

We are friends now. Even though sometimes you hate Me when you commit sin, we are still friends. I will set you free from the corruption of sin and the power of death.

When I put my everlasting life into you at the Second Coming of my Son which is also my Coming in visible glory and that of the Holy Spirit, too, you will be a conqueror over death.

I am the one who gave you life. I am Daddy, and you are my beloved baby. You will live with Me and that will be eternally gorgeous and great.

The Messiah has lifted up His hand before Me and swore solemnly to bring you to Me in heaven. He is making Me known to you as the God and King of this world. Come back to Me, children of Jesus Christ.

He chose you to be my children just as He said here, "You have not chosen me: but I have chosen you; and have appointed you, that you should go and should bring forth fruit; and your fruit should remain: that whatsoever you shall ask of the Father in my name, he may give it you" (John 15:16, DRB).

The Messiah chose you because He is completely delighted and is very happy with you. Actually, He is terribly in love with you so much so that He became an inferior human in order to win your heart.

He brought Me, the Holy Spirit and all the angels from heaven down to earth to save you. You are really precious and loved by Him.

He has appointed you as a co-owner with Him of my kingdom. But you must learn how to govern my kingdom first before I can give it to you. I govern my kingdom by Laws of the Ten Commandments. Learn them.

Practice them. I will help you to live them well. And you will be on your way to owning my kingdom and ruling it perfectly very soon.

The Messiah is the true witness of God. I will do whatever He asks Me to do for you just as He had told you. "And in that day you shall not ask me anything. Amen, amen, I say to you: if you ask the Father anything in my name, he will give it you.

In that day, you shall ask in my name: and I say not to you that I will ask the Father for you. For the

Father himself loveth you, because you have loved me and have believed that I came out from God" (John 16:23, 26, 27, DRB).

In fact, He is God the divine and powerful Creator of the worlds without number. Whatever my promises my Son gives, He will carry them out because He is the Truth. He is a Judge and Conquering Warrior. He will make your salvation come to pass.

He has chosen you to be a brave and courageous soldier of the gospel. So do not give up when the fighting is becoming much more furious and dangerous.

Fight on. The Captain is already ahead of you. He is killing the giants. He has won over sin, death and the devil.

He has won heaven to be your everlasting home. "And I saw heaven opened: and behold a white horse. And he that sat upon him was called faithful and true: and with justice doth he judge and fight.

And his eyes were as a flame of fire: and on his head were many diadems. And he had a name written, which no man knoweth but himself. And he was clothed with a garment sprinkled with blood.

And his name is called: THE WORD OF GOD. And the armies that are in heaven followed him on white horses, clothed in fine linen, white and clean. And out of his mouth proceedeth a sharp two-edged sword, that with it he may strike the nations.

And he shall rule them with a rod of iron: and he treadeth the winepress of the fierceness of the wrath of God the Almighty. And he hath on his garment and on his thigh written: KING OF KINGS AND LORD OF LORDS" (Revelation 19:11–16, DRB).

Those that are fighting you are not strong. You can beat them. So hold onto the faith. I knew from ancient of times that you are a winner. In fact, you are winning. I will exalt you in this world.

One day, they will see you as a prince or princess in my kingdom. They will be outside the walls of New

Jerusalem. They will not even be able to look at you because you will be shining like the sun and blind their eyes.

He is your Father. He made you. Moreover, He bought you from the devil with His own life. He is building you up in my saving faith. Therefore, obey Him implicitly. He experienced all your troubles personally. So He understands your needs.

He might not fulfill all your heart's desires but there is one prayer that He will never fail to answer and that is the need to be saved from eternal death.

That is the best gift He will never fail to give you. The gift is His own self as your beloved Savior and Brother.

He will answer your prayer to be saved from sin so as to give perfect glory to my name as your Dad and not the devil. "Because I go to the Father: and whatsoever you shall ask the Father in my name, that will I do: that the Father may be glorified in the Son" (John 14:13, DRB).

2. The awesome reaction of God when you cry out to Him for help

Enhanced storm

When you are in pain, God the Father gets really angry at the demons, wild nature and anyone who has hurt you so badly. Like any parents who has feelings for his or her children, the Spirit of the heats up when He is angry. He is hurting for His children. Smoke escapes from His nostrils.

They flare into living fires before Him. "There went up a smoke out of his nostrils, and fire out of his mouth devoured: coals were kindled by it" (Psalms 18:8). He breathes very heavily with sorrow because you are suffering.

Since He is All-Powerful, His breathes can turn into fire when He is not happy. As He flies towards you to assist you, His angry mood creates fire that shoot from His mouth.

They are all consuming fires. "A fire goeth before him, and burneth up his enemies round about" (Psalms 97:3). They can burn everything in its path.

The fires are so intense that they can set planets ablaze and turn into burning coals. "Our God shall come, and shall not keep silence: a fire shall devour before him, and it shall be very tempestuous round about him" (Psalms 50:3).

Your God is coming to help you. He will not

listen to your enemies who are telling Him not to help you. But He will listen only to you and fulfill all your needs, if not now, He will fulfill every one of them on the day of the Messiah's Second Coming. Roaring storms of fires spread out all around Him.

They are blown forward as He descends down to the earth to save. They are always ready to devour any obstacle that stands on the way of the Master. They are His burning two-edged very sharp swords. They cut without a miss.

Heaven and the all the universes fall apart when the Lord is hurrying down to assist you. They part ways to the right and left. They make Him a broad highway to pass through. He will do the same thing on the day of the Second Coming of the Messiah.

He will sweep the suns, moon and stars out of His way like clouds being drive by a strong wind. He will come down and rescue you from hell. "He bowed the heavens also, and came down: and darkness was under his feet" (Psalms 18:9). He will descend from heaven like lightning.

He will come surrounded by His holy angels. It will look as if they are carrying Him on their backs because they have surrounded Him as thick as buzzing bees. "Give ear, O Shepherd of Israel, thou that leadest Joseph like a flock; thou that dwellest between the cherubims, shine forth" (Psalms 80:1).

Though you are an insignificant speck of dust that is not noticeable in comparison to the gigantic heaven and universe, the Creator God has made you His equal. He stoops down to listen to your prayers. He, actually, comes down in person to tend to your needs.

He is a dependable Assistant of the human race because He is their Miracle Worker. He has made Himself one of them so that He can take their temptations, diseases, deaths, sorrows, pains, tears, etc. on Himself.

He is the Good Shepherd. He is watching over them and guiding. Though they are as foolish as sheep,

He is changing them into brightly shinning, energetic, and eternal stars so that He can shepherd them in awesome ways from one eternity to another. "Look at the sky and see. Who created these things?

Who brings out the stars one by one? He calls them all by name. Because of the greatness of his might and the strength of his power, not one of them is missing" (Isaiah 40:26, GW).

The Lord is asking you to study and have some knowledge of astronomy. It will build your faith in the existence and power of God in ways you can never imagine. Study His creation and especially the universes with open eyes, mind, and heart.

Do not learn true science with preconceive human theories such as evolution. It will hinder you from learning true sciences very fast in greater details.

You will learn things that will help you all your life and in the next world to come. Make the study of the creation of this world and all the universes as one of the priorities of your life.

If you can afford a telescope, watch the sky during clear night and study the stars, galaxies, constellations, universes, etc. Find as much materials as you can on them and read them. You will realize how great creation really is. It will lift your mind from being consumed with the daily struggles and place it in the hands of God.

He created them in groups as they came out of His hand. And He is making you to be one of them in the future. You are going to be one of the soldiers that will march around the universes like the rolling of the universes as they march forward.

Though He has more children than the number of stars in the universes, He knows you by name. He will call you to by name when He is talking to you. He will never forget your name come all eternities upon eternities without end.

When you cry to Him, He will come down bolting like thunder. He surrounded by whirlwind or tornadoes as if they are the wings of a gigantic bird. "And he rode upon a cherub, and did fly: yea, he did fly upon the wings of the wind" (Psalms 18:10).

His glory is too brilliant for the eyes of mere creatures like angels and people to see. So He has covered Himself up with thick dark clouds of water to absorb some of the tremendous brightly shinning flashes of fire and energy coming out of Him as well as protect the eyes of His children from being burned by them.

He made darkness his secret place; his pavilion round about him were dark waters and thick clouds of the skies. At the brightness that was before him his thick clouds passed, hail stones and coals of fire" (Psalms 18:11, 12).

As He was leaving heaven, brilliant lights preceded Him. They lit up the way ahead of Him because He is the Elder above all. He is God the Creator, and King of the Ages. Thick clouds respect as King of all and bowed at His feet.

They parted ways so that His glories may be seen. Uninhabited planets explode before Him and disintegrate as He rolls down faster than the speed of light. He is the Father of all.

When He hears your cry, He roars in anger from His throne in heaven like a dangerous and angry lion or lioness whose cub is being stolen. He comes charging like a lion to rescue His cub.

Heavens shakes in wonder and awe at the awesome love God has for His children. "And the posts of the door moved at the voice of him that cried, and the house was filled with smoke" (Isaiah 6:4).

God is more powerful than all the powers of heaven put together. When He gives a command, the foundation of heaven would quake with awe and surprise at His greatness.

It is suffers through quaking to try to show respect and love to the Creator of all. As the foundation of heaven quakes, the incense on the altars increase the volume of increase in volume and release thick amounts of sweet smelling smoke.

He speaks from on high and orders that you must be saved from sin and death so that they can give you no further pain. Showers of meteorites break out before Him when He is speaking.

They produced beautiful fireworks of wonder and awe. "The LORD also thundered in the heavens, and the Highest gave his voice; hail stones and coals of fire. Yea, he sent out his arrows, and scattered them; and he shot out lightnings, and discomfited them" (Psalms 18:13, 14).

He sends His angels ahead of Him to root out the demons from before you. He releases His powers. They fly swiftly like lightning and drove the demons far from you. He will rescue from all your sins.

He will give lots of trouble all evil one of these days. He will burn them all up. He will recover you from the land of the dead.

The earth came forward and bowed before the angry Father of the people of the earth. His children are hurting.

The mountains and hills like moved out of His way like strong military forces. They shook back and forth and to their very foundations like really good belly dancers.

They were all afraid of the Creator. "Then the earth shook and trembled; the foundations also of the hills moved and were shaken, because he was wroth" (Psalms 18:7).

He was very angry because you were hurting. "Bow thy heavens, O LORD, and come down: touch the mountains, and they shall smoke" (Psalms 144:5).

He will show all the universes that He is your powerful and caring Father. He will descend down in a blaze of fire that will light up the sky like lightning flashes. When He steps on the top on the mountains, they will explode into pieces. They will burn down.

He will not spare bodies of water either. He will

show them His great powers that He is Someone not to contend with. He who vomited the waters of the oceans, seas, lakes, rivers, etc. out His mouth has the power to dry them up by His fiery breaths. "Then the channels of waters were seen, and the foundations of the world were discovered at thy rebuke, O LORD, at the blast of the breath of thy nostrils" (Psalms 18:15). All eyes will see the bottom of the oceans, seas, lakes, etc. when He dries them up.

He will reach out His hand from hand and grasp you before you fall into that deep abyss awful despair and death. He can dry up all the waters in the world to rescue you from the deepest hole in the earth into which sin, troubles, and/or death have sunk you. "He sent from above, he took me, he drew me out of many waters.

For this shall every one that is godly pray unto thee in a time when thou mayest be found: surely in the floods of great waters they shall not come nigh unto him" (Psalms 18:6; 32:6).

He has prayed for you that your faith may not waver but always stay put on Him. He will smooth the rough places. He will take you into His arms. He will make you a model of peace and joy for all the world and even angels to see and imitate.

He will make you as divinely as possible that human beings can be in their limited capacities as mere creatures. The floods of human conflicts, diseases, sins, etc. will not sweep you away. He will not forget or forsake you.

He will save you from the power of Satan and his stooges. "He delivered me from my strong enemy, and from them which hated me: for they were too strong for me" (Psalms 18:17).

He will not only save you from those monstrous enemies such as demons, sin, and hell but give you great blessings. He will remove from your body harmful and incapacitating things such as diseases, injuries, old age, etc. because they do not allow you to perform your work at your maximum potential. "And my soul shall be joyful in the LORD: it shall rejoice in his salvation.

All my bones shall say, LORD, who is like unto thee, which deliverest the poor from him that is too strong for him, yea, the poor and the needy from him that spoileth him?" (Psalms 35:9).

The Lord will save you. He will give you deep inner joy and peace in the very depth of your spirit. You will shout, dance, run around, jump up, and down, somersault, etc. because it will be very difficult for you to keep your joy all inside. Your bones will be full of life, energy, and vitality. Your physical body will rejoice at the goodness of the Creator. He will reproduce His Spirit and power in you.

You will thank you for dismissing all those monsters that have been harming you from your body and from your life. He will repaired destroyed or wasted lives.

He will return eternal life back into the bodies of those who have been crucified by sin and by death. He will provide for them their food, water, clothes, shelter, eternal life, etc.

The Lord knows the troubles of the wretched men and women of the earth that have been reduced to nothingness by sin. He knows that they are being storm tossed by the forces of evil like ships reeling by blows of wild winds and rough waves of the ocean.

He counts you as one of Himself. He has wrapped His armory around you. He has made you a mountain of strength and power.

The enemy will not overcome you. "They prevented me in the day of my calamity: but the LORD was my stay" (Psalms 18:18).

He is your Defense Forces. He welcomes all refugees to hide in His house. Satan will not destroy their faith or love. "I have set the LORD always before me: because he is at my right hand, I shall not be moved" (Psalms 16:8).

The Messiah is offering His services to you. He wants to help you and make you strong in faith, body, and spirit. He will hold you with His powerful right hand. The earthquakes of trials and temptations will not shake you lose from His firm grasp.

Pain, tears, worry, death, worry, etc. will not divert your attention from Him. He will help you to succeed in your belief and faith in Him.

You will reap the fruits of eternal life. You will sing and praise Him for His tender love and mercy.

He will take you out of all your troubles. He will place you to live within His Everlasting Spirit. He will save you because He loves you very much. You are His son or daughter who looks just like Him. As such, you are completely adorable to Him. "He brought me forth also into a large place; he delivered me, because he delighted in me" (Psalms 4:1).

He will make you grow in intelligence, wisdom, etc. right where you are. He will use your troubles to make you wiser and stronger in faith. You will thrive and rejoice in spite of your troubles. He will enlarge your territories in spite of your obvious limitations.

You are a good person you accept the Messiah as your personal Savior. He will is adopting you as a holy child of His Spirit like someone on earth adopting a child into his or her family and tribe. He will guide each decision you make, each word you speak, and each action you take.

He will be happy and rejoice when you are listening to His voice and obeying good excellent instructions. "The steps of a good man are ordered by the LORD: and he delighteth in his way. The LORD rewarded me according to my righteousness; according to the cleanness of my hands hath he recompensed me" (Psalms 37:23; 18:20).

He loves, respects, and honors all His followers even above His own interests. Love is what sent Him to the Cross. And when you are responding to His instructions, He gets even more excited. He builds you up piece by piece until you are a mature father or mother of righteousness.

He will continue to bless you with greater righteousness as when you continue to allow Him to scrub and wash those fast-holding sins from your heart. He will favor your with continual Presence in your life.

He loves people of integrity. He will put joy into your heart because you an obedient child. You want to be holy and righteous like Him.

4 CHAPTER

SUFFER LITTLE CHILDREN TO COME TO ME

Bernhard Plockhorst, 1825–1907, Let the children come unto Me, in public domain.

Some mothers brought their little children to Jesus to place His hands on them and bless them. He had preached and healed people the whole day. He was very tired. The disciples wated Him to rest. They saw giving blessings was not as important as healing people. But the Messiah rebuked them.

A blessing is the basis for the existence of life. "Then were there brought unto him little children, that he should put his hands on them, and pray: and the disciples rebuked them" (Matthew 19:13).

The mothers' were believers in the Messiah. They knew that He was God in human flesh. When they brought their little children to Him, they were confessing and applauding Him as the Creator God who spread His hands on the floods of water and pronounced blessings of light, space, dry land, plants, animals, birds, luminaries, etc. to come out of nothing. Lifting and spreading a hand out was the symbol of creation.

The mothers asked Jesus to make or recreate their children all over again by placing His hands on them as at the beginning when He touched place where heaven and the universes now stand with His hands and created things out of them.

The prayer that they asked Him to pray for their children was to make things right for them. He was to make them reconcile them to Himself and make things as good as it was at the beginning before sin entered into the world. But the disciples did not ask the mothers to move away from the Messiah in a polite way.

They poured fire on them and their children. They fought them. It displeased the Messiah. He opposed their actions and the cruel words they used on the mothers and children.

He rebuked their unfeeling and selfish spirits that wanted His blessings only for themselves and their fellow adults from whom they stood to gain if they directed them to Him. He rebuked them very sharply for not understanding the real mission of His coming into the earth.

He told them never again to use physical force of adults on children or hurt their feelings with words that adults use on each other. They were hurting the faith the children had in Him. He came to spread His hands over the world and recreate her and her inhabitants again. He came to bless little children as well as adults and make them as good and eternal as Himself.

Children are the kinds of believers He was looking for. "But Jesus said, Suffer little children, and forbid them not, to come unto me: for of such is the kingdom of heaven. And he laid his hands on them, and departed thence" (Matthew 19:14, 15). He spread His hands over them like at the beginning when He was creating heaven and all the universes and blessed them.

In those days and in some cultures in existence when an elder is blessing a person, he or she would spit saliva on the person or spit in his or hand and rub it on the person. In one Middle Eastern language, the word blessing has two words put together.

The first is the sound of spitting saliva and the second word is father. A blessing means that God the Father is spitting saliva on His children in His right of being their Daddy. He is creating them or creating good things for them.

2. The children of God

As a Parent, God is kindly asking children and adults alike to remain His little children for life. He does not want them to grow up proud and independent but to remain sweet, obedient, dependent, and teachable. "Then were there brought unto him little children, that he should put his hands on them, and pray: and the disciples rebuked them" (Matthew 19:13).

After the Messiah had preached, healed very many sick people and brought many to life, He was very tired. He preached the Good News of salvation and did miracles before God His Father and on His behalf. After a long day's work, He was very tired and exhausted.

The parents brought their children to Him for prayer, laying on of hands and blessings them. Horror of horrors! The disciples raised a loud din against the parents and their children.

The Messiah was hurt about the cold heartedness of the disciples. There is no therapeutic treatment as good and healing as the innocent smiles, laughter, and touches of little babies and children.

The Messiah is the Savior of the world. But in His Human frail flesh, He felt tiredness. He was fatigued after a long day's work. He, too, wanted healing from the unconditional love of the children. He wanted them to heal His tired soul after seeing so many sick and dead people and healing them all.

The Messiah cut the rebukes and insults of the disciples short. "But Jesus said, Suffer little children, and forbid them not, to come unto me: for of such is the kingdom of heaven" (Matthew 19:14).

The Messiah ordered that all His Father's children should come to Him. He said that He is the One bringing them in His arms back to Himself. He is escorting them towards great heights of spirituality and excellent morality. He ordered the disciplines and all abusers, offenders, etc. of babies and little children not to level them down with harsh treatments and sin. They must not hurt His beloved babies.

The heaven where God resides is a whole universe in itself. It is the leading kingdom and head of all the kingdoms of the vast and endless universes. The only people who are worthy to enter there are those comparable to beings with child-like faith, trust, hope and love.

The Messiah loves children. They were brought to Him. He held them in His tender and loving arms. He laid hands on each one of them. He prayed for them and blessed them. "And he laid his hands on them, and departed thence" (Matthew 19:15).

Both the Messiah and the children were blessed. Thus loved and adored, He was refreshed to continue to bless the world. They children loved Him forever for loving and blessing them. They were His faithful followers all their lives.

God the Father is very a lovely and sweet. He alone is the loving and Almighty Daddy of the world. He gave this world for His beautiful babies. When they are grown up, they are to marry and raise up more babies for Him.

However, they are still His little tiny and fragile babies who He must nurse day and night for all eternities to come. Though may know it or not, He holds each person in His arms and feeds them.

He gives them water to drink when they are thirsty. He blows air through their nostrils from His mouth to keep them breathing.

It is time for all babies both young and old to praise Him for His unconditional and caring parental love. Congratulate Him for being such an awesome and amazing Parent.

He made a whole world for them. He made them the kings and queens of this earth and beyond. He put the sun, moon and stars under their rule.

When His babies wandered away from Him, they were tempted to sin by His enemy, the serpent. The serpent bit them with the poison of sin. Though the poison was very deadly, He would not allow Adam and Eve to die that very moment. He loved them too much to allow them to reap the consequences of their disobedience.

He had an alternative plan. He adopted the Second Godhead as His firstborn Son and asked Him to come down here on earth and die for His helpless babies. "For God so loved the world, that he gave his only begotten Son, that whosoever believeth in him should not perish, but have everlasting life" (John 3:16).

Every person born into this world is His beloved and adorable baby. He wants them to be saved through His Adopted Firstborn Son, the Messiah.

He is the Way. He will teach you how to love and how to live an eternal life. He is the Law of love and life. He is the Truth by which He is bringing them up into living lives of holiness and righteousness.

The Son spoke about Him whenever He preached. "Jesus saith unto him, I am the way, the truth, and the life: no man cometh unto the Father, but by me" (John 14:6).

He gives wisdom to parents to make a living in order to feed His babies. He feels parents with utmost joy when they can put food on the table, clothes on the back of their children, initiate into how to survive in this world through formal and informal school, etc. And when they children are grown up, meet each other and fall in love.

The parents dressed them up for their wedding gays. They make the boys look very majestic in their wedding gowns like kings. They dressed the girls in brightly shinning clothes and jewels. Their hearts ache with excitements as they hand their daughters into the hands of their bridegrooms.

The parents, too, were married off in the same fashion. Weddings have been taking place from one generation to another. But they are not really the true parents. It is God the Father who is both Daddy and Mommy to these children. All the congratulations that are heaped on the parents for raising children so well should go to Him.

God the Father wants the earthly parents to experience the joy of the unconditional love of children. It is sweet like orange juice. Such dear little people who look up to their parents with eyes wide open like oranges with wonder and awe on their parents! So you can understand why the Parent of all is at war with Satan. He is destroying His beautiful babies!

As a good Parent, God feels very responsible for your welfare. He is watching over you. You are His little helpless baby that needs to be fed, poops and peeing of sin to be removed, bathed with the blood of Christ, clothed in His righteousness, etc.

All the while, He is teaching about character and development into His own image or likeness. He wants you to be like holy and Almighty Daddy in appearance and character. When you are grown up and spiritually mature, He will give you His kingdom to rule and reign over.

Children are so sweet and trusting. They cuddle up to their parents for embraces. They are kissed on the foreheads by their fathers and mothers. They smile from ear to ear with joy. Their love is explosive. The joy on their faces is angelic!

They move closer for more hugs and kisses. These are the kinds of affection seeking that the Heavenly Father wants all His earth children to seek for Him. He wants every one of them to draw closer to Him by faith and love. He wants them to trust Him for love and tender care just like little children trust their parents to always show them love.

As long as a parent and child(ren) are alive, the parent can make daily improvement in the way he or she demonstrate love to his or her offspring(s). So there is no excuse in maintain bad parenting. Everyone can grow in love with God's help.

Every daughter that has been on this world is a beauty queen. They are all Miss Universes. They all have the lovely and gentle features of their Heavenly Father. In the way, every son that is born in this world is very handsome. Each one of them looks handsome and awesome like God their Father.

It is the responsibility of each parent to enhance the beauty of their daughters and sons with love, good food, fresh, and clean water to drink, dry and warm place to sit in, peaceful atmosphere to grow up in, etc.

Raising children is the first duty that the Lord gave to the first parents to do. It is the reason why He gave parents this earth as a gift to live in. The earth belongs to the children. "And God said, Let us make man in our image, after our likeness: and let them have dominion over the fish of the sea, and over the fowl of the air, and over the cattle, and over all the earth, and over every creeping thing that creepeth upon the earth.

So God created man in his own image, in the image of God created he him; male and female created he them. And God blessed them, and God said unto them, Be fruitful, and multiply, and replenish the earth, and subdue it: and have dominion over the fish of the sea, and over the fowl of the air, and over every living thing that moveth upon the earth" (Genesis 1:26-28).

The earth was not given to Adam and Eve as their sole property. It is the property of their descendants. Children owned every good and useful thing on this earth like dry land, water, air, plants, animals, birds, fishes, insects, grubs, etc.

Just as God created this world and gave to His beloved children, progress must make with the children in mind. They are the next generation. All the developments that are made by the adults are the inheritance of the children.

Everyone on this earth was birthed by the Messiah. But He does not want to be the only Parent on earth, so He made both made and women to be parents to the younger children.

He asked all of them to raise the children of the whole earth together. It is for their own good if they can accept to receive the unconditional love of children like drinking sweet fruit juice. Regardless of their races or parentage, all children are capable of developing trust, faith, and love.

The fortunate children who are living in good homes and the unfortunate ones who are being abused need love, respect and honor by all the adults of the world. Both married, singles, barren, etc. adults are capable of loving children. All of them are the parents of the children of this world.

Yes, you are parent once you can love, honor, and respect someone who is younger than you. Parenthood is for everyone whether you have a child(ren) or not. The Lord wants you to take the cups brimming with love that the children are offering you. He wants you to drink and empty the cups.

The children will offer you some more. It will make you a better person. You need children all your life. At the end of your life, the Lord will reward you for a job well done in parenting His children.

So for the time being while this old world is still in existence, let fathers help each other in raising children. And let the mothers do the same. If there is any globes, crowns, prizes, recognitions, Nobel Peace Prize, etc. to be given, they should not be given to actors, actresses, musicians, politicians, athletes, scientists, etc. but to parents and responsible adults who have always been there for their children and for the children of the hold world.

There are children in all the races, tribes, ethnic groups, etc. of the world. There are Arabs, Nubians, White, Yellow, Brown, etc. children. When they are left alone, they see no color, race or any other barrier between the races. They will share their food and water together.

They will give water of love to all who are around them. That is how every adult had once been when they were little children. You had been trustful and loving. But along the way that divine innocence, trustful, faith and love were taken out of you or diminished to some extent.

Had everyone been allowed to grow up with child-like faith and trust, the world would have been one large happy family. Everyone would go out of his or her way to give a cup of love to a brother or sister to drink.

But God the Father has not lost faith in all the adults and hurting children of this world. He said that you can become little children again. Children are not at cut-throats with each other as to who should be the President and Commander-in-Chief. They do not cause World Wars for supremacy in politics, businesses, etc.

The Messiah, aptly, used them to tell all adults to forsake the sin of pride, hate, anger, jealousies, envy, greed, immoralities, etc. He said that unless they become pure, holy and humble, they will never see His face. "But a controversy arose among them as to which of them might be the greatest [surpassing the others in excellence, worth, and authority].

But Jesus, as He perceived the thoughts of their hearts, took a little child and put him at His side And told them, Whoever receives and accepts and welcomes this child in My name and for My sake receives and accepts and welcomes Me; and whoever so receives Me so also receives Him Who sent Me. For he who is least and lowliest among you all--he is [the one who is truly] great" (Luke 9:46–48, AMP).

The bride is the star of the wedding. Like a beautiful dressed bride adorned with glittering jewels, each man, woman, boy or girl is God's star. He looks at you with joy and happiness.

In some homes, the parents like to see outdoors where they can watch their children playing in their compound. They are drawn to their children because they enjoying their company.

Some of them become so excited that they join their children in playing games. They act really childish and foolish when they pretend to be young, too. But both the parents and the children do not care. They love each other.

The parents enjoy the work of parenting little people. God, too, loves parenting you. He is watching over you all the time like an eagle fluttering over its young. "As an eagle stirreth up her nest, fluttereth over her young, spreadeth abroad her wings, taketh them, beareth them on her wings: So the LORD alone did lead him, and there was no strange god with him" (Deuteronomy 32:11, 12). The Lord alone feeds you and trains you in the way of righteousness.

The parents of the world cooperate with each other in raising and protecting the children God has loaned them. Every home in this world is His home. Every family is His family. He is Present in every home of believers and non-believers alike.

Whether He loved or not in the house or not, He counts each house as His house. He is God and Daddy to every person on earth. He fathered them all because He wants to be a loving and caring Daddy and Mommy.

They have formed court system in prosecuting people who hurt their children. They even declare wars on nations who abuse or sell children into slavery. They fight and die to protect their children. They die for the freedom of their children.

They do not want their children to be slaves. And that is exactly what the Messiah did on the Cross of Calvary. He died that He may save His children from demoniac control, sin and death. He wants to give them total liberation from all that is evil and detrimental to their health.

When the parents pass away, such deep sorrow seizes the children. They invite people to mourn their parents. The compounds are filled with mourners.

They spend much money in securing food and drinks for the mourners.

If the parents were alive, many of them would have refused such expensive funerals. They do not want their children to spend too much money on them when they are dead. They do not their children to waste precious resources which they can use to lead more comfortable and happy lives.

God alone loves each one of His children with a new kind of love every day. "It is of the LORD'S mercies that we are not consumed, because his compassions fail not. They are new every morning: great is thy faithfulness" (Lamentations 3:22, 23).

After He has dealt with the issue of sin and death, He will remove all His obedient children from this earth and place them around His throne in heaven. He has built a whole City of gold for them.

He wants to watch over them face to face without any more hindrances like sin coming between them. The children of the earth will be happily surprised to know that He really does love them very much.

All the saints who will surround the throne of their Father are His stars. He will be so happy that they are back that He will crown each one of them to be king or queen.

He will decorate their crowns with beautiful and brightly shinning golden stars. He will dress them in white wedding gowns and ask Jesus Christ to wed them.

He will hand them over to Him as if they are married couples. He will order Him to always love and care for them for all eternities upon endless eternities to come. Jesus will swear that His love for them will never fail throughout His everlasting years.

He knows that the love of spouse is passionate, tender, deep, and really crazy. That is the kind of love He wants each one of His beautiful stars to receive from the Second Godhead.

All parents are the slaves of their children. There

is no exception. Kings, queens, emperors, empresses, soldiers, artisans, farmers, scientists, the jobless, the illiterate, etc. are all the slaves of their children.

Once they look on their children, their faces change. They become soft and tender. Love is the conscience choice to be the eternal slave of some significant other or others. So the Messiah will marry the saints, technically speaking, to be His adorable wife.

He will give them sweet, total, and eternal devotion. "And he saith unto me, Write, Blessed are they which are called unto the marriage supper of the Lamb. And he saith unto me, These are the true sayings of God" (Revelation 19:9).

He will be happy to be their Farmer. He has created the Tree of Life for them. When they eat the fruits, they will never die again. He will create a new earth with fruit trees, grains, vegetables, etc. for them to eat. He will be their Cook. He will make food to ripen for them to eat.

They will only need to harvest them and eat. He will be their Water Boy. He has created the Water of life for them. If they drink it, they will never die again. Etc. He is a total Slave for the sake of His beloved children.

5 CHAPTER

THE LOST

I. The lost sheep

William Holman Hut, 1852, strayed sheep

The people from the streets, prostitutes, and all types of sinners called the Messiah to come to them so that they may listen to His sermons. They were forbidden to approach the respectable people whom the Messiah was living. The respectable people were very angry and bitter with Him when they saw Him listen to the message from the sinners and obey it.

He was going out to the streets to preach to them. "Then drew near unto him all the publicans and sinners for to hear him. And the Pharisees and scribes murmured, saying, This man receiveth sinners, and eateth with them" (Luke 15:1, 2).

Before He left on His preaching tours specifically aimed for the outcasts, He told the respectable people three parables about lost things. They were the parables of the lost sheep, coin, and son.

He told the parable of the lost sheep to describe the deep and boundless love He has for you. "And he spake this parable unto them, saying, What man of you, having an hundred sheep, if he lose one of them, doth not leave the ninety and nine in the wilderness, and go after that which is lost, until he find it?

And when he hath found it, he layeth it on his shoulders, rejoicing. And when he cometh home, he calleth together his friends and neighbours, saying unto them, Rejoice with me; for I have found my sheep which was lost.

Philippe de Champaigne, 1602-1674, the lost sheep

I say unto you, that likewise joy shall be in heaven over one sinner that repenteth, more than over ninety and nine just persons, which need no repentance" (Luke 15:4–7).

Who among you if he has one hundred sheep that look up to him like a beloved brother or sister could live him or her to face death alone when he can save him or her?

Sheep are like brothers and sisters who are facing death everyday unless someone takes care of them.

If one of the one hundred sheep you own happens to get itself into danger and is going through great pains, you will become its God. You will leave the comfort of your home to go out into the wilderness to search for it. There is no truth until one hundred of them are all safe in the house. You cannot live on half-truths. You want all the truths in order to feel safe and at peace.

All truths are found in God. He extended these truths in the creation of His children. If one of them goes missing, He goes out to search for him or her. He brings He lost sheep home to make form a one undivided truth.

So if you lose something precious like a sheep, you too do go out to look for it. You do not mind suffering drought, heat, cold, hunger, thirst, ambushes of enemies, etc. because you want to get back what you love.

The Lord is out looking for the children who got angry with Him because they could not create themselves into Himself as God the Almighty, All-Knowing, and Everlasting. He loves them because they are extensions of Himself. He misses them. He searches for them until He finds them and brings them into the safety of His house.

He has infinite universes and worlds. They are all sinless except for one world. Your world got lost like a sheep that has strayed away from the flock. You were or might still be His lost little sheep.

You are among wild animals that could have eaten you except for His guardianship over you. You could have fallen down the steep hill and be broken into a thousand pieces but I have kept watch over you. You could have died of hunger, thirst, heat, and bitter coldness of the night but He never let down His guard over your life. All the time you were in the wild He kept calling you name to come back home to Him.

At last, your ears picked up His loving voice amidst the wild and angry voices of demons hungering for your blood. You came to Him. It was a sweet exhilarating feeling to have you back in His arms! There was a great celebration party in heaven in His honor because He got you back from the world of sin.

When He finds one of His lost sheep, He puts him or her on the shoulders on which He carries the weight on the whole world. He is recreating him or her again.

He is showing off His children for angels and the sinless world to see and admire. He child rides on His shoulders. He goes around dancing and rejoicing with a loud voice that His baby is safe and at home with Him.

He goes to the house that He himself had built with His own hands with His sheep. He calls His friends, companions, and neighbors and tells them, "Lift up your hearts and voices and rejoice with Me. I have love because I have one of my lost brother (or sister) who was dying and save him." And heaven exploded with joy as if hit by an earthquake.

He concluded, "This is how My joy is expressed in heaven when I give the hand of brotherhood to one lost sheep of Mine. Their Father walks in style because His house if full of children. He is happier that the lost is found than ninety-nine percent of the self-righteous who do not want His salvation.

They will not get help because they think that they are as good and powerful as God the Father Himself. They have refused to mourn and weep for their sins. They call themselves the fathers and mothers of the church.

They are claiming that they know all the truths and are living by it. They do not know what they are talking about. They have not yet found the Trinity. One day, the angels will sing your praise songs again in your hearing when you are at home with Father.

Please do not make the false claim that you are too weak to abandon sin. It has not eaten you through and through yet. You still have a mind to think about God and a heart that longs for Him. "There be many that say, Who will shew us any good? LORD, lift thou up the light of thy countenance upon us" (Psalms 4:6).

There are many people who may claim that you have no good fortunes. You are living from one crisis to another. They may claim that true Christianity is a bare and austere life deprived of all joy and fun.

They point to their drinking and drug parties and

say that they are very happy people. They can make money in any way they like. They shoot to the top through any available routes.

They can change friends like shirts. They claim that you are unhappy and friendless. You have few or none of the things that the world calls good fortunes.

They may go as far as saying that you have nothing because you are cursed by God. He does not love you and that is He is not blessed you like He has blessed the people who do not even care about Him as much as you do.

He knows that you have rejected the pleasures of the world because you love Him. It has touched His heart. It has made Him love you more than ever before. The light of His Presence is shining all over you though you do not see it. He is with you. Their parties may be noisy but you will have gladness in your heart because Jesus lives there. "Thou hast put gladness in my heart, more than in the time that their corn and their wine increased" (Psalms 4:7).

The Lord will put into your heart the gift of being thankfulness. You will be thankful for just being alive even if you do not have all the good things of this life. You will be happier off with Jesus living in heart than the merry seekers who do not have Him.

They may have all the food, clothes, gold, businesses, politics, etc. they want but with Jesus in your heart, you will have what they do not have.

You have the everlasting God of Peace in your life. In the final analysis, you will excel over and above all of them because God is with you.

Seek the Lord all the time during the day or at night. He will live in your heart. He will give you peace. Your life is in good hands. "I will both lay me down in peace, and sleep: for thou, LORD, only makest me dwell in safety" (Psalms 4:8).

The Creator is coming to you not to hurt you but in peace. Receive in Him in your heart so that you can truly live great and excel eternally. He will supply peace in your heart. You are in His arms. You will have it whether you are awake or asleep. No temptation or trial will draw you away from Him.

You will thank Him for His protection and say, "I have set the LORD always before me: because he is at my right hand, I shall not be moved. Therefore my heart is glad, and my glory rejoiceth: my flesh also shall rest in hope" (Psalms 16:8, 9).

Now that you have brought yourself forward and presented yourself before the Lord your Creator and Savior, serve Him with all your heart. He will not be disappointed you.

He is your Comforter in all the sorrows you are facing in this world. He is the Healer of your broken body, heart and spirit. He is standing at the spot of great favors. He is standing at your right hand as your source of power, strength and all other blessings.

He will not leave you alone to be shaken and removed by the earthquakes of troubles. You will be secure and stable because the One who is as solid and immovable as a gigantic mountain of hard rock is with you.

God always blesses the works of His hands. "The Spirit of God hath made me, and the breath of the Almighty hath given me life" (Job 33:4).

He put your body parts together. He put His Spirit into you. "But there is a spirit in man: and the inspiration of the Almighty giveth them understanding" (Job 32:8).

All the people of the earth have the Spirit of God. He is the One giving them intelligence, wisdom, and breaths. "All the while my breath is in me, and the spirit of God is in my nostrils" (Job 27:3).

You are not only flesh that was created out of the soil of the earth but have the Spirit of God also. He put Himself into you through the breath that He breathed in your father, Adam.

There is also corrupt spirits in them that they received from Adam. These are the spirits or intelligence and feelings that lead them to sin. But the Almighty Spirit of the Lord is drawing all humble hearts from the lives of sin.

He is speaking in their hearts and teaching what is right. If they continue to listen to Him, He will walk them away from sin and into the way of holiness.

The Lord listens to the Spirit He placed in your through Adam when you are praying to Him. Because He is your Almighty God, He listens to your prayers. He will answer them.

He will fulfill all your needs whether today or later. He will recreate your spirit again complete with a new body. You are the small spirit and He is the Great, Almighty, and Eternal Spirit.

He loves each one of His children whether they love Him or not, like Him or not or know Him or not. He is their Savior. He saves them from sin. He is their Counselor. He leads them in the path of holiness and righteousness.

The Lord's face is watching you very lovingly and tenderly. "The LORD bless thee, and keep thee" (Numbers 6:24).

God the Father has blessed you more than you will ever know. He is keeping you within His own everlasting Spirit by giving you heart beats, blood to run through your vein, air to breathe, food to eat, water to drink, etc. He does not want the work He has done for you to go to waste.

He wants you to be an eternal child so that He can always pour His love on you. He will keep you eternally close to His by making you the bride of His Son, Jesus Christ. Whenever Jesus will go throughout the paths of the eternal years, you will always be by His side because you are His bride. Whatever He will do will be known by you. You will have a share in all that He create and own.

Even now He has set His face very firmly to always look towards favorably. "The LORD make his face shine upon thee, and be gracious unto thee: The

LORD lift up his countenance upon thee, and give thee peace" (Numbers 6:25, 26).

He is very loving and gracious to you. He is set His face on you as an approval that you are His beloved baby. He will bless you with His own peace that temptations, troubles, wars, conflicts, etc. cannot destroy. He will save you.

II. The lost coin

©Sarah More, the lost coin

Fathers and mothers have brought up good children. Each kept saying, "That person who is good and nice, is with me. He (or she) is growing and getting bigger.

He (or she) is great. God, too, says, "My child(dren) is very important to me. They are wonderful. People say that my children are good. Some are sung in songs.

I am their parent. I taught them my manners. So I keep fighting like a soldier to give them shelter, food, water and clothes on their backs. I give them unconditional love.

I sacrifice My own comfort and pleasures to give life for my children. I gave birth to my home by my power and strength.

My children are the best in the world. They are becoming great like dad (or mom). I gave them life.

Ha-a-a! What a sweet satisfying feeling to be a parent!

If you are a parent, I hope you are now understanding some of the feeling God your Father is having towards you. It was a great feeling when I set the world in motion. I fathered the world and the universes. The most exciting part was when I formed you in the body of Adam and Eve.

When you were born, I was the happiest of all Parents. I made you by the strength of my powers. I make you to live day by day by the greatness of my fatherhood. It is such a good feeling seeing myself in you.

You are resembling Me in your physical features. But the sweetest feelings come when you are reaching out to Me. When you confess your sins and turn away from evil, I explode with joy. I ask the angels to sin your praises.

I have infinite universes and worlds. They are all sinless except for one world. Your world got lost like a sheep that has strayed away from the flock. You were or might still be my lost little sheep. You are among wild animals that could have eaten you except for my guardianship over you.

You could have fallen down the steep hill and be broken into a thousand pieces but I have kept watch over you.

You could have died of hunger, thirst, heat and bitter coldness of the night but I never let down my guard over your life. All the time you were in the wild I kept calling you name to come back home to Me.

At last, your ears picked up my loving voice amidst the wild and angry voices of demons hungering for your blood. You came to Me.

Ha-a-a! It was a sweet exhilarating feeling to have you back in my arms! There was a great celebration party in heaven. The angels sang songs in My praise and in your praise."

The Messiah told another parable, saying, "Either what woman having ten pieces of silver, if she lose one piece, doth not light a candle, and sweep the house, and seek diligently till she find it?

And when she hath found it, she calleth her friends and her neighbours together, saying, Rejoice with me; for I have found the piece which I had lost" (Luke 15:8, 9).

Now, there was this person who made out of a man's rib. She wanted to be made whole again by being united to him in marriage. She worked all her life and save ten beautiful golden coins for her wedding day.

They are watching over her back that she would soon become a wife. But one of them got lost from the bag that had held it like a baby in a mother's womb. It was a very painful lost to the owner.

The owner is now the lost coin's God. She lights the candle and put it to stand on its lampstand. She takes a good broom and sweep every inch of her house looking for that lost coin.

She will give her arm not rest. She will continue sweeping until she finds her lost coin.

Then, she comes across the lost coin. She calls her neighbors and says, "Lift up yourselves in love and joy with me. I have found the one who watches over my back. I had lost it. But now I have love and rest in my house."

The Messiah pointed out the lesson of this parable by saying, "Likewise, I say unto you, there is joy in the presence of the angels of God over one sinner that repenteth" (Luke 15:10). One day, the angels will sing songs in your honor in your hearing when you are at home with Dad.

You are His precious gold coin of great value that no one has enough money to buy. You are His invaluable treasure. But you were or are still lost. You slipped off the pile of His gold coins and ran away.

Actually, the devil broke into His bank and stole you. He stole you from Him. You were lost.

You were hidden in a deep hole in a dark corner

of sin and death. It was pitch dark all around. This is the darkness of sin that has descended into the world.

So God the Father lit light on Christ. He went around searching and looking for you. He you found very cold and covered with dirt and moss of sin. He washed away your sins with the blood of Jesus Christ.

You are a brand new shining dollar. He called the angels to celebrate your recovery. You are back in the deposit in the Lord's heaven back. You are now safe from burglars and thieves called demons and your own sins.

He said, "You are My precious gold coin of great value that no one has enough money to buy. You are my invaluable treasure. But you were or are still lost. You slipped off the pile of my gold coins and ran away.

The devil broke into my bank and stole my money. He stole you. You were lost. You were hidden in a deep hole in a dark corner. It was pitch dark. The darkness of sin has descended the world. So I lit the world with the light of Christ.

I went around searching and looking for you. I found cold and covered with dirt and moss of sin. I washed with the blood of Jesus Christ. You became a new shining dollar again. I called the angels to celebrate that I have recovered my money. My bank is safe from burglars and thieves."

The greatest fortune on earth is divine truth. It is worth being persecuted and dying for. It is the straightway that leads to God.

It forgives and forgets all sins and wrongs. It washes away human sins from their souls. It is the secret that leads to the path of peace.

It is beautiful. It is sweeter than honey. It is all consuming. It is attractive. It is worth seeking after. It must be celebrated. It leads to love. And "God is love" (1 John 4:8).

He is divine and eternal love that gives perfect joy and peace. He is all goodness. "Finally, brethren, whatsoever things are true, whatsoever things are honest, whatsoever things are just, whatsoever things are pure, whatsoever things are lovely, whatsoever things are of good report; if there be any virtue, and if there be any praise, think on these things" (Philippians 4:8). God is good because He loves you. That was why He gave birth to you.

Salvation is a blessing that is too expensive for money, diamonds, gold, etc. to afford. He is washing away your sins with His precious blood. He is filling you with His everlasting Presence. He is writing His Ten Commandments in your heart. One of these days, He will transport you to heaven to live with Him eternally.

His divine love gives you air to breathe, a firm earth to walk on, food to eat, water to drink, shelter to live, family and friends to love, help of strangers, etc. He gives you the ability to love, smile, laugh, etc.

You may not have sight but He will give you the ability to touch. You may limbs but He will give you the ability to think and move with your mind. You may not have human love but you are already saturated with love His love.

You may be dumb but you can talk with your heart. You may be deaf but you can hear with your heart.

The outer person may be aging, handicapped, weak, tired, sick, etc. but the inner person is beautiful, loving, warm, and ageless. You may be healthy or not outwardly, but the inner person is perfect. It has the Spirit of God.

The fact that you are a human being created in His image is a direct result of His love for you. He wants you to look, think, talk, and act like Him. And how much more should you give Him thanks daily for creating you in His image! And best of all is that He died to pay for all your sins.

That is a reason enough for celebration life no matter what good or bad things are taking place in your life. "O give thanks unto the LORD; for he is good: because his mercy endureth for ever" (Psalm 118:1).

He is loving and merciful because He is the eternal truth that gives Sabbath rest. He is the sweetener of human life.

He never fails in showering you with all His goodness. "Charity never faileth: but whether there be prophecies, they shall fail; whether there be tongues, they shall cease; whether there be knowledge, it shall vanish away" (1 Corinthians 13:8).

God's kind of love will never fall silent or die. Prophecies may fail. If they are fulfilled they have done their works and become obsolete. The life of the men and women who speak in tongues is short. They are just mortals. They will die. Education has an end. Educated people do not live forever.

They do die. But he (or she) who has love in his heart will never die. He will be remembered by the Creator on the day of creation because love is eternal. And this eternal love resides in the heart of God.

He is forever faithful in loving you because He is eternal. He is excellent and His love is extremely good.

You may disappoint Him in many ways. But that will not lessen His love for us. In fact, when you fall into sin, He pities you because of your weaknesses and foolish presumptions. "For the LORD is good; his mercy is everlasting; and his truth endureth to all generations" (Psalm 100:5).

He is the sweet and eternal Sabbath rest for all the peoples of the earth. He walks in love and mercy. He is ready to forgive all generations of sinners and bring them back into His truth. This truth is about forgiving love and Sabbath rest that live from everlasting to everlasting.

When you love Him, He loves you even more tenderly than ever before. Even after our death, because of the goodness of His love and faithfulness, He will carry on His covenant of love between you and

Him onto your children.

Sometimes your children may not care much about Him but because of the vow He made to you when He forgave your sins and walked with you day by day, He would always be there for a thousand generations of your children. He will be with your descendants because you love Him. What an awesome love!

Throughout the ages, fathers and mothers have sung the praises of their sons and daughters. They have brought up good children. Each kept saying, "That person who is good and nice to you, is with me.

He (or she) is my child. He is growing and getting bigger. He is great. My child(dren) is very important to me.

They are wonderful. People say that my child is good. People are praising him in songs. I am his parent. I taught him my manners. So I keep fighting for him like a soldier. I give him shelter, food, water, and clothes on him backs.

I give him unconditional love. I am sacrificing my own comfort and pleasures to give life for my baby. He is the best thing in this world to me. He is going to be great like dad (or mom). I have given him my life. What a sweet satisfying feeling to be a parent!"

If you are a parent, at least a good one, you will understand some of the feeling God your Father is having towards you. It was a great feeling when He set the world in motion.

He fathered the world and the universes. The most exciting part was when He formed you in the body of Adam and Eve.

When you were born, He was the happiest of all Parents. He made you by the strength of His powers. He made you to live day by day by the greatness of His fatherhood. It is such a good feeling seeing Himself in you.

You resemble Him physically. But the sweetest feelings come when you are reaching out to Him.

When you confess your sins and turn away from evil, He is happy that the fires around Him explode like bomb with thunderous noises. He asks the angels to sin your praises.

III. The lost child or prodigal son

The Return of the Prodigal Son (1773) by Pompeo Batoni

Now, there was a man who was well known because of a certain story that took place in his house. He had two sons that came out of His body.

The younger one was like young eagle that had refused to be taught by its parents in how to fly. He found no peace or joy in his father's house.

He was in a bad mood all time. He was an angry kid. "And he said, A certain man had two sons: And the younger of them said to his father, Father, give me the portion of goods that falleth to me. And he divided unto them his living" (Luke 15:11, 12).

He asked his father, "Oh you who have given me birth and built me up to this day, give your divisions of the weal that you would leave for me when you pass away."

So his father divided up everything that was feeding them between himself and his younger son.

And not counting many days after what had

transpired between the father and the son, he gathered all his everything that was allocated to him and flew away like an eagle looking for new venture.

He took on a safari to a far country. When he arrived in that country, he made himself the father of the inhabitants who lived there. He tried to give them rest from their hard labors by entertaining them a lavish lifestyle.

He lived like a fabulously rich king. He used his wealth to buy for them a comfortable living. He paid their bills and debts that they owned to one another. He spent all the wealth he had on them.

He was left with a few changes in His pocket that consisted only of coins. But even these were taken away from him by the people of the land. "And not many days after the younger son gathered all together, and took his journey into a far country, and there wasted his substance with riotous living.

And when he had spent all, there arose a mighty famine in that land; and he began to be in want" (Luke 15:13, 14).

When the last change was taken out of his pocket, starvation covered that country like a blanket. It was the worst starvation they had ever seen or heard of.

In fact, it was the story real starvation. The young man was terribly shaken by fear and hunger. His body trembled violent for want of food.

He went job searching and he attached himself as a son to one of the fathers of the land. "And he went and joined himself to a citizen of that country; and he sent him into his fields to feed swine" (Luke 15:15).

He wanted a family or relative that could feed him. This supposed father sent him into the field that fed him and his family. The field had pigs grazing in it. He wanted to live and not die of hunger.

He felt that if he could fill his stomach with the leftovers that were thrown to the pigs, he could leave. But no one offered him anything to eat. "And he would fain have filled his belly with the husks that the swine did eat: and no man gave unto him" (Luke 15:16).

His spirit or thoughts came back into thinking about himself. "And when he came to himself, he said, How many hired servants of my father's have bread enough and to spare, and I perish with hunger!" (Luke 15:17).

He thought about all the young men and women that his father broadcasted all over his large farm like seeds to care for it and yield him plenty of produce. Those workers were, indeed, his father's own seeds.

He took good care of them because he wanted them to be strong so as to be productive workers. None of them died of starvation because there was always bread in his father's house. And yet he himself, the son of the owner of the house, was allowing hunger to cut off his neck and kill him.

He made a decision. "I will arise and go to my father, and will say unto him, Father, I have sinned against heaven, and before thee, And am no more worthy to be called thy son: make me as one of thy hired servants" (Luke 15:18, 19).

This was a little speech that he has planned in his head to win his father father's favor to at least give him an accommodation and food. "Oh, my daddy, "I have cut off myself from heaven and from standing before you as your son.

I am yet to have any truth in me as a loving son that can stand in your presence after all the pain I have given to you. Draw me closer to you as one of those workers who are seeding your land to bring you plenty of harvests."

He left the pig farm and started to come back home to his father. He was still far away on the hill.

But before he could star ascending down the hill towards his father's house, the old man recognized him. "And he arose, and came to his father. But when he was yet a great way off, his father saw him, and had compassion, and ran, and fell on his neck, and kissed him. And the son said unto him, Father, I have sinned against heaven, and in thy sight, and am no more worthy to be called thy son" (Luke 15:20, 21).

He was filled with compassion that also the Triune Godhead had for his lost son. He stood up.

His whole body was shaking as he started to run up the hill. He fell on the neck of his son. He kissed him and brought him back into his bosom. He welcomed him.

The son told him the rehearsed speech just as he had planned in his head. "But the father said to his servants, Bring forth the best robe, and put it on him; and put a ring on his hand, and shoes on his feet:

And bring hither the fatted calf, and kill it; and let us eat, and be merry: For this my son was dead, and is alive again; he was lost, and is found. And they began to be merry" (Luke 15:22–24).

By this time, his mother and the servants had also caught up with them. There was nothing for the father to tell the son.

He loved him too much to utter a word. He talked to his servant instead. "Go back into universe and bring back the long-sleeved and floor length wedding gown and clothed my son. He is the chosen bridegroom of my house so you must put the ring of authority on his finger.

Put shoes on his feet. Bring out the bull we have been fattening on good grass for this occasion and slaughter it. Let us all eat and celebrate with joy. This is my son.

Death had finished him but he has come back to life to eat dinners. He was angry and got lost but I have found him."

They all started to celebrate his son's arrival back home with music, dancing, plenty of drinks, and roasted beef.

You were a lost child but God ran all the way from heaven to the earth and embraced you in my loving arms. He found you.

He covered with the kisses, acceptance, and

reinstatement into your royal heritage. You responded to His love.

He picked up yourself from that dirty and smelly pigsty of sin and washed it away with His precious blood.

God the Father said, "You were or still are My lost child in the wild world of sin. Jesus died for you. The Holy Spirit pleaded with you in your heart to leave your life of sin. Then you responded to His love. You picked up yourself from that dirty and smelly pigsty of sin.

When I saw you turning towards Me I ran all the way from heaven to the earth and embraced you in my loving arms. Jesus was with Me. He covered your dirty and stinging sins with His precious blood.

My heart, the Holy, the angels and I had a huge welcome party in your honor. The angels blew their trumpets. They strummed happily on their harps for hours on end. They praise Jesus for dying for you. They praised the Holy Spirit for wooing you back to Himself. They praised Me for saving you. We are all happy and excited because you are now safe.

You now stand with Me in the holy principles. I will make you greater still in being holiness and righteousness. Some people are praising you for living your life of sin. They say you are religious and good. You are catching up to my greatness.

You are becoming strong in principles and in doing those things which are right. You got your fame from Me since I am famous.

I am the one who gave both physical and spiritual birth to you by my wisdom, intelligence and power. Other people are jealous of you.

They hate you and persecute you because you have refused to join them in their sinful lives. I keep on fighting for you spiritual safety.

I fight demons and your sins minute by minute like a soldier firing at his or her enemies as he or she marches on. I brought the world into existence by my power. And I will save all those who want to be saved by my powerful strength alone.

I keep on parenting my world. I bring sunshine and rain. I blew the winds around the world to give air for my children to breath. I make fresh water to flow on the surface of the earth and underground, too, to provide drinking water for my children.

I make plants to grow to provide food for my children. They are all eating at my table.

And I will save everyone who turns back to Me. I keep them save from the evil one by my power."

Hold onto Him with the arm of faith. He is inviting you saying, "Rejoice and sing about the faith I have given you.

Faith is a piece of the infinite God within your soul. This faith is the complete freedom within heart to be with God and be like Him in everything.

Faith prevents everyone and everything from enslaving your spirit. It gives you the freedom to fly away in your spirit and be with Me all the time even in the midst of temptations and trials.

For now, I have given you the soil of this world as your home. You have not yet inherited the soil of heavenly Canaan.

This has made you not to have complete power over His world yet. But soon you will.

I am the God of Mercy. I am the One who loves you with all of my heart. Sometimes, it is hard for you to conceive it because you are still bound to this sinful world. You have not been given your freedom yet.

Sometimes, you blame me. You accuse me that I have turned your life upside down like a tray or plate that has been put upside down.

You accuse me of trying to crushing your life under my feet. You accuse me of stepping on your hopes, dreams and ambitions and crushing them with my heels. You claim that I am not leading you in a straight path.

All your ways are twisted and uphill all the down.

That is not true. A piece of Me is in you. Though you are eaten up by wars, hate, sin, death, etc., that part of Me will conquer all of them. I am the only in the world who is on your side. Jesus is the only one left to hold onto.

You may be poor. You may wish you have a bank so that you may spend the money as much as you want.

You have a bank in heaven. Your bank is your city. She is made of a solid gold. Your streets are made of every kind of precious jewels and overlaid with gold.

I am giving you this bank as your very own because you are the one my heart loves. As the Merciful Judge, I am repaying you for all your sufferings with riches and very enjoyable life.

I am your Merciful and Loving Judge. I saw that you need a good land. Soil is blood. Men and women have given their blood for their land.

The Messiah also has given His blood so that you may have best of all lands. He bought heaven for you with His own blood. Soil is also grains. It is your food. Your heavenly soil is jewels. They are rare soil. They will support your life for days without end.

As your Dad, I want to guide your feet in the way of prosperity in all things and not just for celestial economic gains. But first of all, you must learn to live by my Moral Laws as stipulated in the Ten Commandments.

They will give your feet to walk in the higher plane of love for God and for all His children. The Decalogue will give you self-respect and love for yourself also."

A huge welcome party was held in heaven in your honor in. The angels blew their trumpets. Some thumbed on their golden harps with joy. They were happy that you have come back home. They praise Jesus for dying for you. They praised the Holy Spirit for wooing you back to Himself. They praised God for saving you. All heaven is happy and excited because you are now safe.

You are now standing on holy principles. Your Father will make you into a greater blessing still. You will be all holy and righteous. Even down here on earth, some people are praising you for leaving your life of sin.

They say you are spiritual and good. You are catching up to the greatness. You are changing. You are growing stronger in principles. You are doing those things that are right in His eyes. You got your fame from Him. He is the most famous Person on earth and in heaven.

He is the one who gave to you physical and spiritual. He is filling you wisdom, intelligence, and power. Other people are jealous of you of your spiritual progress. They hate you because you love Him.

They are persecuting you because you have refused to join them in chasing evil. He is asking you to keep on fighting for you spiritual safety. Fight demons and your sins minute by minute like a soldier firing at his or her enemies as he or she advances forward.

He brought the world into existence by His power. And He will save everyone who runs to Him by His powerful and strength.

He is parenting His world. He brings sunshine and rain. He blows the winds to go around the world to provide air for His children to breath.

He makes fresh water to flow on the surface of the earth and underground, too, to provide drinking water for His children. He makes plants to grow to provide food for His children.

They are all eating at sumptuously at His overflowing table. And He will save everyone who turns back to Him. He keeps them save from the evil one by His power alone.

Rejoice and sing about the faith He has so kindly

provided for you. Faith is a part of the infinite Presence God that is now living within your soul.

This faith is the complete freedom that is within heart to be like your Creator in everything. It blocks everyone and everything from enslaving your spirit. It gives you the freedom to fly away in your spirit and be with your Father in heaven especially in the midst of temptations and trials.

For now, He has given you the soil of this world as your home. You have not yet inherited the soil of heavenly Canaan. This has made you not to have complete power over His world yet. But soon you will.

He has invited Himself into your life to be the Head of your Family. Therefore, He is your Guide, Protector and Provider.

He is your perfect glory of all goodness. He will change your life.

He will make you holy and take you to heaven. "But thou, O LORD, art a shield for me; my glory, and the lifter up of mine head" (Psalms 3:3).).

The wicked will learn the truth that God loves you. They will finally, come to the understanding that He has been with you all along. He made you to lean on Him for strength. He will imbue into you His own holiness to become like Him.

It is wonderful to pray to God your Maker and King. He loves listening to your voice. You bring out warm love out of Him just as any child can bring out of a loving father and mother. You eat breakfast in the morning to have energy for day.

In the same way, when you pray in the morning, you will have spiritual energy to overcome temptations, face trials bravely, and walk closely with your Maker. "Give ear to my words, O LORD, consider my meditation.

Hearken unto the voice of my cry, my King, and my God: for unto thee will I pray. My voice shalt thou hear in the morning, O LORD; in the morning will I direct my prayer unto thee, and will look up" (Psalms

5:1–3).).

He listens to your prayers. He makes them His own. As God the Creator, He is able to use your words as His own and create things that you have asked for. He executes your requests in His capacity as the King of kings and Attorney General of heaven and the earth.

No one can oppose what He does for you because He is the final authority over heaven and the infinite universes. He creates things in answer to your prayers in order to uplift your spirit because you came out of His own Spirit.

He has never stopped answering your prayers. He will answer them throughout the everlastings rolling in. "But know that the LORD hath set apart him that is godly for himself: the LORD will hear when I call unto him" (Psalms 4:3).).

He has selected you to be His baby long before He laid the foundation of the earth. And He will make someone very great and special out of you. He will love you from one eternity to another.

He will demonstrate His love to you by always being faithful. He will supply with plenty of provisions more than you.

Sit still and ponder about all these wonderful things He is going to you. Count them if you can.

They are simply too many to count. Meditate in your beds on His plans for you and especially about His love and greatness.

I call to remembrance my song in the night: I commune with mine own heart: and my spirit made diligent search" (Psalms 77:6).).

Recall into your mind all the good things God has done in your life and in the world. It will build up your faith in Him. It will make you to be sure beyond any possible doubt you have a great future through Him in heaven.

Your heart will cling to Him in love and friendship. You will rejoice that He has such splendid plans for you.

It will keep smile on your face even when things are dark and stormy around you.

If you take time to pray, fast and meditate on the greatness of God, you will be speechless with awe and wonder of how awesome He really is.

Do not be consumed with your own personal needs but reach out to Him and learn about Him. "Stand in awe, and sin not: commune with your own heart upon your bed, and be still. Selah" (Psalms 4:4).).

If you really know how great He is, His love and all the wonderful things He has in mind for you, sin will not appear attractive any more. Keep His love ever burning in your heart. Do not allow sin to extinguish it. You are move forward with Him through eternal years. You will in the embrace of warm love.

The Messiah is the Lamb of God that was slaughtered to cover your sins. He is your holy sacrifice of righteousness that has brought you back into the bosom of God your Father.

You must reciprocate His love by offering yourself as a sacrifice of love. "Offer the sacrifices of righteousness, and put your trust in the LORD" (Psalms 4:5).).

You must die to self in order to be a perfect sacrifice of love and holiness to God your Father. From then on, you must learn to stay put within Him. Do not sin deliberately again.

You are standing on shaking grounds if you presume that you can fall back into willful sin willfully and expected to be righteous and holy and like God overnight, you are kidding yourself. Sanctification is the process of becoming holy which takes your whole.

If you keep slipping back into sin, you will always remain a sinner. You must learn to break yourself lose from the power of sin through fasting and prayer. Walk in the way of the Divinity, and He will help you to be holy like Himself.

Both you and God will be happy if you take those

firm steps in walking towards. He will be happy that you are trying to be like Him.

Doing the right thing will bring joy and peace into your heart. And the fact that you are making your Best Friend happy will spur you on to seek greater holiness for yourself. As you drew closer to Him, He will also get quite desperate about having you live with Him in heaven.

He will take you and all the other saints to heaven. "They shall call the people unto the mountain; there they shall offer sacrifices of righteousness: for they shall suck of the abundance of the seas, and of treasures hid in the sand" (Deuteronomy 33:19).).

The Messiah will give you and all the tribe of the earth that love Him all the mountains of wealth and joy where His throne resides.

When you arrive in heaven, you will offer yourself as a lamb to be slaughtered and your head cut off for the joy of the Lord that love you so much and gave you His home as your very own possession.

You will vow to always live to make Him very happy and pleased. You will sacrifice yourself interests and needs in preference of exalting the Lord with all the mind, heart, and strength you can master.

He will outdo you in showering you with love and other great blessings that are beyond your wildest dreams. Like a baby who enjoys suckling his or her mother's warm milk, you will enjoy the provisions He has prepared for you.

Like a baby who depends on the love and protection of his or her mother, you will throw yourself into the arms on the Lord to enjoy all His goodness immensely.

The supplies He has prepared for you in the sky, land and seas of heaven and the new earth are yours. They will you grow strong, healthy, and eternal.

Since great blessings are waiting for you in heaven, you must learn to walk right. The Messiah will help you to be holy and righteous. "Trust in the

LORD, and do good; so shalt thou dwell in the land, and verily thou shalt be fed. Delight thyself also in the LORD; and he shall give thee the desires of thine heart" (Psalms 37:3, 4).).

Trust the Lord to take care of your life here on earth and in heaven. Spend the rest of your life seeking the good fortunes of love, joy, peace, etc. They are the riches that will make your Creator and bring contentment to your life.

They will make you the inheritor of the Kingdom of the Everlasting King. His freely love will be like food that will give you joy, satisfaction, and strength. It will make your life meaningful and worth living.

He will add more joy into your heart as you draw ever closer to Him. He will teach you how to find added joys by giving awesome things to think about like He does. He will provide you with all the possibilities of accomplishing your dreams.

Make peace with God right now. "Commit thy way unto the LORD; trust also in him; and he shall bring it to pass" (Psalms 37:5).).

Confess all your sins and turn away from them so that the new life of heaven may start to work in your in your soul right away. They will produce results. He is your Life.

Therefore, walk on His way of truth and righteousness all your life. This life is just the beginning of a greater and better waiting for you in the new heaven and earth. He will fulfill all His vows of being your eternal Messiah.

Salvation is not just saving you from sin but making you like the Messiah in order to enjoy a very abundant, blissful, and over flowing life. He will plant blessings in your life like seeds.

They will grow, mature, and produce plenty of sweet and delicious fruits for you to eat and enjoy.

The Messiah will bring you back to Him like He is making the light of the sun to rise in the morning. He will uncover you. He will make the darkness of sin to flee away. That brightness of goodness will burst out of you light the morning sunshine.

You will shine and dazzle in your own person glory like the sun shining over the earth and giving her its full strength of light, energy, and warmth. "And he shall bring forth thy righteousness as the light, and thy judgment as the noonday." (Psalms 37:6).).

You will be a whole planet of joy and warmth like the glowing sun. Truth will shine out of you like the light of the noonday sun to bring judgment on the earth and govern the universes that will be entrusted into your care as their god, king (queen), and lord.

The beloved firstborn of the farmer was coming back from field work. As he drew nearer to their house, he heard heavy drum beats, singing voices, the rhythms of dancing feet. "Now his elder son was in the field: and as he came and drew nigh to the house, he heard musick and dancing" (Luke 15:25).

The musicals sounds and dances are symbols of the rejoicing of human beings. They have heard the truth and arc praising God about it.

The firstborn did not know what was going on. "And he called one of the servants, and asked what these things meant. And he said unto him, Thy brother is come; and thy father hath killed the fatted calf, because he hath received him safe and sound" (Luke 15:26, 27).

He was told that their father had welcomed his lost brother with the unconditional love of God the Father. The prayers of their father for the safe return of his son were answered.

He grew very angry that his worthless brother was giving this royal treatment. "And he was angry, and would not go in: therefore came his father out, and intreated him.

And he answering said to his father, Lo, these many years do I serve thee, neither transgressed I at any time thy commandment: and yet thou never gavest me a kid, that I might make merry with my friends:

But as soon as this thy son was come, which hath devoured thy living with harlots, thou hast killed for him the fatted calf" (Luke 15:28–30).

He complained to his loving father, "Look! I have been serving you very faithfully like a good son and brother all these years. I lived a righteous life just like you. I have never been you enemy and gave you a beating with my own hand.

And I have not married up to now in order that I may take care of you. I have kept all the truths you have taught me. I have lived your life.

You have never given me the true life in order to satisfy my passions for the good life. You did not even give me anything as little as young kid to enjoy the joy of God with my friends.

But when your son came back who had enjoyed himself fully like God to all the things that you have labored so hard for and which had taken your breaths away and made you prematurely old, you are treating him royally. But he spent his passions on prostitutes.

You have cut the throat of the loving heavenly Daddy when you cut the fatted calf for him. The calf is like that healthy and lively Anointed One that will come from the Presence of the Father to anoint us with His salvation."

His Father told his son to calm down. "And he said unto him, Son, thou art ever with me, and all that I have is thine. It was meet that we should make merry, and be glad: for this thy brother was dead, and is alive again; and was lost, and is found" (Luke 15:31, 32).

He told him that everything that God had given them belonged to him because he had suffered with him since he was born. But God being with them, there remained one more thing for them to do for His glory.

They must rejoice and be thankful that his younger brother has returned home. They must love him. He was completely dead.

He was finished. But his breath returned back into him. He is breathing now. He ran away from God but the Lord found him and brought him back home.

There are other sons and daughters of God who are living in other universes, worlds, and planets. They will not be very excited when you are crowned their king or queen.

They will question the fairness of God's love. How could He exalt sinners who had put Him to death into such positions even if they have repented from all their sins? It is outrageous.

Truly, they never sinned. They were created before Adam and Eve were created.

How can the lastborns take such preeminence over the firstborns? But the Father will tell them not to be jealous of their brothers and sisters who were sinners.

They still owned their worlds and everything that are found in them. But the saved human beings must be treated royally because the Fatted Calf, the Messiah, died for them.

He has anointed them with His own blood. And as such, they should be celebrated and taken to live with Him in heaven.

2. Matthew Levi the thief

Jan Sanders van Hemessen - 1536, the call of Matthew

The Pharisees were intolerable of tax collectors, prostitutes, the sick, the poor, etc. The tax collectors were working for the Romans.

They charged their fellow Jews a double or more amount of the tax that was required for each man to pay by the Romans.

They split the money in half. One half was for their masters and they kept the rest for themselves. They grew fabulously rich and wealthy. All the Jewish people hated them for their greed. They were hated for their thoughtlessness about plight of the majority of their fellow Jews who were suffering under the poverty line.

But shock of all shocks! The Messiah called one of these greedy felons to be one of His disciples. The Pharisees were enraged. The discipleship of the Lord belonged to good Jews like themselves and not to thieves, robbers, and prostitutes.

They did not waste time in confronting the disciples about their anger and frustrations at how the Messiah was including open sinners into the sacred government of good Jews. "And as Jesus passed forth from thence, he saw a man, named Matthew, sitting at the receipt of custom: and he saith unto him, Follow me. And he arose, and followed him" (Matthew 9:9).

Matthew was a man. He was not Satan. He was redeemable. He was sitting at tax office filling his pockets with money that did not belong to him. The Messiah called him and asked him to follow His tradition of divinity.

It was the noblest call that is still being given by God to everyone on this earth. Matthew's heart jumped to his mouth. He had longed for an opportunity such as this to be closer to the Lord. He wanted to be like God. He rose up and followed His tradition of holiness and righteousness.

Naturally, the former thief went to his friends who were all thieves to come and see the Man who had changed his life. Some were seeking God and others came out of curiosity. Matthew threw a big and expensive dinner in honor of the Messiah and the disciples.

The thieves turned up in large numbers to hear the word of life. "And it came to pass, as Jesus sat at meat in the house, behold, many publicans and sinners came and sat down with him and his disciples" (Matthew 9:10).

There was great excitement among them to see one of themselves sitting close to the Holy Man and Miracle Worker taking care of His needs and bringing crowds to Him to hear the Gospel. They wanted to hear and touch the Messiah for themselves if He was real and human. What a courageous Man He must be to reach out to them who were the outcasts of Israel!

The Pharisees were observing the Lord's association with thieves very closely. It broke their hearts when he included one of them into His group of evangelists. Though they doubted His divine connection, they acknowledged privately that He was an exceptionally holy and righteous Man.

They wanted to protect Him from bad influences of thieves, robbers, murderers, prostitutes, etc. They wanted to be His god fathers and school Him in the teachings of the traditions of the fathers. They did not have enough courage to complain to the Messiah directly.

So they cornered the disciples and accused them of breaking the traditions of the fathers by associating with ignorant civilians who had no idea about the righteousness of God and thieves. "And when the Pharisees saw it, they said unto his disciples, Why eateth your Master with publicans and sinners?" (Matthew 9:11).

They were not accusing disciples but the Messiah Himself. They said that the tax collectors were not true Jews. According to them, a good Jew must always follow the traditions of the fathers or the oral laws. Jews like the tax collectors who do not practice them are street urchins and prostitutes.

Hence, the name: the publicans. They were ignorant and unschooled civilians who did not understand the Law and requirements of God. Some of them like the tax collectors were thieves. There were also some who walked the streets for a living. They were the prostitutes. No Jewish man or woman in his or her right mind associated with street people.

The Messiah was watching them hanging around Him and His disciples like hungry vultures ready to sweep down on them and eat their flesh.

"But when Jesus heard that, he said unto them, They that be whole need not a physician, but they that are sick" (Matthew 9:12).

People who consider themselves righteous do not need the great Physician. Sick people who are feeling horrible pain and are afraid to die in hell seek out the Messiah and He heals them. Some of those sick people were thieves and prostitutes. They had a right to be healed of their sin diseases and made whole.

But the Pharisees were too righteous for salvation. However, some of the thieves and prostitutes knew that they were breaking the Law of God. They were sinners. They were reaching out to God for forgiveness, acceptance, and love.

He gave them this strong rebuke for their heartless against sinners. "But go ye and learn what that meaneth, I will have mercy, and not sacrifice: for I am not come to call the righteous, but sinners to repentance" (Matthew 9:13).

God only accepts people who show mercy to weak sinners and invite to the Messiah to receive salvation. He does not like being bribed with tithes, offerings, and other sacrifices. He is looking for love and not works.

He is not calling self-righteous people but those who knew they have cut off their heads because of their sins, and they are crying and mourning about committing suicide. They want to be saved, and He will save them.

The Messiah received flying colors when He recruited Matthew as one of the leaders of His kingdom. The man was searching for God but he was excluded from the community by the strict Pharisees. His conversion has appealed to millions of thieves, prostitutes, and all kinds of sinners to abandoned their sinful life and come to the Messiah.

II. But new wine must be put into new wineskins

While in Matthew's party, the Messiah told the Pharisees and doctors of the laws to accept the new wine of truth that He is offering for everybody to drink. They should no longer drink the wine of sin from the hand of the devil.

wineskin

"And he spoke also a similitude to them: That no man putteth a piece from a new garment upon an old garment: otherwise he both rendeth the new, and the piece taken from the new agreeth not with the old" (Luke 5:36, DRB).

He said, "There is yet to be the love and righteousness of God in a man that thinks he is loving but reaches out his hand and cuts a piece of a new veil and uses it to patch up a tear in an old veil whose strength has all gone.

The new patch would make a worse tear in the old veil because it is very strong. A brand new inheritance cannot be stored in an old. It is not strong enough to hold the brand new and heavy inheritance.

It will tear apart. The old veil will receive no benefit from the new one. Moreover, they will not match each other."

He gave another illustration of divine teachings that are embodied in the Messiah in comparison to the worn-out teachings the Jews were receiving from the laws of ceremonies and rituals sacrificial system. "And no one pours new wine into old wineskins; if he does, the fresh wine will burst the skins and it will be spilled and the skins will be ruined (destroyed).

But new wine must be put into fresh wineskins. And no one after drinking old wine immediately desires new wine, for he says, The old is good or better" (Luke 5:37–39, AMP).

He said, "There is yet to be the love and righteousness of God in a man that thinks he is loving but reaches out his hand and puts new wine into an old bag. (The bags were made from skins of goats for carrying wine, water, etc.).

The bag is too old to be reused again. It has done

its work of storing wine.

If new wine is put into an old bag, it will burst it. The wine will be poured into the ground. What a loss of both wine and the bag!

But new wine is like God. It is put into new bags. God does not like living in a heart that is filled with sin. He loves living in a new heart that is free of sin.

There is yet righteousness of God in a man who claims that he is loving when he is still drinking the old wine that has been giving him support and power. (The old wine is sin).

When he still has his mouth into the cup and is still drinking it, and at that moment, you tell him to drink the new wine being offered to him by the hand of God, he will tell you, "No! I am leaning on this powerful life. It is my father. It is giving me life."

The Holy Spirit is asking to fill you with His new wine or teachings. "Trust in the LORD with all thine heart; and lean not unto thine own understanding.

In all thy ways acknowledge him, and he shall direct thy paths. Be not wise in thine own eyes: fear the LORD, and depart from evil. It shall be health to thy navel, and marrow to thy bones" (Proverbs 3:5–8).

He is saying, "You must leave everything in hands of God. Hand yourself over to Me, the God of your life.

Give everything that is in your heart which you think is God to Me. Do not worship your own intellect, wisdom, and understanding.

Do not present yourself to them as their slave. Your thoughts, feelings, motives are not your God.

All the ways that the Lord has opened up for you are the proofs that He knows you very well. He is the Love. He will give you life. He will make you strong. He will help you to stand strong on your own feet on the foundation that He Himself has built on God the eternal and righteous Father.

You must not love your own wisdom over and above that of the Lord. Do not worship your own self-rule. Do not be passionate in your soul about your government with which you are ruling yourself as being very righteous and holy. Do not keep stare at it as being very lovely and beautiful.

Come to the Lord your God and Daddy for your intellect, wisdom, and power. Lean on Him alone and not on yourself, other people or things. You must reject all evil. They are not God. They did not give birth to you.

God Himself will be your Healer in the very depth of your being or bosom. He will breathe His eternal life into you. He will watch over. He will be your Bone marrow. He will create a beautiful, righteous, and holy person for you from His bone marrow. He will give you strong and eternal soul."

The Lord will create new wine or life out of you. " Thus says the Lord: As the juice [of the grape] is found in the cluster, and one says, Do not destroy it, for there is a blessing in it, so will I do for My servants' sake, that I may not destroy them all" (Isaiah 65:8, AMP).

The Lord does not allow your sins to hang you because there is something good in you. You are still His child. You are still looking like Him. That is why He sent His Son to die for your sins. He will not allow the Law to crucify you because you have broken them.

Unfortunately, the majority of the people of the world have rejected the Cross of Calvary. The fresh juices of the grapes or character that the Lord has put into the heads of human beings have been ruined. Many of them have added too much yeasts of sin and all kinds of lusts into the fresh juice.

They have fermented into very strong concentrated alcohol. The cups are frothing with mixed wine are sedating them into stupor. They encourage each other to commit sin like drinking water.

Anyone who does not listen to the Messiah is drinking dirty knowledge from the cup of sin. It is a concentrated, mixed with many different kinds of sins and, therefore, highly toxic. It is fatal. Anyone who drinks it is committing suicide.

God cannot force people not to drink. He has no choice. He will allow anyone who forces himself or herself to drink it. He or she can drink all of it until his or her cup is empty.

They can drink their fill from the cups frothing with the sin of rebellion and lawlessness. They love to shut up the mouth of the Law because they think they have the power to do it. Let them try to do it, and it will not warn them again about their sins.

The Lord has a cup brimming with mixed drinks that are highly fatal. He will invite demons and diehard sinners to drink it. "For in the hand of the LORD there is a cup, and the wine is red; it is full of mixture; and he poureth out of the same: but the dregs thereof, all the wicked of the earth shall wring them out, and drink them" (Psalms 75:8). They will drink it whether they like it or not.

It is a cup that is boiling with the wine of fires. The sorcerers, witches, and all kinds of rebels who love the darkness of sin will humiliate themselves by drinking from the cup of fires.

The Messiah will empty hot liquor of sulfuric acid that is dry and burning hot on them from His cup. They love the liquor of sin and they will get far more than they bargained for.

He is the hot Brother. And He will discipline his rebellious brothers and sisters by allowing them to drink from cup containing the alcohol of sin that they love very much.

But the alcohol is too concentrated and is literally burning with deadly fires. "The LORD trieth the righteous: but the wicked and him that loveth violence his soul hateth. Upon the wicked he shall rain snares, fire and brimstone, and an horrible tempest: this shall be the portion of their cup" (Psalms 11:5, 6). But He will comfort His companions on the Day of Judgment. He will shield them from the fires of hell.

The fires will get out of hand. They will have minds of their own. They will be the kings and conquerors of the earth. Wild and very strong winds that have much reserved energy like fats or cholesterol to wreck havocs will drive the fires everywhere.

They will cover the whole earth. They will burn sin, diseases, etc. and dry them up completely like water that has been left to boil too long over the fires. The fire will burn the water until it is all evaporated.

It will leave the container empty. It will look as if there was no water in the container in the first place. No one will be able to go around collect those gases of hydrogen and oxygen that had formed the water in the cup and return them into their original state.

It will be even worse for the demons and human sinners when they have all been burned and completely evaporated. They cannot be put back together again. "For as ye have drunk upon my holy mountain, so shall all the heathen drink continually, yea, they shall drink, and they shall swallow down, and they shall be as though they had not been" (Obadiah 1:16).

They will drink fires the cups of fires. They will burn out and never live again. It will be as if they had never been created and lived on this earth. They will never return again tempt, harass, and kill anyone.

But you will be safe. You will spread the Gospel of your salvation around the universes. You will tell them that your Messiah is an All-Powerful and All-Loving Savior. "But I will declare for ever; I will sing praises to the God of Jacob. All the horns of the wicked also will I cut off; but the horns of the righteous shall be exalted" (Psalms 75:9, 10).

But all the people who lived as if they are their own God will die out. They were lawless. They tried to lay spells on people. They tried to confuse their minds of the righteous ones in order to mislead them. They claimed that the world was their own country when she belongs to the Creator God.

They were proud of their powers. They worshipped power as God. They made friendship with violence as their best mates. They ran at the Creator with their ironed horns to gore Him to death. But He broke their horns and defeated them.

He demolished them. They will never be found existing somewhere in the universes. You will never see, hear or touch them again throughout God's eternal years.

III. They that are whole need not a physician; but they that are sick

Matthew could not believe that the Messiah would make him one of his disciples. He had been a thief all his life. But the Messiah saw his miserable life. He was not enjoying the good life he thought he would get by being rich through swindling people. He was hated. His only friends were his fellow thieves.

They, too, were hated by the common community of Jewry. There was little to go for them except the Romans who despised them for stealing from their countrymen in order to make themselves comfortable. They always charged double taxes. One part was for the Roman government and the other belongs to them. Their fellow Jews were not terribly rich people.

The majority of them were peasant farmers. Their over taxation was grinding them to death but they did not care. They wanted to live rich and happy lives. Yes, they were rich but he, Matthew in particular, was not happy. He was depressed but he hid his sorrow from the eyes of the world.

The Messiah saw that he was sorrowing for his sins. He was ready to be a decent and holy man. So He called him to be his disciple. He was enjoying his new found faith, discipleship, and the friendship with the Messiah immensely.

So he threw a big party in His honor in his house. He called all his fellow tax-collectors to meet his new

Friend. They, too, might find the peace that he was now enjoying. Those friends came along with some of their dates.

They were street girls who were as much deceived by the devil as themselves for trying to look for joy in the wrong places. "And it came to pass as he sat at meat in his house, many Publicans and sinners sat down together with Jesus and his disciples. For they, with Jesus who also followed him. For they were many, who also followed him" (Mark 2:15, DRB).

Crooks and prostitutes are not particularly the best group of friends anyone with a normal mind would choose. It alarmed the teachers of the law, scribes, and Pharisees that the Messiah and His disciples should sit down with these sinners to lunch.

They can cast a bad influence on Him and His disciples. "And the scribes and the Pharisees, seeing that he ate with publicans and sinners, said to his disciples: Why doth your master eat and drink with publicans and sinners?" (Mark 2:16, DRB).

They asked His disciples, "Are you really following God the loving Daddy? Why are you are spending your lives eating and drinking together with street men and prostitutes?"

The Messiah overheard them quarrelling His disciples. They were accusing them of not following God very strictly and also of being too friendly with sinners. "But Jesus hearing it, said: They that are in health need not a physician, but they that are ill. Go then and learn what this meaneth, I will have mercy and not sacrifice. For I am not come to call the just, but sinners" (Matthew 9:12, 13, DRB).

He was saying, "No brother (or sister) who has all the love and truths of God spends his life loving and chasing a physician to father him and birth life into him but those who have been dragged away by the god of this world.

So now go and learn about He who is love. I have deep passions for watching and placing My hand on care, love, and mercy and not on murdering the loving Daddy that your sacrifices point to.

My passion for coming into the world is not to place the hand of God on you, the righteous fathers, who know it all but on sinners and help them to mourn and sorrow for their sins."

God the Father is your Physician. He is also your Commander-in-Chief who cannot get hurt or die. Even the best among the military depend on Him for safety. He is your soldier and cop. The 9-1-1 line to reach Him is open twenty four hours a day and seven days a week. In fact, He is the 9-1-1 emergency phone line. He is the hot line.

He is already with you before you make that emergency call. If you get injured in the conflicts, He will send an ambulance to rescue you. He Himself is the Head of the rescue team.

He is your Doctor and Nurse all put into one. He is the best of all the medical team in the world. He can resurrect dead people back to life. "Jesus said unto her, I am the resurrection, and the life: he that believeth in me, though he were dead, yet shall he live" (John 11:25).

He said that He is who is called the Resurrection. He is who is called Life. Anyone who places his or her active faith in Him will not be disappointed. Though he or she may fall dead and gone from the surface of the earth, yet in Him, he or she will breathe again.

Call on the Lord who arms are always stretched out to receive you. Run into His welcoming arms and be safe. He has promised to save you from all your enemies. "I will call upon the LORD, who is worthy to be praised: so shall I be saved from mine enemies" (Psalms 18:3).

You will thank and congratulate yourself for good decision you made in making the Rock your place of refuge. And you praise Him for discovering that He is what He says He is. He is God the Almighty Defender and Protector. He is beyond comparison in power, wisdom, intelligence, love, etc.

His own fingers created you in the body of Adam. He put His own Spirit into you in order to give you life, intelligence, wisdom, and righteousness. "And he said: Let us make man to our image and likeness: and let him have dominion over the fishes of the sea, and the fowls of the air, and the beasts, and the whole earth, and every creeping creature that moveth upon the earth. And God created man to his own image: to the image of God he created him: male and female he created them" (Genesis 1:26, 27, DRB).

He is caring for you every minute of your life otherwise you will cease to exist. He is inside your body to make the brains think, heart to pump, and bones and muscles to work.

Therefore, He knows how to cure your mind, heart, body, and spirit when you fall sick. He said that He is your Healer in the last words of Exodus 15:26, DRB, "I am the Lord thy Healer." His entire everlasting life is deeply loving and passionate about you.

He wants to breathe new and eternal life into you the same way He had breathe His Spirit into a piece of clay and it turned into a living being. He was Adam your father. "And the Lord God formed man of the slime of the earth: and breathed into his face the breath of life, and man became a living soul" (Genesis 2:7, DRB).

You are being bombarded with all kinds of virulent disease-causing agents on your skin, mouth, eyes, ears, etc. every second of your life. Had it not been for the mercy of the Lord in preventing them from infecting you, not only you but the whole inhabitants of the earth would have been wiped out by them.

There are many dangerous objects all around you. Each of them has the power to destroy your life. But the Lord is standing Guard over you to protect you from them all. He has been your Healer from conception to this day.

He has always been there throughout your temptations and trials. "Or know you not that your members are the temple of the Holy Ghost, who is in you, whom you have from God: and you are not your own? For you are bought with a great price. Glorify and bear God in your body" (1 Corinthians 6:19, 20, DRB).

You have not met God through His beloved Son, the Messiah. Know for sure that you are now His royal residence. You are the temple of the Holy Spirit. He has come to live in your heart for all eternal years to come. You cannot live for your own interests any more. That is unrighteousness.

The Lord has laid His hand on you and blessed you. He chose you by buying you back from sin and death with His own blood. You have inherited your Father's blood in order that you may be His child in every way. Your body is longer your own because His divine blood is flowing through your veins.

So now offer your body to Him as an eternal gift of love. Use it for living right and for loving Him in your thoughts, words, and actions. The Lord is inviting you to ask Him for help if you are not well or need help of any kind "Ask, and it shall be given you: seek, and you shall find: knock, and it shall be opened to you" (Matthew 7:7, DRB).

Ask Him for help because He is the Way. He is your Righteousness. He will give you help. Offer yourself to Him because He is your Daddy. He will you add for you more blessings that what you have asked Him for. He will promote you greatly. He asking you to your all your strength and powers to knock on His door, and He will open to you the way to His heart. He will love all of you eternally.

God is with you all. So if you ask for the needs of life and for righteousness, you will get the Brother to be your Eternal Friend. "For every one that asketh, receiveth: and he that seeketh, findeth: and to him that knocketh, it shall be opened" (Matthew 7:8, DRB).

Anyone who asks Him to be his or her God and Daddy, will receive great and eternal successes. Anyone who knocks at His door with all his or her strength and powers will have the door opened for him or her. He will receive that God of love to be His eternal Friend.

3. Zacchaeus

James Tissot, 1836-1902, Zacchaeus in the Sycamore

The Messiah entered into the City of Jericho as God her Brother. He passed through the city winning the war against the forces of darkness. He showed the people that He loved them. He came to give them eternal life. He was watching their backs. There came a man amongst the crowds who was made in the image of God.

His parents had given him the Names of God. They were the Names of "the Just, the Pure, the Holy" or "the Clean." In Hebrews, He was called Zacchaeus.

The parents prayed that their little boy may grow up to holy and righteous like God. Unfortunately, their dreams for him did not materialize at first. They dream was that their little boy would turn out to be a loving and pious man. He was a street leader.

His dubious ways of doing business made him very rich and wealthy. "And Jesus entered and passed through Jericho. And, behold, there was a man named Zacchaeus, which was the chief among the publicans, and he was rich" (Luke 19:1, 2).

He prayed and bound God with an oath to help him see the Messiah with his own two eyes. He wanted to see He who was called Love from the beginning of the world.

But God was still with him even though all the powers he had employed to push his way through the crowds could not get him any closer to the Messiah. "And he sought to see Jesus who he was; and could not for the press, because he was little of stature" (Luke 19:3).

It was not so much as his height that made it impossible for him to see the face of the Messiah but the lack of the knowledge of truth in his heart that kept Him away. He did not have God in his heart all his life.

The crowds formed a rock block on him. He could not push his way through them to see the Messiah. So he rose up and started running ahead of the moving crowds that had surrounded the Messiah as fast as he could.

There was a tree that stood just ahead of him. It was like God who wanted him to know the truth. So he helped himself to its services. He climbed high up and sat on one of its branches. He parted the leaves to peep down on the street on which He hoped the Son of God would pass.

He had seen that the Messiah had commanded the people who were ahead of Him to walk that way. When God had arrived, He stood under the tree. He looked up steadily and studied him. "And he ran before, and climbed up into a sycamore tree to see him: for he was to pass that way. And when Jesus came to the place, he looked up, and saw him, and said unto him, Zacchaeus, make haste, and come down; for today I must abide at thy house" (Luke 19:4, 5).

He spoke to him with love as only the God of love could. He called out loudly to him, "My dear Just One! Come down quickly like God descending from the sky and show Me your real self. In My capacity as the God of love, I have humbled My Omnipotent Fatherhood and made Myself nothing so that I run My office to supply inheritances to the world from your house today."

The man hurried down from the tree like God descending from the sky. He showed himself to the

Messiah. "And he made haste, and came down, and received him joyfully" (Luke 19:6). He welcomed Him with the welcome God the Father gives to people. It was the welcome of much joy and love.

Now, when the many multitudes of peoples of the Lord witnessed what was happening with their own eyes, they were not happy. In fact, they were very angry with God. "And when they saw it, they all murmured, saying, That he was gone to be guest with a man that is a sinner" (Luke 19:7).

They rose up against the Lord and quarreled Him, saying, "Isn't He called Love? Why is He going into the house of His adversary who has been fighting Him so terribly? Why is God and Brother of His enemy?

Zacchaeus stood tall before the Lord with all the strength of his body could command. "And Zacchaeus stood, and said unto the Lord; Behold, Lord, the half of my goods I give to the poor; and if I have taken anything from any man by false accusation, I restore him fourfold" (Luke 19:8).

He spoke to Him with the authority of God, saying, "As long as I am alive, my dear Lord and Daddy, I will give half of the wealth I own to the poor. If I remember in my heart that I had laid a strong hand on someone and tore his life apart with false accusations that he did not pay his taxes, I am now and hereby vowing to repay him four times the amount of money that I stole from him."

The loving God spoke with power and authority. "And Jesus said unto him, This day is salvation come to this house, forsomuch as he also is a son of Abraham. For the Son of man is come to seek and to save that which was lost" (Luke 19:9, 10).

He said to Zacchaeus in the hearing of all the gathered multitudes, "Today, the God of truth has brought divine love and truth into the house of the man He loves. He, too, is the life that Abraham built out of himself.

In My capacity as God and the Son of God, the

Righteous Person, I have already vowed with My uplifted and omnipotent hand to save the people who have abandoned the God of life. And as God their Brother, I will save them by filling them with eternal life and truth."

He is the Good Shepherd. He is searching for you, His lost sheep. "I will seek that which was lost and bring back that which has strayed, and I will bandage the hurt and the crippled and will strengthen the weak and the sick, but I will destroy the fat and the strong [who have become hardhearted and perverse]; I will feed them with judgment and punishment" (Ezekiel 34:16, AMP).

Sin had bruised you terribly with all sorts of physical, mental, spiritual, social, economic, political, security, etc. fears and pains. And worst of all, it has infected you with death.

But the Messiah has come today into your house to save you from them all. He will feel you with His own divine and eternal good health. You will never suffer, cry or die again.

4. The rich young ruler

Johann Michael Ferdinand Heinrich Hofmann (March 19, 1824 - June 23, 1911), the younger ruler

A young ruler or senator had been watching the Messiah for a long time. He saw healing and performing miracles. He listened to his sermons. But what impressed him most was his loving treatment of children. Mothers had brought their children for the Messiah to bless.

He took them in His arms and prayed over them. The whole scene was very moving. He was not much older that some of the youth who came to the Lord to be blessed.

The Messiah looked very pious and holy when the little children in His arms and blessed them. He put His hands on the youth and prayed for them.

The young senator or parliamentarian envied the Messiah very much. He wanted to be gracious especially to the children and youth, the future of his nation.

He wanted to perform miracles for them and pray great blessings over them. If heaven was this beautiful where children are put first before the adults, he wanted it now.

When the Lord had finished blessing the children, He rose up and began to leave. It was getting dark, and

He was going home. "And when he was gone forth into the way, there came one running, and kneeled to him, and asked him, Good Master, what shall I do that I may inherit eternal life?" (Mark 10:17).

When the young ruler saw the Messiah walking away, he rose up from his place and began to run after Him. When he caught up with Him, he fell down with his face to the ground before and asked for a favor,

"Oh You, Most Excellent Teacher of truth who creates life! What things must I do to inherit Your life that has absolutely no beginning or end?"

People of the world like that brilliant, rich, and young senator. They all look very awesome. They are majestic. Their greatness increases when their powerful and wealthy. Their intelligence won them their powers and riches. They are the envy of many who have not achieved their amazing statuses.

Most people do not lend you their ears if you tell them that power, wealth, fame, etc. are not everything. "Hear this, all ye people; give ear, all ye inhabitants of the world: Both low and high, rich and poor, together" (Psalms 49:1, 2).

Whether you are successful or not, there are times when you will think about life, death, and the life beyond the grave.

You will think what really constitutes living in this world. What is the most important thing in your life that is even better than having a family?

The Messiah rebuked the rich young man for calling Him God when he did not love for Him. He just wanted to use Him to promote his own political agendas. "And he said unto him, Why callest thou me good? there is none good but one, that is, God: but if thou wilt enter into life, keep the commandments" (Matthew 19:17).

He was telling the man, "Why did you come here to call Me, 'Most Excellent Teacher of truth who creates life' when you do love Me?

There is yet to be the Most Excellent Teacher and

Creator of life except this God you are looking at. But if you want to walk and enter into life, take the Law and keep it in your heart as the most precious treasure you will ever find."

There is nothing more important in this world than to live in awe and admiration of the Lord. You were created for worship. Worship involves love, adoration, faith, trust, obedience, loyalty, etc. The other things will fall in their right priorities. But God must always come first. "Let all the earth fear the LORD: let all the inhabitants of the world stand in awe of him" (Psalms 33:8).

The world where you are living belongs to Him. In fact, He owns your very life. When you put Him first, He will tell you exact how to spend your life. You are His glory.

Whatever you achieve or fail to achieve is His glory. You are all winners at the end of your lives when you put Him first. He is awesome. He deserves your admiration and love.

Try to put your thoughts into words when you are thinking about God. At least, write them down. What does life mean to you?

Are you one of those people who just live to eat and die? "But instead, you celebrated by feasting on beef and lamb and by drinking wine, because you said, "Let's eat and drink! Tomorrow we may die" (Isaiah 22:13, CEV).

You may be a vegetarian or may you are not. That is not the point. The question is: what exactly are you living for? Whom are you praising? Are you praising yourself in everything that you do?

You are giving yourself as a gift to yourself instead of to God. Do you love, socialize, work, eat, drink, etc. for your sole pleasure? Should you not be praising God instead of worshipping yourself?

The young senator ran his mind through the letters of the Ten Commandments and felt that he had kept all of them perfectly. He asked the Messiah what He was talking about. "He saith unto him, Which? Jesus said, Thou shalt do no murder, Thou shalt not commit adultery, Thou shalt not steal, Thou shalt not bear false witness, Honour thy father and thy mother: and, Thou shalt love thy neighbour as thyself" (Matthew 19:18, 19).

The Messiah mentioned the Commandments most young people struggle with. And this young man was no exception. He mentioned their adulteries, fornications, thefts, lies, and disobedience to parents and other authorities.

But the young man was lying when he said, "The young man saith unto him, All these things have I kept from my youth up: what lack I yet?" (Matthew 19:20).

He said he had kept all the Ten Commandments holy since when he began to learn the stories of the Bible on his mother's knees when he was a little child. Were there any other things that still needed him after all the good things he had done for the Ten Commandments?

God knew what He was accusing youth and children about. They were a bunch of adulterers, adulteresses, fornicators, thieves, liars and disobedient people. He came into the world to save them from their sins because He loved them.

He still loved children and youth. "Then Jesus beholding him loved him, and said unto him, One thing thou lackest: go thy way, sell whatsoever thou hast, and give to the poor, and thou shalt have treasure in heaven: and come, take up the cross, and follow me" (Mark 10:21).

The Lord took a second look at the young. He looked him over carefully. He liked the youth and energy of the young man. He was already a senator or member of the Sanhedrin or council of the elders that governed Israel at a very age.

He had multiplied the inheritance his father left him through hard work and intelligence. He was young and married with children though he was barely a youth. What a youth! He could make an excellent disciple.

He said, "There is still one thing that needs you to attend to if you want to be perfectly holy and righteous. Go straight to your businesses, sell all of them, and give the money to the poor that you are treating like filth.

You will have a whole treasure box in heaven filled with the rarest jewels. Then come back to Me and follow My traditions of preaching, healing, performing miracles, and blessing little children and youth. Complete your journey of carrying My Cross."

The truth is that no human beings own this life. Each of them came into this world for a short season. They will all die. The good and bad all meet the same fate. It is the grave.

They will not be buried with their bulls. The bulls were symbols of all wealth and riches. The people they have left behind want them to help them defray their expenses.

Some rich people have not learned from the mistakes of those people who have passed on. They have very strong feelings in their wombs that they rich houses are eternal powerhouses. They think that their future generations will carry on their names forever.

They have this idea that their descendants will always be grateful to them for making them rich people. Their descendants will go around the world to tell people who they were, how they did their businesses, and how much inheritances they had left for their families. In that way, they will always be famous and awe the world even after their deaths.

But the living are busy trying to live than spend all their celebrating the glories of dead people. It is better to give your life to God that to riches. He will remember you forever. He will resurrect you on the last day. And you will live with people who will not forget that you are also a human being and very special.

Sin has cut the lives of people short. Though you are one kind of a man (woman included), families and friends will not celebrate your greatness and/or goodness forever.

You are not going to be the house of honor forever. "Nevertheless man being in honour abideth not: he is like the beasts that perish" (Psalms 49:12).

You breathe the same air with the animals. You all eat plants and flesh like them. The only one who can make you to be of superior intelligence and wisdom than them is God. After this life is over, He will make you live forever. But the animals of this world will be dead and gone forever.

There are two groups of people in this world: the human beings and the animals. Jesus lives in the hearts of the human beings. The animals have crazy brains. Unfortunately, they are the ones who are loved and admired more than the human beings.

They can make money in any way they want whether it is in the right way or wrong way. They worship wealth. And almost everyone on earth likes wealth and riches. They admire the gorgeous ways the rich live. No wonder many of them have easier times in courts than the poor folks.

When poor people are teaching others how to get rich, they are listened to very politely. But when the rich are advising the poor how to reach to the top, they pay attention. Their counsels are passed on from mouth to mouth and from generation to generation.

In spite of their riches and wisdom, they are just sheep like everybody else. Sooner or later, everyone will be led to the slaughter house by death. All the universe of human beings around you will die each in his or her time.

So do not waste your life trying to impress them with riches, powers, intellectual reasoning, wisdom, fame, etc. They are mere passing shadows. They will soon keep company with death like playmates. It will walk all over their bodies.

It will swallow their beauties, majesties, powers, intelligence, wisdom and everything. "This their way is their folly: yet their posterity approve their sayings. Selah. Like sheep they are laid in the grave; death shall feed on them; and the upright shall have dominion over them in the morning; and their beauty shall consume in the grave from their dwelling" (Psalms 49:13, 14).

If you want to live after the grave, invite Jesus into your heart. "But God will redeem my soul from the power of the grave: for he shall receive me. Selah" (Psalms 49:15).

On the day of His Second Coming, He will breathe eternal life into your nostrils like He did into the clay, and it turned into a warm blooded person whom He called Adam. This breathe is the new and eternal spirit you will receive into your new body.

There will be a whole universe of the people with new spirits and bodies. He will recreate them all over again because He is their Brother. He will take them out of their graves and recreate them again. Pursue that new life with all your mind, heart, spirit, time, and energy.

Impress the Messiah with love, faith, trust, riches, powers, fame, etc. and not your neighbors, and you will live forever. He will help you enjoy true riches in heaven. You stand tall, brave, and strong forever. You will feast on eternal life.

The ears of the young man heard all the words of the Messiah and almost had a heart attack. He, and not the young man, is the All-Powerful, richest and wealthiest Person in heaven and on the earth. He could have given the young man true riches that earthly money cannot buy.

They are priceless and eternal in value. But this young senator had never matured since he was a selfish little toddler. Though he boasted he always lived by the Law since he was a toddler, he never did.

He had never taken those baby steps of walking

righteously in the truth. "But when the young man heard that saying, he went away sorrowful: for he had great possessions" (Matthew 19:22).

The words of Jesus not only broke his heart but his body was all beaten up. He was deep grieved. He went away mourning about losing the pride of his life. The love of riches had stolen his heart away from his Creator and Messiah. He was a very wealthy more than the average rich people.

The Messiah was sad to see this man crying and mourning about his riches as if he was falling dead. He was holding his own funeral party. He was deceived by the riches of the world. He refused to listen to God who gave him to wealth.

The Benefactor wanted him to be a disciple and senior king above the rest of the world, and he refused because of dirt that he called wealth. How sad! "And when Jesus saw that he was very sorrowful, he said, How hardly shall they that have riches enter into the kingdom of God! For it is easier for a camel to go through a needle's eye, than for a rich man to enter into the kingdom of God" (Luke 18:24, 25).

It is impossible for rich people who have rejected the Ten Commandments to enter into heaven. If they refuse to obey the Law of love, they will not see the face of the Messiah. If they make a heaven out of their wealth, it will be impossible for them to enter into the real heaven. The real heaven is where God their Creator and the richest Person in heaven and on the earth lives.

Some rich people bet their lives on their wealth. They think that their riches can take through anything. They put all their weights on them. They worshipped them as God Almighty that can do anything they wanted. They cover themselves with wealth like garments.

They see through the eyes of riches. They only see things that are of value to them. They look at their wealth and riches as young calves only. They want them to grow into bigger and stronger bulls.

Even strong bulls get sick or injured. They can die. Wealth cannot solve all the problems of this world. And this brother or sister can injured himself or herself instead of saving himself when he puts his or her wealth above his or her Creator. And another rich brother (or sister) cannot buy the mercy of God to help the other brother save himself from troubles.

The Messiah sorrows for lost rich people. Other rich brothers (or sisters) cannot comfort His heart by giving Him gifts. He needs their hearts. They are the only things that will make Him happy.

He wants to celebrate their lives from births to eternity. They are very precious children. He wants to give them better riches in heaven that they can enjoy throughout eternities that stretch back to back.

He is asking them not to worship the riches of this world. They should put more values on their lives than on riches.

They are not going to live forever. They will die like everybody else. And their money will not bring them back to life.

There is no life in the grave. "For he seeth that wise men die, likewise the fool and the brutish person perish, and leave their wealth to others. Their inward thought is, that their houses shall continue for ever, and their dwelling places to all generations; they call their lands after their own names" (Psalms 49:10, 11).

Take a few moments and look at the world around you. You will be shocked in seeing that human beings are not really more powerful than their Maker. They may spend their lives trying to run away from Him but they are just fooling themselves.

They are not powerful. They will die in their wisdom which they think are better than that of the Savior.

There are people who are prisoners of their own intelligence. They will not see other wisdom except their own. They will die because of intellectual pride and/or spiritual arrogance.

They wall themselves by their education, expertise, philosophies, etc. They refuse to see a world that is far greater and better than their familiar surroundings.

Violent people are idolaters. They are the children of Baal, the prince of all demons. They live as if they were not been born by God the Father. They are suicidal because they live by violence.

They ignore that the swords they are welding against other people can turn against them. They have refused to celebrate the greatness, powers, and goodness of God their Father every day.

There used to be small gates beside the big ones around Jerusalem. The big gates are closed just before sun down every Friday afternoons.

Late comers used the small gates to enter into Jerusalem. And if a man comes in time but finds the big gates closed, he would make his camel to kneel down.

He would coax it to crawl on its belly slowly and laboriously through the small gate. Hence, the small gates came to be known as the eye of the needle.

The Messiah warned rich people to be careful about the attractiveness of wealth. It must in no way blind them to the truth wealth that is waiting for them in heaven.

The devil will surround them with many temptations. And these will hamper their way to heaven.

It will be hard getting to heaven because of the temptations and trials that riches usually bring. But if they can get on their knees like camels going through the eyes of the needles and pray all the time, they will make it to heaven.

The disciples were surprised to hear the Lord saying that riches were not everything. In some Semitic Bibles, the word called "fortune" is used in many verses.

But in the English Bible, almost all of the statements where the word "fortune" is used were replaced by the word called "blessing".

"And they were astonished out of measure, saying among themselves, Who then can be saved?" (Mark 10:26).

The jaws of the disciples dropped low as they gaped at amazement at the words the Lord just said. They could not believe their ears. They discussed about the greatness of riches among themselves and wondered why the Lord was not impressed about wealth.

They asked each other, "And now, who will be given salvation?"

The priests were stressing only one type of fortunes. They were preaching only about the riches of this world. Thus, they misled the people in thinking that earthly wealth went together hand-in-hand with heavenly fortunes. In fact, you had earthly fortunes, and you were well on your way to receiving the heavenly fortunes.

They had rejected to preach about the true Fortune that the world needed. He is God the Creator of everything. Fortunes are God and His salvation for the world. God used the word fortunes to include everything and especially His eternal blessings.

Whether you are rich or not, you are still the child of God. He loves you for who you are and not for your wealth. He is, therefore, saving you and not your riches. "And Jesus looking upon them saith, With men it is impossible, but not with God: for with God all things are possible" (Mark 10:27).

He looked straight into their eyes and told them, "Holy feast days like the Passover and the Day of Atonement are celebrated because God is able to give His full powers on His enemies and level them down. He is able to save His children. But such works of salvation and miracles are impossible for men and women to carry out.

God can celebrate victories over His enemies because He is able to vent His full force on His enemies and save you all. He can do the impossible."

Do not envy people who are richer than you or who use dubious methods to accumulate their wealth. The poor also should stop envying people that the Lord has blessed with wealth.

Do not rob, kill, rape, insult, etc. them. "Be not thou afraid when one is made rich, when the glory of his house is increased; For when he dieth he shall carry nothing away: his glory shall not descend after him.

Though while he lived he blessed his soul: and men will praise thee, when thou doest well to thyself. He shall go to the generation of his fathers; they shall never see light. Man that is in honour, and understandeth not, is like the beasts that perish" (Psalms 49:16–20).

Do not be afraid of who live off their wealth. It is true. Their houses are more powerful than of the poor people. They have achieved the glories of the earth. But do talk to them.

Befriend them as your fellow human beings who also need love and affection. Do not be impressed with their riches to make you treat them better than you treat yourself and other poor people.

Do not stop breathing as if your head has been cut off when they are around. Do not state at them as if they are some special specimens of human beings. Be casual and normal. Treat them like you will treat everybody else.

Rich people are not different from you. They, too, have heartaches and temptations just like you. Death will feast on them just like it does on the poor folks. It will not give them better treatment than the poor. It will steal their lives just like it steals of the common people.

The rich will not descend into their graves in full glory and surrounded by wealth and comfort. When they fall dead, their bodies will be as dead as of the poor who fall dead.

The dead bodies of the men may be dressed in expensive tuxedos and of the women in jeweled wedding gowns but they are as dead just like the rest of the dead bodies of other people whether they were rich or poor.

People chased them for their riches when they were alive. They were worshipped. Doors of opportunities were opened for them even when they have not asked for those business ventures.

Everybody blessed them. And you, too, blessed them in your spirit. You loved them. You were always polite and gracious to them.

You will receive the same reverence when you get rich. You will be treated with awe and reverence as if you are God. They will think that you are far better than them because you are rich.

But in no way must you allow your riches to get into your head and take full control of your mind. You will soon be thrown into jail where all your ancestors have been cast. There is no life there. It is a land of perpetual darkness.

Celebrate God with all that you have while you are still alive and not yourself. Wealth is not everything. God is everything. Live for Him and not for your animal lusts.

If you love Him all the days of your life, He will save you. If you live like an animal, you will not be resurrected after the second death.

Some wise people have been asking about the real issues of life. You have also meditated about the same things more or less. "Why should I be afraid in times of trouble, when I am surrounded by vicious enemies? They trust in their riches and brag about all of their wealth.

You cannot buy back your life or pay off God! It costs far too much to buy back your life. You can never pay God enough to stay alive forever and safe from death" (Psalms 49:5–9, CEV).

Do not go trembling and fearing terribly during the days when Satan has his eyes upon you to destroy you. He will hold a feast just like when you hold holy feast days to the Lord to celebrate your suffering and death. But do not be afraid of him.

He loves and his supporters like to see you suffer. Do not be scared to death because of them.

They are evil. They will oppose everything you say or do out of malice. Their hat and anger against you show that their hearts are evil.

Be prepared to see such kinds of evil against. So you do not faint because of their evil behaviors towards you.

Peter was the first to recover from the shock. "Then answered Peter and said unto him, Behold, we have forsaken all, and followed thee; what shall we have therefore?" (Matthew 19:27).

Well, if the rich do not have first place in entering into heaven. What about the disciples?

They had left their lucrative fishing, tax collectors, etc. businesses to follow Him. It was not easy for them to break away from the business that they loved.

But they had left everything. They were now dirt poor just as the Messiah wanted.

They were beggars for the sake of the kingdom of God. They were now following the Lord's tradition of being poor men in order to serve and save the whole world. What kinds of riches, wealth, positions, powers, etc. were they going to get in heaven?

The Lord stressed the real truth to the whole world. It did not lay in being rich and/or powerful. Truth is the salvation of the world. "And every one that hath forsaken houses, or brethren, or sisters, or father, or mother, or wife, or children, or lands, for my name's sake, shall receive an hundredfold, and shall inherit everlasting life" (Matthew 19:29).

Everyone among you who breaks away from things that they hold dear will not be forgotten. They are the houses which they themselves built very lovingly with their own hands as if they were raising their gentle and loving daughters. They are the brothers that take care of you.

They are the sisters that love them as their only true brothers. They are the fathers who stand tall and proud because they have given births to them. They are the dear and lovely mothers who travailed with great pains when they were giving births to you.

They are the people who were taken out from your ribs. (They are the men who united you back into their flesh). They are the children you gave your flesh and spirits to. They are the fields that give you your sustenance.

If you follow God today, He will give all the houses of the believers. They will welcome you into their homes because their houses belong to you. All fathers, mothers, brothers, sisters, and children of the believers will be your family.

Their lands and businesses will belong to you. The saints will pay you tithes and offerings out of what they own. But you must remember that Satan hates you because you are rich through the businesses and works of the believers.

You have a very large family because all the believers are your family. The devil will persecute and even murder you out of jealousy.

Those put personal interests first will miss heaven. But those who put God and His kingdom first will be the first to be welcomed back home in heaven. "But many that are first shall be last; and the last first" (Mark 10:31).

If you live the life that you have known behind for the beautiful Name of the Messiah, you will receive more than a hundred percent rewards in heaven. Infinite blessings will be poured into your hands together with inheritance of the Kingdom of God and eternal life.

"And Jesus said unto them, Verily I say unto you, That ye which have followed me, in the regeneration when the Son of man shall sit in the throne of his glory, ye also shall sit upon twelve thrones, judging the twelve tribes of Israel" (Matthew 19:28).

He said that anyone who has faith in His divine culture and lived like Him will be among the resurrected ones. They will be taken to place where the Son of God sits as the ruling and reigning God, King, and Lord with great powers, authority, glories beyond descriptions.

You will also sit on your own throne. You will pass judgments in how to bless the children of God.

5. Come unto me, all ye that labour and are heavy laden

Carl Heinrich Bloch (May 23, 1834 – February 22, 1890), Jesus Christ the Consolator of all worlds

The Messiah invites all the overburdened people of this world to come to Him to find rest. He promised, "Come unto me, all ye that labour and are heavy laden, and I will give you rest" (Matthew 11:28).

He was saying, "Come all of you who are on this earth to the Lord. I am the God of life. You are Mine.

All of you, who are being now being harassed by all kinds of temptations and trials, came out of My life. Everyone who is burdens that the Lord alone ought to carry, come to Me.

I will fill you with the love and completeness of God. I will watch over you. I will love you and live within each one of your hearts."

He has infinite passions of watching over your life always and eternally. He is said that He will delegate the responsibility of looking after to someone but will watch over you personally.

He will make His All-Powerful, Eternal, All-Knowing, and All-Benevolent life to flow from Him and into your soul until you are overflowing with His Spirit. He will end all the suffering people of the earth with His Spirit. He is not selecting a few people favorite people will save anyone who asks Him for help.

A yoke is wooden structure that is put on the next of oxen to force them to go in one direction according to the dictates of the driver. A number of them can be harness together so that their combined powers may do a bigger and more thorough job.

Satan has put heavy yokes of sin, death, sicknesses, old age, hatred, pride, selfishness, etc. on all the people of this earth. These yokes are simply too heavy for them to carry.

The Messiah promised, "Take my yoke upon you, and learn of me; for I am meek and lowly in heart: and ye shall find rest unto your souls. For my yoke is easy, and my burden is light" (Matthew 11:29, 30).

He will each of you with His love. Love is an easy yoke to carry. Actually, it is pleasurable. It is the real and true life that He had planned that you should have lived had sin He will treat you with love and kindness. Learn about His passions for life and love. He will bring peace and rest in your heart. "For this is the love of God, that we keep his commandments: and his commandments are not grievous" (1 John 5:3).

The Ten Commandments are gentle like good mothers. They have very loving and compassionate. You will not find them too burdensome to obey.

They will love you and show you how to love God and your fellow human beings unselfishly. The joys of this world have limits.

Before you have really begun to enjoy it, it has flown away from you like an eagle into the sky. "And in my prosperity I said, I shall never be moved" (Psalms 30:6).

But the joys of the Lord your God is eternal in nature. "He only is my rock and my salvation; he is my defence; I shall not be greatly moved" (Psalms 62:2).

No matter what problems are facing you in this world, the Lord God is your rock solid peace and joy. He has already saved you and filled you with His all-powerful glories.

He will not allow pain and sorrow to hurt you here and there forever. Your sorrows are increasing now but they are about to end. They will never trouble you again.

It is the greatest desire of the Messiah to be your Comforter in this troublesome life you are going through here on this earth. And He is powerful. He will save you. "Save thy people, and bless thine inheritance: feed them also, and lift them up forever" (Psalms 28:9).

He will save His wise and intelligent people in whom is His Spirit. He will not forget His own descendants.

He will wash away their sins and reinstate them into greater glories than they had before they fell into sin. He will always move them forward. He will fill them with His own Supernatural Self.

Your lips will never leave offering Him praises and thanksgiving. He, indeed, is your glory and peace. You live and thrive through the generous life He has given. But He has a better life ahead of you.

It is perfect, awesome, and everlasting. He wants you to reach out for it. He will give it to you because you are His inheritance that He made out of Himself.

The Lord will give you the wings of an eagle to fly high up to the top of the Rock of Ages. "The LORD is my rock, and my fortress, and my deliverer; my God, my strength, in whom I will trust; my buckler, and the horn of my salvation, and my high tower" (Psalms 18:2).

Your Savior will reveal the glory of His tremendous, fiery and infinite powers to you that is able to save you. He is the power of your salvation. He is your undefeatable Defender.

He will cover you with His all-consuming fires and no devil will destroy your soul. He will hide you in the rock until all the troubles of this world are over.

He is your safe house as well as vacation house. Trust Him. He is a strong fortress. Nothing that is eternally dangerous such as sin or death will get you when you are hiding in Him.

He will personally lead and guide you throughout this life and into the next one because you are His lovely dove. He is your loveliness and all goodness.

He is the Shepherd, and you are His beloved sheep that He is tenderly caring for day and night. He feels you sorrows, pain, sickness, death, etc. more than you do.

"In all their affliction he was afflicted, and the angel of his presence saved them: in his love and in his pity he redeemed them; and he bare them, and carried them all the days of old" (Isaiah 63:9).

He is with you when you are oppressed and/or overwhelmed. He is your guardian Angel.

He is a faithful Friend. He is your overflowing blessings.

He is the Savior of all. He is your Liberator from sin, demoniac powers, death, and all other troubles of this world.

Eternal Love has lifted all you very high so that you may completely filled with His All-Powerful, All-Knowing, All-Benevolent, and Everlasting Supernatural Spirit from eternity to eternity.

6 CHAPTER

THE GREATEST LAW IN THE TEN COMMANDMENT

One God

The Pharisees were Bible scholars. Their faults lay in misinterpreting the Bible to fit their own wishes and dreams. They multiplied the Ten Commandments into many frivolous laws. Since they an agrarian society, most of the tradition of the fathers or oral laws are inapplicable today.

The Sadducees were self-seekers and influenced too much by Hellenism (Greek culture), the Pharisees believed the world of God. They believed in the existence of God. They preached about moralities by keeping the Ten Commandments holy.

They taught the doctrines of judgment that will reward good people but punish sinners. They believe in the existence of heaven as the place where good people would go. They believe sinners will be punished in hell.

They also believe in good angels and demons. "For the Sadducees say that there is no resurrection, neither angel, nor spirit: but the Pharisees confess both" (Acts 23:8). The Pharisees spread the message of the coming of the Messiah as the hope for all the peoples of the earth.

The Pharisees made an error in claiming that the soul never dies. They believed that somewhat good person could be saved. He would be burned in hell a brief period and then be transferred into heaven.

They were influenced by pagan religions. Though they believe in predestinate, fatalities, etc. they also believe that God has endowed each human being with a free will to choose to follow good or bad ways.

They believed in one God but could not explain the Triune Godhead. One of them asked the Messiah if there was one Law that was more important the rest.

They asked Him whether keeping just that Law could take them to heaven. "And one of the scribes came, and having heard them reasoning together, and perceiving that he had answered them well, asked him, Which is the first commandment of all? And Jesus answered him,

The first of all the commandments is, Hear, O Israel; The Lord our God is one Lord: And thou shalt love the Lord thy God with all thy heart, and with all thy soul, and with all thy mind, and with all thy strength: this is the first commandment" (Mark 12:28–30).

Jesus replied in the affirmative. He told them, indeed there was a Law that was above every other Law in heaven and on the earth.

The first Law for everyone to keep is the Law of worshipping the one and only God the Creator who made heaven, worlds, and universes.

He owns everything including the inhabitants who live on those planets. He is, therefore, their Lord. They are caring for those planets on His behalf.

They must give accounts about how they are conducting their lives and the places that He has entrusted into their care.

The Law of love

God the Creator made people of the world because He wanted to be a caring and loving Daddy. Love is the law in His family.

Love Him as much as He loves you. "And thou shalt love the Lord thy God with all thy heart, and with all thy soul, and with all thy mind, and with all thy strength: this is the first commandment" (Mark 12:30).

He said that you are expected to love the Lord of all. And there is no question that you must love Him at all times.

There is no maneuvering your way around the Law of love. And He must always be to you your only God in heaven and on the earth.

You must love Him from all the rooms, corners, nooks, etc. of your heart. You must love Him with all the strength and passions of your heart. You must love Him with all your spirit as long as it is able to breathe.

You must love Him all your thinking capacities. You must love Him with all the strength you can must. Love for God is the most important Law that He has given you. They are embodied in the first four Commandments that were written in Exodus 20:1–11.

The Messiah said that the second important commandment is love for the neighbors. He said, "And the second is like, namely this, Thou shalt love thy neighbour as thyself. There is none other commandment greater than these" (Mark 12:31).

Loving the neighbor is like loving the spirit that gives you. It is like loving the spirit that helps you to breathe. The Law of love is stipulated in the last six Commandments as written in Exodus 20:12–17.

The Pharisee declared that the Messiah spoke the truth. He said that there is only one God in heaven and on the earth. There is yet to appear a new God beside Him. "And the scribe said unto him, Well, Master, thou hast said the truth: for there is one God; and there is none other but he:

And to love him with all the heart, and with all the understanding, and with all the soul, and with all the strength, and to love his neighbour as himself, is more than all whole burnt offerings and sacrifices" (Mark 12:32, 32).

The scribe seconded the Messiah words about love. He repeated Christ's words. And He added that love for God and for the neighbors is more important than all the sacrifices and burnings of all the animals and birds that Israel was sacrificing to the Lord.

The Lord gave Him His blessings. He said that he

would be saved if kept on believing and obeying the truth that he had just seconded. "And when Jesus saw that he answered discreetly, he said unto him, Thou art not far from the kingdom of God. And no man after that durst ask him any question" (Mark 12:34).

All the Pharisees, Sadducees, scribes, and lawyers never dared ask Jesus any more questions. He knew the Bible very well. He was more intelligent and wiser than any man or woman ever born on this earth.

Make a covenant of love with God

All of you need to transfer yourselves on the side of the Creator. It is only then will you be able to see the wonders of creation in its fullness.

And the greatest workmanship He performed was when He made you. "Come and see the works of God: he is terrible in his doing toward the children of men" (Psalms 66:5).

He took a part of His Spirit and birthed Himself into you. You and your fellow human beings are very awesome. "For we are his workmanship, created in Christ Jesus unto good works, which God hath before ordained that we should walk in them" (Ephesians 2:10).

He did birth all of you looking and sounding exactly like Him. He wants to create the brains of the Messiah in you so that you can truly be His brothers and sisters.

All these wonderful things will come through the excellent works the Cross in performing in each of your lives. He wants you to be in every way like God your Father.

He calls you to live to live as a people belong only to Him. As such, you must live righteously just like Him.

The All-Powerful flooded the whole earth with the great Floods with water during the days of Noah and his family. The rest of the people worshipped demons.

After He taught them a lesson to the people of that world until all of them were conquered by the waters, He blew His breath on the earth and dried her up again just like He did during creation. "He ruleth by his power for ever; his eyes behold the nations: let not the rebellious exalt themselves. Selah" (Psalms 66:7).

He will move you forward by His powers. He brings out one generation after another by His strength. His eyes are all over the nations to see if anyone is ready to come back to Him.

He who does not love Him will beat killed by the disease of sin. It will teach them that sin is evil. The proud and unrepentant will die because of their bad decisions.

Make an eternal covenant of love and loyalty with God, and He will save you. You will go around singing because you know that your life and future are safe in His powerful hands. Everyone on this earth has a chance to be saved.

He (or she) will find true joy in Him. Rest and compassion will follow Him (or her) whenever he goes. He will come and place His powerful on him.

Whoever praises His holy name receives eternal blessings from His omnipotent right hand. "Make a joyful noise unto God, all ye lands: Sing forth the honour of his name: make his praise glorious" (Psalms 66:1, 2).

He came into this world for purpose of being your eternal Friend. Learn how to exalt His name very high like you are sending rockets into highest universe.

Keep on exalting higher and higher still above yourself and everything in this life. Praise Him when you are praying.

Sing songs of exaltations about Him. The most beautiful voices come from dumb people or those who lost their voices due to accidents or hereditary diseases.

Their joy and enthusiasm as they praise the Lord with any sounds that come out of them are heartwarming. They encourage people who still have good voices to sing and not be ashamed of praising the Lord in some places where people tend to stare at them with disapprovals.

Give full love, honor, respect, and awe to Him because He deserves it. He gives you faith to believe in Him that He exists. He blesses you with His Presence. He walks with you from the birth and on into eternity. He loves your company very much.

His rest, love, and compassion are greater than the joy of keeping one's self alive. There is no meaning to life without God who loves you and is saving. He heals you from all your diseases of sin.

He wants you to be healthy and exactly just like Him. "Say unto God, How terrible art thou in thy works! through the greatness of thy power shall thine enemies submit themselves unto thee" (Psalms 66:3).

He is All-Powerful and does not tolerate sin and demons occupying your body. He will drive them out. He will liberate your completely. "By terrible things in righteousness wilt thou answer us, O God of our salvation; who art the confidence of all the ends of the earth, and of them that are afar off upon the sea" (Psalms 65:5).

He will deal with those sins and demons that are bringing down very drastically. He will drive them out of your heart and kill them.

He will make your mind to think straight. He will make you all attractively and lovely eternally. Your recreation will completely and awesome.

This is He into whose arms the honest people all over the world have thrown themselves. He guides them gently and patiently with His staff of love and compassion.

They all declare that He is God the Omnipotent or the All-Powerful. Many listeners are encouraged to also put their faith in Him. He does not disappoint them. He is saving them.

God your Father will give you the blessing of rest.

He will make you strong people when you give all your hearts to Him.

You must allow your voices to be heard in this world because you are His friends. "O bless our God, ye people, and make the voice of his praise to be heard: Which holdeth our soul in life, and suffereth not our feet to be moved" (Psalms 66:8, 9).

He did come and chose you to be His beautiful bride to be wedded only to Himself and not to demons, pride, and all your other sins. He will fill you with His everlasting life and joy that will never end.

He asks that you should not allow your feet to slip into sin again. Do not walk on shaky grounds that are infected with sin. You may sink into them again.

Gold and silver are burned with fire to remove their impurities. "Diamonds are cut in good shape and polished to make them shine and glitter very brightly. "But he knoweth the way that I take: when he hath tried me, I shall come forth as gold" (Job 23:10).

The Lord does allow trials to come your way in order to strengthen and make you strong. He wants to live and not die. The fires of trials and temptations will not kill you.

The Messiah will save you. He wants you to join His eternal kingdom. The afflictions of sin and demons will be things of the past. They will not exist in the new heaven and earth.

Obey the Law because you love God

The Ten Commandments will be very enjoyable to keep if you first love Him. You will keep them perfectly because you love Him. Do not pretend to be like Him by forcing yourself to keep the Commandments correctly. Keeping the Commandments for the sole purpose of avoiding hell will breed too much worries and fears in you.

You will begin to think that He is after your blood instead of being after your soul in order to save you from hell. He is saving you because He loves you. If He did not love you, He will have told you nothing about Himself leave alone choosing to die for your sins, too.

You cannot keep the Ten Commandments perfectly because you are not God. Worst of all, you are a sinner. Therefore, you are a law breaker by nature.

He is kindly inviting you to base your relationship with Him on mutual love and trust. Love Him and He will show you how to be holy. You will then enjoy yourself in following Him very, very much.

The Ten Commandments will not be burdensome, anymore. He will teach you how to keep them holy. You will work on them together. You will not struggle to keep them perfectly alone.

You will have peace in the Messiah. In the world, you will be burdened by allurements, guilt, and shame. You might not be perfect as you walk the way of the Cross but He will breathe peace in your heart. He will give you the assurance that your sins are forgiven right after you have committed them.

So you will not feel overwhelmed by your weaknesses. Even if people deride you for your failings, you will have the peace of God in your heart. You will not feel alone and miserable with your own thoughts but reach out to Him for forgiveness.

His over-abundant grace will surround you with deep peace and exuberant joy. "Therefore if any man be in Christ, he is a new creature: old things are passed away; behold, all things are become new" (2 Corinthians 5:17).

Instead of only dwelling on forgiveness of your sins all your life, He is encouraging you to move into higher spirituality. Focus your mind on the good God. Learn about His greatness.

Study about His supernatural nature and love. "Now thanks be unto God, which always causeth us to triumph in Christ, and maketh manifest the savour of his knowledge by us in every place" (2 Corinthians 2:14).

Thank Him all the time for empowering you to ride in the golden chariot of the Messiah. You are sitting beside with Him and moving from glory to glory. He is teaching you deep truths that are known only by Him.

As you increase knowledge about His nature and character through Bible studies, your faith will increase, too. You will grow wiser and stronger in following Him. For your focus will be on your glorious God and Savior and not on your personal weaknesses and many failings.

There will be a positive and holier change in your character. It will affect the people who are around you. Your holy character will be like sweet aromatic perfumes that they will not help sniffing and enjoying.

You will grow very close to the Messiah when you begin to understand that even the bad stories, especially in the Old Testament, are about His love for the world and, in particular, for you. He will keep your mind off yourself and your weaknesses and center it on Himself.

You will absorb the right knowledge about Him. You will begin to enjoy the real abundant spiritual life He has planned for you before the world begun.

Love will free your mind from worrying about your sins. It will lay hold of Him. You will grow stronger, bolder, and confident in the real truth about your salvation based on His love.

Truth will help you to grow up in Him very righteously. And life everlasting will spring up in your soul like underground water bubbling up, filling, and overflowing from the well.

The well will always be full of water and will never run dry. "But whosoever drinketh of the water that I shall give him shall never thirst; but the water that I shall give him shall be in him a well of water springing up into everlasting life" (John 4:14).

You will no longer believe the lies of Satan that the Messiah is after your blood. He did not die on the Cross of Calvary to put you to death but to save you.

You will know beyond any possible doubt that He is saving you because He loves you. You will love to keep the Ten Commandments because you love Him and want to be like Dad.

God your Father says that the divine blood of the Messiah as sufficient to cleanse you from all your sins. He recommends Him highly as the only way of salvation and not your own concept of how to save yourself from hell.

If you want to come to heaven based on the fact that you don't want to go to hell, Christianity will become a burden to you and not a joy.

Eliminate pride and feelings of self-sufficiency from your heart by surrendering your heart to the Messiah. Do not try to keep the Ten Commandments holy by your own personal efforts again. It does not work.

Let your fellowship with God be based on love for Him and not the fear of being burnt up in hell if you don't obey Him. Be humble and ask for love and understanding of who He is and how He wants to save you.

He blesses you every day. He is filling you up with Himself because He is God your salvation. He is the truth that is creating you by His Spirit. "Blessed be the Lord, Who bears our burdens and carries us day by day, even the God Who is our salvation! Selah [pause, and calmly think of that]!" (Psalms 68:19, AMP).

He sent my Son to preach and live the gospel of peace and love from His heart to you. He is the bridge between heaven and the earth. When you heard Him speaking to you through the Bible, sermons, nature, etc. you began to change. You allowed the Holy Spirit to convict you of your enormous and terrible sins.

He convinced you to leave the works of darkness and follow Him. "And when he is come, he will reprove the world of sin, and of righteousness, and of judgment" (John 16:8).

He has come to make the world weep for cutting themselves away from God with the swords of their sins. He convinced you that you will answer to God your Father for every thought you are cherishing, every word you speak, and every action you do.

He wants to do right because you fell in love with Him. You gave your life to Him as peace offering. He will make you righteous. He will pass the judgment of peace on repentant sinners and of condemnations on all those who refused to repent.

Your heart is responding very warmly to His gospel of peace. He is increasing your faith in Him daily.

Please do not be afraid of Him anymore. Do not be overcome with the fear of the judgment and hell. Just love Him, and He will show you how to be like Him.

7 CHAPTER

THE DARKNESS OF SIN

I. The first darkness where demons are chained

Lucifer thought he could unseat the Almighty and take the throne of power and awesome majesty. "For thou hast said in thine heart, I will ascend into heaven, I will exalt my throne above the stars of God: I will sit also upon the mount of the congregation, in the sides of the north: I will ascend above the heights of the clouds; I will be like the most High" (Isaiah 14:13, 14).

Satan claimed all heavens to be his own heavens and not of the Creator God longer any more. He declared that all the angels were his worshippers. All riches, wealth and powers of all heavens and universes belonged to him. He declared that he would help himself onto the throne of the Lord God Almighty and rule as God.

Only angels can understand the needs of angels. He claimed that they needed him to be their god in order to increase their power, wealth and joy. He will carry his throne high up into the highest heaven where God Himself sits in full glory of power and majesty as the Lord God Almighty, Creator and Sustainer of all.

He would set his throne on top of the highest mountain in heaven that is located on the northern side from where all resources come from for the good of heaven and all the universes.

He declared that all the myriads clouds of angels are his personal properties. Therefore, he would be on top of them all. He would seat his throne above their heads in the highest heaven. He would be the perfect example of how even an angel can turned into a god.

He set out to win the support of all the angels. One third agreed with him. They declared that only angels can rule angels.

One third was not sure whether that was a good idea. Another third declared that angels are mere breaths of the Creator. They will amount to nothing if they did not hold onto the One who can sustain their breaths through His own life. They side with their Father.

They were led by Gabriel. "And there was war in heaven: Michael and his angels fought against the dragon; and the dragon fought and his angels, And prevailed not; neither was their place found any more in heaven" (Revelation 12:7, 8).

There was a collision of wills. On one side stood Michael the Prince and His supporters declaring that heaven must be ran on the Ten Commandments which are expressed in one word: love.

Satan declared that anyone can seat on the throne of God even if he is a creature because serving self as of the greatest importance that putting the needs of other beings first. So love, mercy, joy, peace and all divine graces war against pride, selfish, hatred, stealing, immortality, lies, etc.

Truth and error locked themselves in a deadly combat. And Satan started war began in God's perfect heaven. But he had no power or strength to withstand the might of the All-Powerful God.

He could not hold onto his seat any more after he sinned in himself and lured one third of the angels to commit sin like him. They were too impure to stand before the holy God.

They were expelled before the holy fires coming from the Presence of the Almighty and Righteous One would consume their sin and consume them also in the process. They were ordered to leave until they had repented of their sins and then they would be reinstated back into their positions.

Jesus is Michael. He described the fall of Satan this way: "I beheld Satan as lightning fall from heaven" (Luke 10:18.

He kicked Satan out because of the evil nature of sin. Satan could have gotten burnt in His presence if He had not shown him mercy. He gave Satan more than 4,000 years to repent but he refused. "And the great dragon was cast out, that old serpent, called the Devil, and Satan, which deceiveth the whole world: he was cast out into the earth, and his angels were cast out with him" (Revelation 12:10).

The great monster or dragon whose evil nature never changes though he may look innocent and cute is deadly. He is the old serpent who crept into the Garden of Eden and bite innocent and holy Adam and Eve with his deadly poison.

The world is slowly bleeding to death. People are born only to suffer and die. He is the Devil because he is fiend, mean, cruel and evil spirited. He is Satan, meaning an adversary or enemy of God and mankind. He took the whole world by deceit and most of them are still obeying him.

No angel, man or woman can win a war against. He is victor of all. He made men and women to have intelligence, wisdom and strength that will make them superhuman.

He came down to the earth to bring them into greater glory than He had given them originally when He created Adam and Eve. "And I heard a loud voice saying in heaven, Now is come salvation, and strength, and the kingdom of our God, and the power of his Christ: for the accuser of our brethren is cast down, which accused them before our God day and night" (Revelation 12:10).

Salvation has appeared in the form of God Jesus Christ among men and women. He has set His kingdom of heaven within their midst and in their hearts, too.

Each man, woman or child need to adopt Him and

His kingdom that are already in their hearts and they will become one in mind, heart and Spirit.

He has given each person chieftainship in Christ's kingdom which is already within their minds and heart to make decisions for their progress, and He will carry them out. Satan is an outcast.

He has no control over the mind and heart of anyone unless they give him permission to do so. The only thing he can do is grumbled that God loves them too much when they are also sinners.

But they are not as bad as he is. Even the worst ones among them still have hearts and can do quite good stuff for each other and for God.

This wonderful God was completely misunderstood by Satan. He thought that because their Creator is very humble, kind, and gracious and loving that he thought he could unseat Him from His throne and drive Him out of heaven quite easily. But true power creates deep humility. The humblest Person in heaven and earth is God the Almighty.

He uses His unlimited power to create and save and never for the joy of destroying His good workmanship. Satan miscalculated God. He cannot be controlled much less by mere creatures like angels and people. He is holy, loving and perfect. Therefore, He is All-Powerful.

Satan is quarantined down here on this earth. God has ordered him never to set foot in heaven again or visit other worlds where there are no sin or suffering. He is chained down in this world of sin.

He cannot roam around all over the universes much less in heaven. "And the angels which kept not their first estate, but left their own habitation, he hath reserved in everlasting chains under darkness unto the judgment of the great day" (Jude 1:6).

The disobedient angels were once serving the God Lord and King Jesus Christ as governors of the universes. They failed to manage the huge positions given to them efficiently and effectively. They did not protect the sacred duties given them over all universes.

But because of their insatiable lust for power, they tried to use lies, discord and physical force to force themselves as members of the Triune God or even better as their gods. Their greed, selfish, pride and foolishness cut them off from their Creator.

Sin means to "cut off" in some Semitic languages. They lost the awesome privilege to live within sight of God's Presence. A judgment in payment for their disobedience was passed against them.

They were cut off from His Presence and thrown down to this lost as prisoners chained in total darkness of sin and death until the great days when they will burnt up completely. This sinful world is the first prison.

They chose the lowliest of all creatures to symbolize them – venomous crawling serpents or snakes. Indeed, their characters and the awful things they have done to the inhabitants of this earth make them venomous snakes.

The Lord their Creator uttered this solemn lamentation over Satan and his followers: "How art thou fallen from heaven, O Lucifer, son of the morning! how art thou cut down to the ground, which didst weaken the nations!" (Isaiah 14:12).

His voice has fallen silent in the court of heaven. He is not recognized any more as the leaders of all the angels. He does not shine brightly any more like the morning star.

He is now the prince of darkness. "Wherein in time past ye walked according to the course of this world, according to the prince of the power of the air, the spirit that now worketh in the children of disobedience" (Ephesians 2:2. He is not the prince of light but of the darkness of sin and death. No one commits sin error like him.

The Lord Jesus described him, thus: "Ye are of your father the devil, and the lusts of your father ye will do. He was a murderer from the beginning, and abode not in the truth, because there is no truth in him. When he speaketh a lie, he speaketh of his own: for he is a liar, and the father of it" (John 8:44).

His passions and nature are lying, cheating, confusing, demoralizing, profanities, abominations, immoralities, murdering, etc. people and everything on this earth very much. Truth is not his thought, language or life. He hates truth because it reminds him that God is truth and he must be obedient to Him and worship.

He is the inventor of all the lies and errors as if they are special treasures like gold, diamonds, clothes, steel, etc. that he must manufacture and sell in the market for profits. "By the multitude of thy merchandise they have filled the midst of thee with violence, and thou hast sinned: therefore I will cast thee as profane out of the mountain of God: and I will destroy thee, O covering cherub, from the midst of the stones of fire" (Ezekiel 28:17).

He has multiplied lies against God like seeds. They germinated and produced giant plants with deadly fruits of sin that will consume him in hell. His all-consuming sin has made him very violent.

He is now bent on destroying the world completely. He has covered the whole world with the darkness of sin. While human beings still have some goodness in them though they are sinners, he has become sin itself. There is nothing in him except sin. It drove him from the beautiful, joy and Lovely Mountain of your God as infectious garbage.

This proud angel will be destroyed one of these days. The fire that makes the gold and other jewels on the pavements of heaven glow very brilliantly and among whom he had once walked will fall down on him and consume him up.

Satan caused his own downfall. He was created as the biggest creature of all. It made him stand out as the most awesome, brilliant and beautiful. But he was created a giant to stand out in order to lead the heavenly host in worshipping God.

It was not for his own personal glory but that of God. He thought that appearance is what made God to be God, and he wanted his absolute authority over heaven and earth. He grew bigger because of pride that he really was.

His claims of also being God drove him away from the presence of the one and only true God of heaven and the earth. "Thine heart was lifted up because of thy beauty, thou hast corrupted thy wisdom by reason of thy brightness: I will cast thee to the ground, I will lay thee before kings, that they may behold thee" (Ezekiel 28:17.

His heart grew proud because of the blessings the Lord poured on him. As a leader, he was to be wise. His wisdom was to be employed in worshipping God and building a greater joy and love for the angels. But he failed to handle the share of the Lord's government entrusted into his care with wisdom, intelligence and good manners. His corrupted his fortunes because of greed.

He wanted everything and especially the throne of God for Himself. Instead, his greed and selfishness landed him in the deepest hell imaginable. He is a spectacle of indecency and mockery to the saints, holy angels and all the citizens of other planets.

II. The second darkness where demons are chained

On the day of Jesus' Second Coming, He will resurrect the saints from the grave and together with the living ones; He will change them into immortal and glorious beings.

He will take them to heaven. "And I saw thrones, and they sat upon them, and judgment was given unto them: and I saw the souls of them that were beheaded for the witness of Jesus, and for the word of God, and which had not worshipped the beast, neither his image, neither had received his mark upon their foreheads, or in their hands; and they lived and reigned with Christ a thousand years" (Revelation 20:4).

You will sit on thrones of judgment and power. And you will pass judgments on demons and lost sinners by going through their records. You will approve their burning by fire. Those who suffered martyrdom will be given special honors. Their thrones will be next to that of the One whom they had witnessed for and upheld very high.

They died for His glory. But all those who never repented from betraying, torturing and murdering Jude-Christians and all the other unrepentant sinners will be dead on this earth. Those who had declared Satan to be their God will be cut off from the true God.

All those who died still fighting and killing Sabbath-keepers and ordering the whole world to worship on a false Lord's Day or Sunday on the pain of death will not be among the saints. They will not be there to welcome the arrival of heaven in their midst.

All the evil people would be dead. Satan will have no one to tempt or destroy. Every animal, bird, fish, plants, etc. would be dead. The lights of the sun, moon and stars will be put out.

There will be total darkness. Satan and his fellow angels will be the only living beings on the earth. It will be worse than being chained down physically.

Indeed, he is chained down because he is not allowed to move out from this world to another world. He must live here alone with his fellow demons to think over of all the evil he done to them. "And he laid hold on the dragon, that old serpent, which is the Devil, and Satan, and bound him a thousand years,

And cast him into the bottomless pit, and shut him up, and set a seal upon him, that he should deceive the nations no more, till the thousand years should be fulfilled: and after that he must be loosed a little season" (Revelation 20:2, 3). God will show His wisdom by locking Satan and his fellow demons up in this world in total darkness for one thousand years.

III. The third and final darkness that will cover Satan

After the one thousand years, all the dead sinners will be resurrected only to be given the final judgment of death by burning alive until death with fire. "But the rest of the dead lived not again until the thousand years were finished. This is the first resurrection" (Revelation 20:5).

Satan will be active again when he sees the resurrected sinners. In other words, his chains of inactivity would be loosened. "And when the thousand years are expired, Satan shall be loosed out of his prison" (Revelation 20:7.  Satan

He will mobilize them. He will try to attack the New City of God in which His saints had taken shelter but fire will descend from heaven and put the sinners out of their evil lives.

The Lord passed a death sentence on Him for murdering the people of the earth beginning with the death of Abel who was slaughtered by his own older brother over how to worship the Lord. "Thou hast defiled thy sanctuaries by the multitude of thine iniquities, by the iniquity of thy traffick; therefore will

I bring forth a fire from the midst of thee, it shall devour thee, and I will bring thee to ashes upon the earth in the sight of all them that behold thee.

All they that know thee among the people shall be astonished at thee: thou shalt be a terror, and never shalt thou be any more" (Ezekiel 28:18, 19).

Satan brought death on himself. He was created a perfect and holy sanctuary for the abode of the Spirit of his Creator. Instead, he welcomed sin into his heart and drove the Lord away.

Sin is a slow death. Though it may take time, the sinner will eventually die and not just the natural death but eternal death by being burnt up with holy fire that can kill spirits. "For the wages of sin is death" (Romans 6:23. Sin is the fruit of disobedience to the heavenly. And the fruit has seeds of death in it.

The final and last darkness is extinction of sinners by hell fire. They will be chained into bosom of eternal death where there is no life, breathing or anything. Everyone will forget them except God whose knowledge is everlasting. "And the devil that deceived them was cast into the lake of fire and brimstone, where the beast and the false prophet are, and shall be tormented day and night for ever and ever."

Sin, death and hell will also be put to death by holy fire. "And death and hell were cast into the lake of fire. This is the second death. And whosoever was not found written in the book of life was cast into the lake of fire" (Revelation 20:10, 14, 15).

The fire will be lit only for the extermination of demons. But if anyone likes them, he or she can join them in hell.

This is Jesus own words concerning the end of demons and all everyone who is full of sin and nothing else. "Then shall he say also unto them on the left hand, Depart from me, ye cursed, into everlasting fire, prepared for the devil and his angels" (Matthew 25:41).

The serpent and his fellow evil spirits will be in the middle of the fires will be lit by heavenly fires. He had taken the world away from their Creator and caused the suffering of all the inhabitants of the earth.

He must suffer for what he did to them.

Next to them will be false Christs and false prophets and then rest of the gullible sinners who followed the ways of the devil. Each person will be according to the length of time determined by the amount of his or her sins.

Satan will burn the longest because he brought this trouble on the earth. He will be punished for the sins of the saints, too. With his extinction, the work of the second would be complete and final. No sin or death will ever exist again after that.

All the saints will be astonished at the fall of the devil burning before their very eyes. He had terrorized them mercilessly.

At one time, they had loved him and were his diehard slaves. Then, they saw through his lies and rebelled against. Shock and amazement will run through their ranks.

He wasn't as powerful as they thought that he was. "Yet thou shalt be brought down to hell, to the sides of the pit. They that see thee shall narrowly look upon thee, and consider thee, saying, Is this the man that made the earth to tremble, that did shake kingdoms;

That made the world as a wilderness, and destroyed the cities thereof; that opened not the house of his prisoners? All the kings of the nations, even all of them, lie in glory, everyone in his own house.

But thou art cast out of thy grave like an abominable branch, and as the raiment of those that are slain, thrust through with a sword, that go down to the stones of the pit; as a carcass trodden under feet. Thou shalt not be joined with them in burial, because thou hast destroyed thy land, and slain thy people: the seed of evildoers shall never be renowned" (Isaiah 14:15-20).

Satan will be stoned with burning brimstones and charcoals. This is the life he had chosen: to die by stoning and burning in the pit of hell.

The saints will exclaim with astonishment: "He had showed off to us with great pride and arrogance that he was a god. Is this the person who caused earthquakes on the earth?

Is he the one who shook the Nations of the Gentiles and made them obey him? He made the world nothingness before heaven and the universes."

The kings and queens and all the people of the earth were buried honorably when they died but his death was awful. He died a slow death by stoning and of the heat of the fire in sight of angels and saints whom he had harassed terribly.

The place where he will burn will cause a deep crater on the earth like the Dead Sea where Sodom and Gomorrah and the other cities of the homosexuals got scorched including the soil they had had used.

He will be like a dried branched that can never be green and bear fruit again. He will be forever gone from the life that comes from Jesus the true Tree of Life.

Thus will be the end of all liars who claim themselves God. He murdered the world and must pay for his crimes against her in full.

He will be cut down with flame sword of God and never live again. He will be burnt on this very earth that he destroyed. He murdered human beings who were better than him.

The survivors will desecrate his memory by walking on it and remembering him no more. This will be the end of Satan and his fellow demons.

8 CHAPTER

I AM THE LIGHT OF THE WORLD

Carl Heinrich Bloch (May 23, 1834 – February 22, 1890, the Messiah is inviting you to come to Him

The Messiah said, "My heart loves you very much because I am your Daddy. Everlasting love is My nature. When I say, "I love you," it means that I am sharing My almighty life with you forever and ever without end.

It is the highest and most important life that you cannot create for yourself. I am giving a part of it to you because of My tremendous live for you. It is what is called "your blessings."

It is a gift. I have given you a tiny part of it by fathering you on this earth and giving you a part of My life to live as a human being. I am the boundless and almighty source of creative of power.

I am hot, and I am your Daddy. I am blazing with the fires of love that no firefighter can put them out. I am All-Light.

I am the true and only Daddy you got in heaven and on the earth. We are a family for My name's sake as the Creator of heaven and the earth. As the only and only All-Powerful and All-Loving Daddy, I will never leave you or forsake you.

Without Me there never was a creation and never will be. And also, I alone am the Savior of this lost world.

No other God or gods can save you from sin and eternal death. Speak to Me about anything you want because I am honest and true to My word of saving you from sin.

I am the light of life, joy, peace, love and all kinds of limitless goodness. I am the light because I am God Almighty." "Then spake Jesus again unto them, saying, I am the light of the world: he that followeth me shall not walk in darkness, but shall have the light of life" (John 8:12).

"Do not follow the traditions of your fathers and mothers that have been down to you through the ages. They are corrupted by sin.

They will lead you into deeper darkness of sin. Follow My ageless tradition that I wrote down for you in the Ten Commandments and in the righteous way I lived among you on the earth as one of you."

His enemies accused Him of self-love. "The Pharisees therefore said unto him, Thou bearest record of thyself; thy record is not true" (John 8:13).

They said that He was beating His chest to show off that He was the Helper of the world and the Lord of all. In short, He was proud. As such, His doctrines were false because they were based on self-promotion.

The Messiah accused them of being judgmental. "Jesus answered and said unto them, Though I bear record of myself, yet my record is true: for I know whence I came, and whither I go; but ye cannot tell whence I come, and whither I go.

Ye judge after the flesh; I judge no man. And yet if I judge, my judgment is true: for I am not alone, but I and the Father that sent me. It is also written in your law, that the testimony of two men is true. I am one that bear witness of myself, and the Father that sent me beareth witness of me" (John 8:14–18).

He said, "Even if I am My own Witness about My eternally Righteous Spirit, it is about My having breathed eternal life (as the Everlasting God). The truth about God is that He breathes love and omnipotence. His hand is powerful. It has brought you truth to you.

As God, I am very passionate about where I came from. I can see My everlasting past. And I am going forward powerfully in My capacity as the God of life. I can see the eternal years before which I will live as the Everlasting Father.

But as for all of you, you have not met God. You do not know Me. You can see where I came from. And because you are not being together with God, your eyes can see where I came from as the God of life or where I will go from here as the Father who gives births to life.

All of you judge and carry our revenge and counter-revenge because your sinful flesh tells you so. As for Me, I am the Righteous God who never revenges on My enemies some personal hurts they did to Me.

Even if I should judge, I will judge based on the power of evidence and on love. As God, I have these passions to never be an unrighteous God. My judgment is based on truth and love for sinners.

I do not lay My hand on passing judgments alone. God the Father who sent Me to you because I am very passionate I am you judges each case with Me.

Even in your Mosaic laws, it is written that the eye witnesses of two men must be true. But I have right to bear witness about My Righteous and Eternal Spirit because I always speak the truth.

I am the Truth. I have the God of life as My Daddy. His witness about Me is the truth. He is the One who sent Me to save you because I love you very passionately."

The Jews asked Him, "Where can our eyes behold Him who is Love, your Eternal Father?"

He told them He was who He was. "Then said they unto him, Where is thy Father? Jesus answered, Ye neither know me, nor my Father: if ye had known me, ye should have known my Father also" (John 8:19).

He replied them and said, "You still do not have the righteousness of God to know who I really am and to exalt Me very highly. You do not have My Father living in your hearts.

That is why you do not know Him and are exalting Him. Had you know who I am and are exalting Me highly, you would have known My Daddy also."

He spoke to them point blank that He was God. According to their Jewish laws, that would have amounted to blasphemy. It carried a death sentence.

But they did not arrest Him because His time of be crucified had not arrived. "These words spake Jesus in the treasury, as he taught in the temple: and no man laid hands on him; for his hour was not yet come" (John 8:20).

Yes, the Messiah is the Light of the world because He is God the Creator of both natural and spiritual lights. His first creation was the light. "And God said, Let there be light: and there was light. And God saw the light, that it was good: and God divided the light from the darkness" (Genesis 1:3, 4).

He created the lights of the sun, moon, and stars. "And God said, Let there be lights in the firmament of the heaven to divide the day from the night; and let them be for signs, and for seasons, and for days, and years:

And let them be for lights in the firmament of the heaven to give light upon the earth: and it was so. And God made two great lights; the greater light to rule the day, and the lesser light to rule the night: he made the stars also.

And God set them in the firmament of the heaven to give light upon the earth, And to rule over the day and over the night, and to divide the light from the darkness: and God saw that it was good. And the evening and the morning were the fourth day"

(Genesis 1:14–19). He will create spiritual light in you. It will drive away the darkness of sin from your heart. He will make you holy and righteous.

V. The war is between God and Satan and not between you and Satan

Many a time, you take the struggle between evil in very bad ways. You claim that there is a war between you and God when it is between Him and the devil.

You keep asking, "Where is God?"

Is He really on your side when you are facing so much trouble? Why is He hitting your home area so much? You conclude that it is a war between your race and God.

There is no other race or family that suffers as much as yours. You have no sharp man or woman who is standing up for your people. Nobody loves you or wants you around. You would love to hear some answers from Him.

Listen friend, God entered into this world to give you faith to believe in the impossible. Run to Him as fast as the wind.

He is rising over you like the morning sun to give you faith and hope. Run to Him who is rising like the morning sun. He has salvation that will give you a new life.

You have too many powerful enemies if you decide to live it alone on this earth. They have defeated the human race since the beginning of time. Even physicians cannot heal themselves when the diseases or injuries are fatal. No human being has ever conquered death.

Your eyes are searching for love. You believe that you will find it in God. You want to look on His Spirit to find assurances of unconditional love.

You want the kind of love that the fleeting world has failed to give. So you made yourself a slave of faith.

You stood looking at the Eastern horizon to catch a glimpse of the descending Lord and King. It is no more a war between you and the devil, sin, pain, tears or death. It is a war between you and God.

"And Jesus answered and said unto him, Get thee behind me, Satan: for it is written, Thou shalt worship the Lord thy God, and him only shalt thou serve" (Luke 4:8).

The Messiah commanded Satan to get away from His Presence not only on His behalf but especially for you.

Carl Heinrich Bloch (May 23, 1834 – February 22, 1890), Get thee behind Me, Satan

You would love to see the love in His eyes and His welcoming smile that will invite you into His eternal home. He, indeed, is the only One on this earth who absolutely good, perfect, and loving.

Wasn't He the One who said He gave you the Law of love to live by? Didn't He demonstrate it by dying for you on the Cross of Calvary? He spoke to you in your heart.

But you are still hurting. How can the world isolate you from true love and companionship so much? Perhaps, she really has nothing to offer you.

There is no unconditional and everlasting love without God. And the world chose to live without her Maker. She died spiritually. But there is hope in God. The war for more love, understanding, comfort, and other blessings is between you and Him.

After your meditation, you face your family to

face yet again the war of who has dominion over who? Who is more loving than the other? Many times, you feel that your house is lost.

There is no denying the fact that the love in your home is not divine and unconditional. Some people advised you to let your spirit hire a taxi and run away from trying and trying again to love your family and friends like God do.

As for you, your spirit considers cowardice an unacceptable choice. So you strive daily to find the true meaning of love and friendship in your home.

You know that you will find your true self in serving your family and other people even when they are enslaving you in order to be happy. After they have finished wandering the world looking for true love, they will return and find you still waiting at home to express that divine and absolute love you learned at the feet of the Messiah.

The world may never know that someone who really cares about unconditional love once lived down here. They failed you. They were not able to receive the kind of love you were ready to give them. But as a responsible person, you vow to live like God all your life.

However, you will never cry or mourn for human love. They are not able to understand it, anyway. Crying will not help. Live it with them whenever they are receptive. But never cry when they are not receptive. They have no idea about how much you can love or how much God loves them.

When they are thoughtless, you also throw in some punches. You declare that you do not care about their love any more if they do not love you. Why do you trust mere creatures so much? Why are you always complaining that people do not love you enough? You are always saying that you are missing on love.

Don't you know you're your loved ones are also complaining about the careless and/or thoughtless way you are treating them? They are saying that you do not love them as much as you should. You know that all of you are sinners. Their yardstick of love may be too short to reach you, and yours is short, too.

Stop blaming people. Stop bringing more confusion into the family and between friends by complaints about lack of interests or love. Take your heart to the King of love, and He will fill it up. You will have more love to share with your family and friends after you have met with the King of love.

The real war is between you and God and not between you and your loved ones and the rest of the world. You always complain to Him that you were ready to give love. And your loved ones are the cream of the world.

Sometimes, they do reach down deep into your heart. But still there is a yearning in your heart for love and understanding that is out of this world.

You are longing and pining for the love of your Creator and Messiah. You will find Him.

The days are coming when you will enjoy unconditional love from Him every day. They will be feast days of love, joy, and blissful happiness forever and ever without end.

When this world is over, He will take you to heaven to live with Him forever where all is joy, love, peace, etc. "Violence shall no more be heard in thy land, wasting nor destruction within thy borders; but thou shalt call thy walls Salvation, and thy gates Praise" (Isaiah 60:18).

You will no longer die violent deaths. There is no violence in the Holy Land where the Lord resides in great glories and powers beyond description. No one will lift up a spear or any other kind of weapon against you.

This is because sin and Satan no longer rule in human heart. Every inch of the land of heaven belongs to you and to God. Your heavenly home is filled with godliness.

There is no evil there that will do you harm. God

is your loving Daddy. Everyone will be your loving and devoted brother or sister. None of them will have evil thoughts against you.

They hate, curse or mistreat you again. Out of your own free will, you will accept them as your bosom friends. You will be surrounded by God your Salvation from one eternity to another. Out of your own mouth, you will admit that He is always loving and marvelous to you.

God the Father's throne will be inside the Golden City. He is so holy and powerful that He shines brighter than the sun.

His Presence will make the City even more beautiful and brighter than the light reflected by the sun and gold. "And the city had no need of the sun, neither of the moon, to shine in it: for the glory of God did lighten it, and the Lamb is the light thereof" (Revelation 21:23).

You will not see the rising of the sun in the City of God during the day or of the moon and stars at night. The brightly shinning glories of God the Father, God the Son or the Lamb and God the Holy Spirit are the city lights by day and by night.

You will never go through the awful and dreary nights of this world again. There will be no demons and criminals hiding in the shadows. You will not need electric, candle, gasoline, etc. lights to brighten up the night again.

Even the lights of the sun, moon, and stars are not that important. God's Presence will light up day and night.

The luminaries will serve more or less as decorations in the sky. "And there shall be no night there; and they need no candle, neither light of the sun; for the Lord God giveth them light: and they shall reign for ever and ever" (Revelation 22:5).

Your Daddy is your eternal light in the new heaven and earth. He will light up everything for you so that you can see very clearly and distinctively. You will sit at His right hand to rule worlds without end at your good pleasure.

The saints will be strong and powerful men and women in their minds, bodies, and spirits. They will come from the nations of the earth. They will march like a great army in the light of God's love and righteousness. They will work for Him.

They will employ all their intelligence, powers, and strength to make their Father happy. He will be honored and respected before all the angels and beings of all the universes because of the love and devotion His human children will give Him.

"And the nations of them which are saved shall walk in the light of it: and the kings of the earth do bring their glory and honour into it" (Revelation 21:24).

9 CHAPTER

THE BREAD OF LIFE

1. Wait patient for your bread and water from the Lord

Elim was a beautiful resort or vacation place. It had twelve wells bubbling with clear, cool, and refreshing water. The house that Israel built out of his own body vacationed there. There were seventy large palm trees that provided cools shade for the people to lull to sleep during the day.

They munched on the fresh and sweet dates very happily and contently. It was a perfect life that was beyond the wildest of the newly liberated slaves.

But Canaan was still a long way to go. So the Lord gave the command that the march should begin once again. They marched forward until they arrived at the wilderness of sin. It was the complete opposite of Elim. It had no life.

It was barren and wild. "And they took their journey from Elim, and all the congregation of the children of Israel came unto the wilderness of Sin, which is between Elim and Sinai, on the fifteenth day of the second month after their departing out of the land of Egypt" (Exodus 16:1).

There were no wells bubbling with cool refreshing water. There were no palm trees with ripped fruits to eat and shade for people to sit under and enjoy fresh air.

To make matters worse, the food they had brought from Egypt was finished. Hunger was gnawing their stomachs. Much as they had tried, they could not figure out the ways in which the Lord was going to provide them with bread. The place was lifeless, barren, wild, and still. It was dead.

In what way was the Lord going to provide for bread? "And the whole congregation of the children of Israel murmured against Moses and Aaron in the wilderness: And the children of Israel said unto them,

Would to God we had died by the hand of the LORD in the land of Egypt, when we sat by the flesh pots, and when we did eat bread to the full; for ye have brought us forth into this wilderness, to kill this whole assembly with hunger" (Exodus 16:2, 3).

The people were bitter with the way things were turning out. They thought that the Lord would provide water and food for them before they would arrive at place of camping. The family that Israel built was angry and bitter with Moses and Aaron in that land that was out there in the wild where life could not exist.

They let their minds be known to their leaders, complaining very bitterly, "Why did God run us through with His sword while we were still in Egypt. We could have died by His hand while we were still there.

Deaths by running our hearts through with spears, arrows or swords would be kindness. The slow and painful deaths caused by hunger are inhumane. We used to sit around pots of flesh.

We feasted on meat with all out strength. We ate bread, too. But you and the Lord have made us leave the plentiful land of Egypt to come to this land of fear and want so that you can have the opportunity to be the cause of the death of this independent nation through hunger."

Although they accused the Lord of intend to commit murder, He did not defend Himself in any way.

He loved them very much. He took the insult quietly. "Then said the LORD unto Moses, Behold, I will rain bread from heaven for you; and the people shall go out and gather a certain rate every day, that I may prove them, whether they will walk in my law, or no.

And it shall come to pass, that on the sixth day they shall prepare that which they bring in; and it shall be twice as much as they gather daily" (Exodus 16:4, 5).

He told them that they would see what real life and power was the following day. As the Ever Living One, He would rain down bread from heaven.

The people should go out and measure out the fields with their feet for each family. The fields would be covered very thick with grains. They should collect them in containers and eat them.

They should gather enough only enough for one day. He would give them provisions for one day at a time to find out if they had faith in Him. If they had faith in Him, it meant that they were compassionate and gracious people. Those are very important qualities.

He would keep them alive by the food that He would provide for them. On the sixth day or Friday, they were to gather food that would last them for two days. They should grind the grains and make lumps of flour.

They should do all their bakeries on Friday. No fire must be lit on Saturday. It is the Lord's Sabbath Day. They must devote the day for prayer and worshipping Him.

Moses and Aaron told the house of Israel what to expect the following day. The Lord was going to rain for them plenty of bread from heaven.

They could not miss chiding them for their lack of faith by pointing out to them that it was they, the two brothers, who liberated them from slavery and got them out of the hands of their master but their Maker.

When they would see grains sent from heaven, they would know that the Lord loved them. He was with them all along. He brought them out of Egypt. He was taking excellent care of them.

They had no rights to accuse Him of murder because they did not have provisions for the following day. "And Moses and Aaron said unto all the children of Israel, At even, then ye shall know that the LORD hath brought you out from the land of Egypt:

And in the morning, then ye shall see the glory of the LORD; for that he heareth your murmurings against the LORD: and what are we, that ye murmur against us?" (Exodus 16:6, 7).

Moses told the people that in the morning the Lord will give them a sign to show them that He knew about all the battles they were wagging against Him. They were pushing Him around. They were commanding Him to do whatever they ordered Him to do.

They were too angry and bitter with Him. His glorious Presence will appear in the sky and cover the Ten of Meeting where the Ark of the Covenant was placed.

Just like the house of Israel of old, God is holding you by the hand and is walking with you day by day. That is why you are still alive today.

He is making you into a powerful and intelligent spirit that is His own make. And He receives the full credit as the Creator of a wonderful person.

He will take out of this world. You are going to heaven to live with Him forever.

Things may not be go well sometimes but He is with you. He birthed you and is working out your salvation. So please do not cry and mourn that you are all alone.

He is with you. He is taking care of you. Please be patient when the going gets harder.

You will soon break out of this cocoon into a beautiful and eternal butterfly. You will go fluttering around heaven and the universes with joy. So hold onto Him with all your strength. "For yet a little while, and he that shall come will come, and will not tarry"

(Hebrews 10:37).

He is missing face to face relationship with you more than you are missing Him. He is not trying to torture you by waiting for so long. He hates this separation.

It is also too long for Him. He will return from heaven at any time from now. You will reunite and never part again.

They were some people among the Israelites who were light in weight spiritually. They could never be trusted. They had a habit of changing with the weather.

They were the slaves of unholy passions. This time it was the lust for meat that took over their over the reasoning capacities.

Even the usually reasonable elders joined the crowds that had uncontrollable passions in weeping and crying as if the whole camp was being wiped out by a plague. "And the mixt multitude that was among them fell a lusting: and the children of Israel also wept again, and said, Who shall give us flesh to eat?

We remember the fish, which we did eat in Egypt freely; the cucumbers, and the melons, and the leeks, and the onions, and the garlick: But now our soul is dried away: there is nothing at all, beside this manna, before our eyes" (Numbers 11:4–6).

They were weeping and mourning as if they were mourning for the dead. Men and women, young and old wept very loudly, crying, "Who will give us a real life?

Who is merciful to us by giving us flesh to eat? We are now sitting here in the desert with nothing to eat.

We have been recalling the fish that we used to eat in Egypt. And it was all for free. We never paid a cent for them. We used to enjoying cutting those big, fleshy, and sweet cucumbers and melons and eat them.

The leeks were very appetizing. The onions and garlic were so aromatic their sweet smell covered us like veils. Now, we have all lost weights. We are thin, dry, and dying for want of good food. There is yet to appear food here in this desert before our very eyes apart from this manna."

God was already giving them grains called manna. He would rain it from heaven every morning. Sunday to Thursday, they would gather enough of it in the morning to feed them for the day.

One Friday, they would gather a double amount. One portion of the grains was to be eaten on Friday and the other for the Sabbath (Saturday) day.

No manna fell on the Sabbath day. "And the manna was as coriander seed, and the colour thereof as the colour of bdellium.

And the people went about, and gathered it, and ground it in mills, or beat it in a mortar, and baked it in pans, and made cakes of it: and the taste of it was as the taste of fresh oil. And when the dew fell upon the camp in the night, the manna fell upon it" (Numbers 11:7–9).

©James Tisso, 1836-1902, Manna. But it is enhanced.

The manna had all the nutrients the people needed. It was a whole meal.

But now the people were very ungrateful to their heavenly Benefactor. "Then Moses heard the people weep throughout their families, every man in the door of his tent: and the anger of the LORD was kindled greatly; Moses also was displeased" (Numbers 11:10).

Israel sat by their families in front of their tents and began to weep heartbrokenly as if for the dead. They lost all their common senses.

They were terrible food addicts. Their food of choice for that time was meat. They were wailing and crying about it.

The Lord felt a deep parental concern for them. They were behaving like three-year olds. They needed a spank on their backs very badly to arrest their attentions and bring them back to common sense.

Even Moses was unsympathetic to their cravings for meat. They were not asking for it in the right way.

They had turned into three-year old unreasonable children who were wailing with loud voices and demanding to have their own ways.

Unfortunately, Moses took their fights against him very personal. One is never to take problems at work or in the church personal. It will crush you.

You will burn out and abandon your post. Every work-related problem must be presented to the Lord.

He will carry the burdens and heartaches for you. "And Moses said unto the LORD, Wherefore hast thou afflicted thy servant? and wherefore have I not found favour in thy sight, that thou layest the burden of all this people upon me?

Have I conceived all this people? have I begotten them, that thou shouldest say unto me, Carry them in thy bosom, as a nursing father beareth the sucking child, unto the land which thou swarest unto their fathers? Whence should I have flesh to give unto all this people? for they weep unto me, saying, Give us flesh, that we may eat.

I am not able to bear all this people alone, because it is too heavy for me. And if thou deal thus with me, kill me, I pray thee, out of hand, if I have found favour in thy sight; and let me not see my wretchedness" (Numbers 11:11–15).

Moses was saying, "Why are you not dealing truthfully with Your slave? Why have I not found grace in your eyes? You are killing me. You have put the heavy weights of all these powerful people on me.

They are too heavy for me. I am not their mother. I did not conceive and give births to all these very strong-headed people. They are Your children. You bred them. You are their Mother.

How can you turn around and claim that I am the one who conceived and gave births to them and now I must bear my own burdens? You have put all of these people who behave like selfish babies into my lap to console as if I am a baby breeder mother.

You have ordered me to carry them on my back to the Lord that You vowed to their fathers that You would rather hang Yourself than not give them.

Where is the flesh that I can see with my own two eyes in this desert that I can supply for all these powerful people? They are weeping very deeply and angrily to me. They are ordering me to give them meat to eat.

I am not able to conceive all these powerful people in my womb. They are too heavy for me to carry in my womb.

If there is something very special You would want to do for me. I ask for only one thing: put me to death with Your own hands. And I give you the glory of my death.

I want it to make You look very kind and gracious in Your own eyes. It is against God to see the people remove my loincloth and see my nakedness when they are stoning me to death. Let me die a dignified death in Your hands."

It was the Second Godhead who was talking to Moses. He asked him not to be ashamed of dying a shameful death.

He would be the One to be hanged on a Tree without His clothes for the sins of the people. He would bear the burdens of the stubbornness, pride, selfishness, addictions, etc. of the world Himself.

For now, He would give seventy elders to share the burdens of Moses with him. "And the LORD said unto Moses, Gather unto me seventy men of the elders of Israel, whom thou knowest to be the elders of the people, and officers over them; and bring them unto the tabernacle of the congregation, that they may stand there with thee.

And I will come down and talk with thee there: and I will take of the spirit which is upon thee, and will put it upon them; and they shall bear the burden of the people with thee, that thou bear it not thyself alone" (Numbers 11:16, 17).

He asked Moses to select seventy men from amongst the elders of Israel. He should select people whom he knew very well as responsible men. He should include senior military officers among them.

He should bring them in front of the tabernacle where the congregation usually meets for prayers. They should all stand together with him before the Tent of Meeting.

He would descend down from the sky and talk to them. He would take some of the power of the Holy Spirit He had put into Moses and create it in them also. He would empower them with courage, strength, intelligence, and wisdom.

They would conceive the burdens of the children of Israel in their wombs just like Moses. He would not be the only man in the camp who was pregnant with the sorrows of carrying the children of Israel in his womb.

He gave a direct message for the children of Israel through the mouth of Moses. "And say thou unto the people, Sanctify yourselves against to morrow, and ye shall eat flesh: for ye have wept in the ears of the LORD, saying, Who shall give us flesh to eat? for it was well with us in Egypt: therefore the LORD will give you flesh, and ye shall eat.

Ye shall not eat one day, nor two days, nor five

days, neither ten days, nor twenty days; But even a whole month, until it come out at your nostrils, and it be loathsome unto you: because that ye have despised the LORD which is among you, and have wept before him, saying, Why came we forth out of Egypt?" (Numbers 11:18-20).

The Lord was saying, "I am ordering you must stand strong and trample your sins down. Accept truth in your heart, and I will make you holy today.

You will eat meat for lunch tomorrow. I will provide meat for you because you had been weeping very loudly in My ears. You have challenged Me by asking Me whether I can real life that you used to enjoy in Egypt.

You asked whether I am really a merciful who can have pity on you and provide for you the things that you are want. You said that you it was simply fortunes abundant for all of you in Egypt.

I am now going to provide for all of you meat and you will eat it. You are not going to eat the whole for only one day.

You will eat not only for two or five days. You will not eat it for ten or twenty days although will be wonderful. It would be very long.

I will feed you with meat for breakfast, lunch, and supper for a whole month. You will loath it so much that you will vomit it out. And it will come out not only through your mouths but from your nostrils, too.

You will treat it like filth. I will oversupply you until you will vomit at the sight of meat. You will treat it like filth.

You have despised Me. I, God living in your midst, am despised by you so much that you even question if I am powerful. You ordered Me to explain Myself to you as why I delivered you from your slavery in Egypt."

Moses had believed in God in Egypt. He could do those ten signs. He believed that He could make a path through the Red Sea for the people to cross over. But this time He doubted the ability of God. "And Moses said, The people, among whom I am, are six hundred thousand footmen; and thou hast said, I will give them flesh, that they may eat a whole month.

Shall the flocks and the herds be slain for them, to suffice them? or shall all the fish of the sea be gathered together for them, to suffice them?" (Numbers 11:21, 22).

He tried to remind Him that He seemed to forget that He had 600,000 foot soldiers and still going and not even counting the ladies, the older, and the younger generations in His hands.

Was God sure of what He was promising them that tomorrow He would give the multitudes of people meat to eat for a whole month?

He told God that even if He could slaughter all the livestock they had in the camp to feed them people it would be barely enough for each person to take a bite leave alone feeding them for a whole month. Even if He would collect all the fish in the sea and feed them with it, it would not be enough.

Moses was afraid for the Lord. He did not want the Lord to ashamed Himself before the people by failing to provide for them enough meat even for just one day leave alone for thirty days. "And the LORD said unto Moses, Is the LORD'S hand waxed short? thou shalt see now whether my word shall come to pass unto thee or not" (Numbers 11:23).

He asked the doubter, "Are you standing up against Me? Are you able to break My hand?

You will see how I will untie My package and give them My gift. But whether I will actually give it to them or not is My decision."

He is encouraging not to be a doubter but to believe that He can untie the packages He has brought to you. Your gifts are already with you. He only needs to untie them and give them to you.

So stop doubting that He cannot until simple ribbons in order to unload your treasures and supply you with whatever you may need. "Wherefore, when I came, was there no man? when I called, was there none to answer?

Is my hand shortened at all, that it cannot redeem? or have I no power to deliver? behold, at my rebuke I dry up the sea, I make the rivers a wilderness: their fish stinketh, because there is no water, and dieth for thirst" (Isaiah 50:2).

There is yet anyone among you who has total faith in you when He is all around you. Throughout His eternal years, there never has been a time when He broke His hands and was handicapped. His hands are outstretched over you in blessings and protection. He has never been an idiot who could not think or willed a blessing for you.

When He curved a path through the heart of the Red Sea even her fish died for lack of water so that He could move the children who had faith in Him to the other side. He sends droughts and all-year round rivers dry up. Their fish die for want of water.

Then He has pity on the inhabitants of the land and the fishes. He pours water on them like floods. If He could all these fits, what makes you think that He cannot help you?

He also makes the sun to rise and clothes the sky with light. He makes it to set and clothes the sky again but this time with blackness.

If He could do such simple things, how could He forget His own kid that came out of His Spirit? "I clothe the heavens with blackness, and I make sackcloth their covering" (Isaiah 50:3).

Moses went back to the people. He sounded the horn to call them for a meeting. He told them everything the Lord had promised.

He ordered them to purify themselves by confessing their sins, washing all their clothes, cleaning their tents, bathing, and fast for that day. They would have plenty of meat to eat for lunch the following day.

They would eat meat for one whole month until they would not stand the sight of it any more. They will never crave for meat again.

He selected seventy men from amongst the elders to form the council of elders or senate to help him govern Israel just as the Lord had instructed. "And Moses went out, and told the people the words of the LORD, and gathered the seventy men of the elders of the people, and set them round about the tabernacle.

And the LORD came down in a cloud, and spake unto him, and took of the spirit that was upon him, and gave it unto the seventy elders: and it came to pass, that, when the spirit rested upon them, they prophesied, and did not cease" (Numbers 11:24, 25).

While he was addressing to the newly formed parliament, the cloud that hid the Presence of God descended on them and filled them with the Holy Spirit.

They all prophesied. But they did not prophesy again because of unbelief. They could have walked on the land of Canaan on their feet like Joshua and Caleb who trusted God all the way.

They died among the elders who perished in the desert because they refused prophets, councilors, and faithful followers of the Lord. But things looked very promising on that day for each of them. They had given their hearts to God, and they were ordained to be prophets.

Two elders were very angry with God and Moses. They wanted their meat right away. They refused to receive even the wonderful gifts of the Holy Spirit of prophesying, working miracles, healing, speaking in tongues, loving people passionately and unselfishly, etc.

"But there remained two of the men in the camp, the name of the one was Eldad, and the name of the other Medad: and the spirit rested upon them; and they were of them that were written, but went not out unto the tabernacle: and they prophesied in the camp"

(Numbers 11:26, 27).

The two men who remained were not called the usually persons or powerful people. They were just called men. Perhaps, flesh was controlling them so much that they refused to come to pray in front of the temple to receive the Holy Spirit and become prophets.

Moses had promoted Eldah and Medad as members of the senate. But they refused to report for their duties. They also received the Holy Spirit and prophesied.

The Lord has not finished pouring the Holy Spirit yet. Towards the end of this present age, He will pour His eternal life and power more than He ever did from the beginning of the world up to that time.

Your hearts will well with joy when you will see your children prophesying, preaching, healing, etc.

He will show that He is the life of the world through the dreams He will give to the older folks. He will appear to your sons and daughters.

They will see visions of Him. He will walk together with them.

He will pour His Spirit on your slaves and on your baby sitters. "And it shall come to pass afterward, that

I will pour out my spirit upon all flesh; and your sons and your daughters shall prophesy, your old men shall dream dreams, your young men shall see visions: And also upon the servants and upon the handmaids in those days will I pour out my spirit" (Joel 2:28, 29).

A young adult was shocked when he saw these two rebels turning into prophets and prophesying very passionately and accurately. He took off running to the council of elders, fell at the feet of Moses and told him of what was going on in the camp.

"And there ran a young man, and told Moses, and said, Eldad and Medad do prophesy in the camp. And Joshua the son of Nun, the servant of Moses, one of his young men, answered and said, My lord Moses, forbid them" (Numbers 11:27, 28).

But Moses' slave who happened to be his personal

bodyguard objected very strongly that rebels should also be filled with the Holy Spirit. In his military mind, rebels should be punished and not given any blessings especially of the Holy Spirit at all.

He begged his master to show them that his hand was powerful and teach them a lesson. He should teach them a lesson that the Nation of Israel would never forget. He should punish them.

Moses asked the young soldier not to be heartbroken for him. His prayer was that everyone in the camp would be the chosen people of the Holy Spirit just like bridegroom would choose their brides.

He was welcomed to anoint them as His prophets. He should help them to prophesy. He wanted to share his leadership with all of them.

Then, they would truly become the Lord's powerful, wisdom, and intelligent people. "And Moses said unto him, Enviest thou for my sake? would God that all the LORD'S people were prophets, and that the LORD would put his spirit upon them!" (Numbers 11:29).

Joshua was like the disciples who tried to stop the spread of the Gospel by ordering none members to stop calling on the Messiah's name and healing the people. The worst thing that could happen to a person is to be devil-possessed.

The disciples were unsympathetic when they saw people who were not the inner friends of the Messiah using His name to relieve the suffering of the world in the hands of demons.

They ordered the people to prove their loyalty to the Messiah first just like they did. They should abandon their homes, businesses, etc. and follow the Messiah before He could allow them to have His powers.

And the sad thing was that they stopped the other messengers of the Messiah who were not a part of the inner camp from preaching and healing the people.

They told Him that those people were not their

followers. "And John answered him, saying, Master, we saw one casting out devils in thy name, and he followeth not us: and we forbad him, because he followeth not us" (Mark 9:38).

It was true. Those men were not the followers of the disciples. They were the disciples of the Messiah, too, just as the twelve men were.

He was very angry with the disciples for hindering His mission work. "But Jesus said, Forbid him not: for there is no man which shall do a miracle in my name, that can lightly speak evil of me" (Mark 9:39).

He warned the disciples never to beat and finish off the people who are preaching about Him even if they are not baptized or attend church. Those creative powers they are using in healing people are being be delivered by using His name.

The people who know His secret powers and are using them cannot hate and curse His name as Satan at the same time.

He concluded by warning all persecutors to back off from killing Him through His disciples who are scattered around the world and are not church members, "For he that is not against us is on our part" (Mark 9:40).

He said that people who do not hate Him or persecute Him are His friends even if they are not church members.

The Lord promised a double blessing for the house of Israel. "And Moses said, This shall be, when the LORD shall give you in the evening flesh to eat, and in the morning bread to the full; for that the LORD heareth your murmurings which ye murmur against him: and what are we? your murmurings are not against us, but against the LORD" (Exodus 16:8).

He promised give them the bread of heaven that angels eat in the morning. In the evening, He would send for them quails to slaughter, cook, and eat.

They would bread and poultry until they were all satisfied. But Moses could not help telling the people off for having terrible quarrelsome attitudes.

They were always ready to pick stones and hurl at people they did not like. He and his brother, Aaron, were being victimized on behalf of God. And he hated it. He ordered to stop victimizing them.

They were just human beings just like them. In what ways were they to help feed people who were so many?

Moses asked his brother to make a loud announcement to the people to draw closer to the Tent of Meeting. He did. They were told that they Lord heard everything that they had said against Him.

He was going to reveal to them that He was ever present with them and heard everything even though they could see or hear Him.

They people came closer to the Tabernacle. Their attention was drawn towards the barren landscape. The clouds over their heads were blazing very brightly.

Thunders were rolling and lightning were flashing from the brilliantly glowing clouds. "And Moses spake unto Aaron, Say unto all the congregation of the children of Israel, Come near before the LORD: for he hath heard your murmurings.

And it came to pass, as Aaron spake unto the whole congregation of the children of Israel, that they looked toward the wilderness, and, behold, the glory of the LORD appeared in the cloud" (Exodus 16:9, 10).

The Lord thundered from the clouds and addressed Moses only. He and his brother were the only men in the camp who were spiritually prepared to meet with Him.

The other men were mean and hateful towards Him. So He ignored them. "I have heard the murmurings of the children of Israel: speak unto them, saying, At even ye shall eat flesh, and in the morning ye shall be filled with bread; and ye shall know that I am the LORD your God" (Exodus 16:12).

He said that He saw with His own eyes and heard with His own ears how angry and bitter was the family of Israel against Him for bringing them out of Egypt. He told them they would have bread for breakfast and lunch.

They would have meat to eat that evening. They would know that He, their God, loved them and was taking good care of them.

The following day, a great miracle took place in the camp of Israel the likes of which has never occurred in this world again. He did send plenty of quails for the people to eat that very evening. They covered the camp like swarms of than bees.

"And there went forth a wind from the LORD, and brought quails from the sea, and let them fall by the camp, as it were a day's journey on this side, and as it were a day's journey on the other side, round about the camp, and as it were two cubits high upon the face of the earth.

And the people stood up all that day, and all that night, and all the next day, and they gathered the quails: he that gathered least gathered ten homers: and they spread them all abroad for themselves round about the camp" (Numbers 11:31, 32).

Powerful winds went out from the stores houses of the Lord. He welcomed them to blow on the earth. The people thought that they were seeing black sandstorms coming from the desert in the East but they were quails.

They also saw storms coming from sea. They thought they were hurricanes but they were quails. The quails blanketed the sky. They could not see the sun. They could not see the sun for two days. The quails covered the sky completely.

He channeled the winds to drive the quails into the camp of the children of Israel. "He caused an east wind to blow in the heaven: and by his power he brought in the south wind.

He rained flesh also upon them as dust, and feathered fowls like as the sand of the sea: And he let it fall in the midst of their camp, round about their habitations" (Psalms 78:26–28).

Quail, public domain

He drove in quails from their breeding ground along the shores of Red Sea region. They came as thick as rain all around the camp.

They encircled the camp for a distance of a day's journey on all sides. There were piled high about one meter or three feet high from the ground so that even little children could catch them.

They people helped themselves to the generosity of the Lord plentifully supply and freely provided. They spent the whole night gathering the quails and slaughtering, cooking, and eating.

They caged many birds to eat at later dates. "And it came to pass, that at even the quails came up, and covered the camp: and in the morning the dew lay round about the host" (Exodus 16:13).

They fell on them like rainwater. They covered the whole place and many miles (kilometers) around the camp like fine dust that was brought by a sandstorm.

They covered the ground several meters high like the sand on the seashore. They waded knee-deep in the sea of poultry ready for the harvesting.

They filled the camp and would not move as if they were paralyzed. They looked as if they were dead. They waited for the people to pick them up. It was like that ever around their camp.

They walked into their tents and utensils to be slaughtered, cleaned, and roasted or boiled. They were very healthy birds.

Up rose the men and women of Israel to hunt the

birds. For the next two days and nights and nights, they caught quails and filled their tents with meat.

1896 By Providence Lithograph Company, God provided meat in the desert

Each person caught about sixty bushels for gorging. "The people asked, and he brought quails, and satisfied them with the bread of heaven" (Psalms 105:40). He fed them royally more than king or queen has been able to feed his or her kingdom.

Wild birds such as the quails and guinea fowls are more delicious than domesticated poultry. Moreover, they are healthier than larger animals such as cattle, goats, sheep, etc. The Lord did give them the best flesh to eat.

In the morning, the air was foggy. Dew lay thick on the ground. When it cleared, ground was covered thick with grains.

They were several feet high like flour mill. But they were grains. "And when the dew that lay was gone up, behold, upon the face of the wilderness there lay a small round thing, as small as the hoar frost on the ground.

And when the children of Israel saw it, they said one to another, It is manna: for they wist not what it was. And Moses said unto them, This is the bread which the LORD hath given you to eat" (Exodus 16:14, 15).

The bread of heaven had never been seen on earth before. So it had no name. It was simply called manna because they people kept asking each other in Hebrew, "What is it?" Moses told them it was the bread of heaven sent by the Lord their God.

He is called Jehovah-jireh. "So Abraham called the name of that place The Lord Will Provide. And it is said to this day, On the mount of the Lord it will be provided" (Genesis 22:14).

He will provide for your needs. He knows that that you need food to keep alive. Just ask Him, and He will give your food and water.

Unfortunately, the people of Israel were not true friends in their hearts to God. They were His enemies. They beat their own Holy Brother.

He is the All-Powerful God of truth. "And they sinned yet more against him by provoking the most High in the wilderness. And they tempted God in their heart by asking meat for their lust" (Psalms 78:17, 18).

He made them and was keeping them alive. They sinned against Him in that dried land. He imagined that they were stoning Him to death. And technically they murdered Him. They stoned Him to death in their hearts.

They cornered Him with questions that were too difficult to answer. They finished Him by driving Him away from their hearts. Instead, they offered their bodies are breeding grounds of lusts and uncontrollable passions.

They were bad boys and girls. They tempted Him to see if He could retaliate on them and fight them, too. As if that was not enough, "Yea, they spake against God; they said, Can God furnish a table in the wilderness?" (Psalms 78:19).

The people fell on Him and strangled Him, demanding, "God, are you alive? Does your hand have the power of the Spirit to show us trays of food on tables that your own hand has prepared in this outback of a wasteland?"

God is blessing you with far greater blessings than your immediate needs require. He is doing it right in front of Satan. And there is nothing He can do about it. He is anointing you with the blood of the Messiah until you are all saturated with His Spirit.

You will have abundant fortunes, rest, love, and compassion more than you need. They are your slaves. They will suffer in caring for you all the days of your eternal life.

The only thing you will do will be to sit quietly in heaven at the feet of the Lord and enjoy yourself. "Thou preparest a table before me in the presence of mine enemies: thou anointest my head with oil; my cup runneth over.

Surely goodness and mercy shall follow me all the days of my life: and I will dwell in the house of the LORD for ever" (Psalms 23:5).

The Israelites who were in the desert at that time were clearly in the wrong. They saw Him doing wonders in Egypt and rescuing them from the hands of men who were too strong for them. He then led them through the Red Sea.

They walked on dry ground through the heart of the sea. "When your fathers tempted me, proved me, and saw my work" (Psalms 95:9).

He was already raining grains down from heaven. They were making bread, cakes, cookies, etc. It was whole grains that had carbohydrates, proteins, fats, vitamins, minerals, etc. They were eating it every day.

They were not starving. But they picked up stones, anyway, and were stoning Him intending to kill Him in their hearts. They wished He could die a violent death in their hands.

He already quenched their thirst with miraculous water. "Behold, he smote the rock, that the waters gushed out, and the streams overflowed; can he give bread also? can he provide flesh for his people?" (Psalms 78:20).

It was not Moses who gave a cracking sound to the rock with his stick. It was Himself. The rock was pregnant with water.

Its womb broke out and cool refreshing water gushed out like a river. His hand is the only one that can perform such a miracle.

He had already given them bread. It did not need meat or fish to accompany it. It had all the nutritious values they needed.

How could matured people behave like toddlers? Their Maker was not amused by their thoughtlessness. He was disappointed. "Therefore the LORD heard this, and was wroth: so a fire was kindled against Jacob, and anger also came up against Israel; Because they believed not in God, and trusted not in his salvation:

Though he had commanded the clouds from above, and opened the doors of heaven, And had rained down manna upon them to eat, and had given them of the corn of heaven. Man did eat angels' food: he sent them meat to the full" (Psalms 78:21-25).

He was forced to straighten up in order to save their souls from further destructions that were being egged on them by their lusts for unprofitable things. Their lusts invited fires into their bodies and burned some of them to death. They were faithless in the Creator who made them out Himself.

He had sworn to save them from the hand of the devil and all their hardships. They had refused to throw all their weights on Him. They did want to be His brothers and sisters. They refused to follow the truth that could have saved them.

All the time, He was still raining for them bread from heaven like heavy rainfalls. They were scooping, boiling, cooking, roasting, etc. them every day and eating bread to their hearts fill.

He opened all the store houses of heaven to provide for them all that they needed. They were not paying Him taxes. But He was paying taxes to them like He was doing to all the heavenly angels.

He provided them good and secured lives in the desert. He gave picked food from the table of the angels and rained it down to them.

He gave them more meat than they craved for. "So they did eat, and were well filled: for he gave them their own desire; They were not estranged from their lust.

But while their meat was yet in their mouths, The wrath of God came upon them, and slew the fattest of them, and smote down the chosen men of Israel" (Psalms 78:29-31).

They ate to their full to show that they were powerful people who can gorge large amounts of meats. They believed that the truth by which they could live by lay in putting large amounts of food away. But it is not matter that makes people saints but the Spirit of the Creator.

They got the meats that they were ready to kill God for. The meat addicts refuse to believe that eating more meat will not cure their addictions to it.

Even when they were satisfied, they were still sucking on the bones of the birds. "And while the flesh was yet between their teeth, ere it was chewed, the wrath of the LORD was kindled against the people, and the LORD smote the people with a very great plague" (Numbers 11:33).

They were overfed with cholesterol and got bloated. No digestion could take place. There was too much fat in their stomachs. They could not break down fast to help them to breathe. The suffocated and died in great masses.

The fat people among them who loved food ate more than their bodies could handle. The meat turned poisonous and started killing them. They whimpered half-hearted to God to cure them from and remove the fatty meats from their stomachs.

He refused to listen to nonsense prayers that

addictions brought on themselves. He did beat them with heavy lashes by ignoring their prayers for healing completely. They died and were burning in mass graves.

God helped Himself to what happened to them as wrath for Him. What could He do? They overfed themselves and caused them to die.

Too much fat is dangerous, and it killed them. It first killed the overweight people because their bodies could not handle additional fats.

There were too much fats in their stomachs and too little fatty enzymes to emulsify them, break them into small amounts, and digest them. There were too little rooms for the stomach contents to move and relief them of pains. They died of bloated stomachs, obesities, heart attacks, etc.

Moses called the place Kibroth-hattaavah. It means the graves of lusts or sensuous desires. "And he called the name of that place Kibrothhattaavah: because there they buried the people that lusted" (Numbers 11:34). The graves of the sensual people are warnings to all nations in all generations not allow themselves to be controlled by any form of lust or it will kill them.

Unfortunately, Israel never learned anything about the dangers of tempting their bodies to commit forbidden things. Even after the sad events that took place in Kibroth-hattaavah, they sinned again. They refused to have faith in the Savior.

They refused to study His work in nature that is attractive and magnetic. Had they been good students and studious, they could have built tremendous faith in the Savior.

They would have resurrected from their graves just like Moses and been taking to heaven. He has all the powers to meet their physical, social, economic, and spiritual needs. They do not want their needs to be satisfied.

They hated the Law and loved the lawlessness.

"For all this they sinned still, and believed not for his wondrous works. Therefore their days did he consume in vanity, and their years in trouble. When he slew them, then they sought him: and they returned and enquired early after God" (Psalms 78:32-34).

More than a million people died in the desert because of lusts. Moses, too, had lusts for temper. He struck the rock twice instead of once. The only adults who managed to cross the border into Canaan were Joshua and Caleb.

Be careful that you do not behave like those hypocrites. Do not cut off yourself from the grace of your own Eternal Father. They went off track because they had no faith in the most magnetic and beautiful love.

Do love anything more than God. If you do, you are sensuous person. You are controlled by lusts. You are deceiving yourself that you are in love if the person or thing you love is not God. "Love not the world, neither the things that are in the world. If any man love the world, the love of the Father is not in him.

For all that is in the world, the lust of the flesh, and the lust of the eyes, and the pride of life, is not of the Father, but is of the world. And the world passeth away, and the lust thereof: but he that doeth the will of God abideth for ever" (1 John 2:15-17).

You are sensuous and, therefore, dirty in mind and heart. It does not matter what kind of addictions you love to obey, you are an animal.

You cannot claim that you are a Christian when you have other things that are first in your heart. You have not yet fallen in love with God your Father.

The so-called love for this world is simply the lusts of the body. It is not love at all. They are having sensuous eyes that are never satisfied by watching forbidden things.

They have sunk deep into your bones and are pulling them towards forbidden things. Such activities are not from the holy God but from the prince of this world called Satan.

The world is already on the fast track towards her final end. She is being driven by her lusts to commit suicide any time from now.

And anyone who is controlled by her lusts is committing suicide. But anyone who adopts the holy and righteous culture of God will have eternal life.

The story of the ancient of times ended with orders being given by the Lord to executed people with uncontrollable passions from infecting the whole world with their sins. And so those whose lusts drove them crazy were the first to die.

They are a warning to all the people who live by their lusts instead of common sense to wake up and stop fighting for things that are not beneficial for their bodies and spiritual advancements.

Lawlessness will definitely result in eternal death. "Now these things were our examples, to the intent we should not lust after evil things, as they also lusted" (1 Corinthians 10:6).

The Holy Spirit is warning every one not to make their hearts hard like rocks through unbelief. They must not be like those people who rebelled against Him on the day of that awful rebellion.

He is complaining that those people tried to overpower Him and maim Him so that He could never function again. When your fathers were tempting Him they were, actually, throwing stones at Him to kill Him. Temptation is murder.

They had no fear or shame of hurting Him and even killing if they could get their hands on Him. "Wherefore (as the Holy Ghost saith, To day if ye will hear his voice, Harden not your hearts, as in the provocation, in the day of temptation in the wilderness: When your fathers tempted me, proved me, and saw my works forty years" (Hebrews 3:7–9).

He said that He was completely heartbroken by the disrespectful ways that evil generation treated Him. He did all His works by truth.

Truth created heaven and earth. He wanted to teach them that truth has infinite creative powers in order to save them from the fires of hell. He suffered endless tortures in their hands for forty years.

He could not stand that generation of evil doers anymore. They were weak-willed. Their hearts were easily led astray. They never knew the beautiful ways in which He always lived and acted.

And since He is the Ever Tough One who cannot put up with nonsense forever, He refused for them to enter into His rest and have peace. "Wherefore I was grieved with that generation, and said, They do alway err in their heart; and they have not known my ways.

So I sware in my wrath, They shall not enter into my rest.) Take heed, brethren, lest there be in any of you an evil heart of unbelief, in departing from the living God" (Hebrews 3:10–12).

The Messiah is warning His brothers and sisters to watch out. Each person must check out himself or herself to make sure that his or her heart is not strong and unbreakable like steel.

Such a heart belongs to a sorcerer. Do not be like your father, Adam, who rejected living by faith. He tried to show off to everlasting God that he was somebody great.

Unless the devil will cut your days short, it is the plan of your Maker that you must die from old age. He wants to live for many years.

He wants all of you to grow into grayed hair old men and women. Do not kill your remaining days due to lusts or uncontrollable.

If you put bad substances in your body, get involved in body languages outside your marriages, etc. you will murder yourself. You will put your remaining years to death.

The Lord will respect your choice of committing suicide by your thoughtless and selfish acts.

Anybody discomfitures are symptoms of dying. If you do not feel right about certain things, your body is crying out to its Maker for help. Pray to Him. He will help you overcome those stupid addictions.

How long are you going to be hyenas? Stop eating rotten and smelling meat of your lusts and addictions. You see those things that your bodies are craving for, you either roaring or laughing like hyenas to entice them.

You are terrible hyenas that want to even eat your God because you are angry with Him for telling you to quit all those sensuous.

You are the powerful, intelligent, and wise people made in the features of God complete with His brain powers. You have no excuse sinning like that.

2. **God is your food and water in the desert of this life**

God loved His children very much. No one was starving. He provided plenty of food in that barren land for forty years. He did not provide them with water for irrigation in order to grow food in the desert. But He did all the hard and provided them with His grains.

He made them to stand strong. They were breathing the air of heaven of the love of their Creator. He really did love His brothers and sisters. He blessed them with everything that they needed. They knew that

He loved them because their stomachs were always full. They did nothing else but munch on food and take a walk from one place to another which they called marching. He was their meat, bread, and water.

They did need the natural food of the earth. It is corrupted with sin. They were all healthy. No one got sick or died or naturally diseases.

If they died at all, it was either due to old age or some rebellions that brought punishments upon them. "And the children of Israel did eat manna forty years, until they came to a land inhabited; they did eat manna, until they came unto the borders of the land of Canaan" (Exodus 16:35).

When they arrived in the Promised Land, they were surrounded with fields of ripped corn. When they went out, harvested, cooked and ate them, the work of the Lord of providing daily bread for them personally stopped.

He promises to care for you just like He did for the children of Israel in the wilderness. He gave them bread, water, security, etc. "Thou gavest also thy good spirit to instruct them, and withheldest not thy manna from their mouth, and gavest them water for their thirst. Yea, forty years didst thou sustain them in the wilderness, so that they lacked nothing; their clothes waxed not old, and their feet swelled not" (Nehemiah

9:20, 32).

He will fill you with His loving, eternal, intelligent, all powerful, creative, and excellent Spirit. It is the Spirit of truth. He is your Teacher.

You may be living in a land where nothing can grow. But He will feed you. You may live in a land of plenty but are too poor to buy a piece of bread. But God will feed you.

He is your Bread of life. You will not starve to death for lack of food. He is your Water of life. You will not die of thirst.

You may have only one piece of cloth on your back. But they will not fall into shreds that you cannot put on again until He has brought you a replacement. He is sweeter than honey. He will remove your fears and loneliness.

He is your Physician. He cures you from over 3,000 deadly viruses every day. He is your Bodyguard. That is why you are still alive today. He has kept the deadly diseases away. He has given you limbs so that you can ambulate around in order to help yourself. He has supplied means of survival to those who are handicapped.

You will have times of hardships that will force you to live by faith. And during those difficult times, you will come to understand the real value of life.

Life is not about clothes, food, water, peace, security, shelter or even belonging and loves of the world. It is about God and union with Him.

Think of all the times when you were thrown like bird that has fallen from the tree into the enemy's trap. You were squeezed between a rock and hard place and could hardly breathe.

The merciful God appeared to you at the nick of time. He led you through all those difficult days when you were overwhelmed with fear and brought you to this place in time.

He was throwing rocks of problems at you. He broke your bones. He wounded you in order to harden you and make you a strong and resilient person.

He forced you to evaluate your life very thoroughly. He made you to discover what your real intentions, motives, and goals in the life are. He forced you to reveal your inner most thoughts as to what constituted real living in your heart.

He is really after your life even today and especially during these hard and difficult times. He is hurting your ego very much. And you do not like it at all.

You hate embarrassments before people you care about. But now you are beginning to let go of proud. Other times, you hated Him for shaming you before the eyes of the worthy ones. But slowly and surely, you have begun to learn humility.

You love it better than that foolish pride that always got you into trouble with other people and hurt your feelings. "And thou shalt remember all the way which the LORD thy God led thee these forty years in the wilderness, to humble thee, and to prove thee, to know what was in thine heart, whether thou wildest keep his commandments, or no" (Deuteronomy 8:2).

He has allowed the devil to take away your health, food, water, resources, family, etc. He is giving you enough substances to barely keep you alive. At other times, you do not know where your next meal was going to come from.

You may be feeling deep pain from the terrible disease that easily slows eating your life away. But healing is on the way. Even if you may not be healed, you will die in the arms of the Lord. You may be dying of thirst. But He will quench your thirst.

You may be feeling very merciless hunger gnawing in your stomach. The Lord will give food that you have no idea about. He will rain for you manna from heaven.

Everyone's miracle is a little bit different from that of the next person. But it is still a miracle.

He will not answer your prayers exactly like He

answered those of your father and mother. He will put personal touches on the miracles and gifts that He will provide to you. You know that they are coming from a heart that loves and cares for you very much.

The Israelites receive manna from heaven and water from the rock. Your miracles may not be so dramatic but they are miracles none the less. They are supplied by the same hands of the One who loves very tenderly as much as He loved the Israelites in the desert.

He wants you to know life is not are your needs being met fully and on time but it is about feasting on His word as the most delicious food and water on earth.

"And he humbled thee, and suffered thee to hunger, and fed thee with manna, which thou knewest not, neither did thy fathers know; that he might make thee know that man doth not live by bread only, but by every word that proceedeth out of the mouth of the LORD doth man live" (Deuteronomy 8:3).

It is the relationship with God that counts above everything your hold dear. It is dearer than even your own life. It is the Spirit of God that created human beings and can, therefore, make them intelligent, wise, powerful, and eternal.

You have begun to ask certain difficult questions. "What do I live for? Is life merely about meeting mental, physical, and social needs?" How are you spending your life?

Is there anything better to do with your life than spending it by celebrating the greatness of the nature and character of God? It is about keeping the Ten Commandments holy, accepting the Messiah as your personal Savior, and living righteously by the power of the Holy Spirit.

Food, water, shelter, earthly love, etc. though very important and one should have them if possible, are not God Himself. They are not All-Powerful, All-Knowing, All-Loving, and All-Present.

They are inferior and cannot even save you from dying when your times come. But the Lord can resurrect you. He will give you food and water that have better qualities in heaven. They are substances that have the excellent qualities of eternal and joyous life.

The words that are falling from the mouth of Lord are your bread, water, shelter, social life, etc. They are love, joy, peace, eternal life, etc. "I call heaven and earth to record this day against you, that I have set before you life and death, blessing and cursing: therefore choose life, that both thou and thy seed may live" (Deuteronomy 30:19).

The One who gave life to the inhabitants and earth has place two bridegrooms in front of you. He is asking you to choose one of them to marry you. You have no choice but to get married. There are no singles in this life and in the next one to come. Choose whom you want to marry for all eternities.

One bridegroom is called eternal death. Its love is called sin. The other Bridegroom is your own Creator. He is unconditional love, peace, joy, eternal life, etc.

He is the blessed and eternal Savior. But His rival is under a curse. It is called eternal death that is being advocated by Satan.

If your choose the Man of Calvary to be your Husband, He will fill you with His own powerful, steady, intelligent, wise, holy, righteous, and eternal life. He will bless both you and your children forever if you choose Him to be your Husband. Obey His word.

It is creative, and it is life eternal. You and your children will excel in this life and in the next one to come in wisdom and intelligence because you are His brother or sister.

The word will help you to love the Lord your God very deeply, eternally, and unconditionally. "That thou mayest love the LORD thy God, and that thou mayest obey his voice, and that thou mayest cleave unto him: for he is thy life, and the length of thy days: that thou mayest dwell in the land which the LORD sware unto thy fathers, to Abraham, to Isaac, and to Jacob, to give them" (Deuteronomy 30:20).

Listen to His voice very intently. Give your entire mind into understanding what He is telling in the Bible, your conscience, nature, etc. Get out of your comfort zone.

Get out of arrogance, pride, and self-concept and get developed mentally and spiritually by Him. He will make your mind very holy, and righteous.

He will make you a very sharp axe that He will drive into Himself, and you will never fall into sin again. The truth is a very sharp sword.

It is in your hand. Drive it deep into the life of God to suck all the good and everlasting juices that are inherent in Him.

You got to have His life because He is your life. He is the reason why you were born in this world. He has given you days to live on earth by His power.

Make yourself ready to exist in the next one to come, too. He swear that He would rather be hanged on the tree by His neck should He not give you a decent life here on earth and a better life in heaven.

He is your Father who is greater in power and intelligence than Abraham because He is the Creator. He can give you rest, life, and grace that Abraham cannot give you.

He is greater Father than Isaac because He is the eternal truth and life. He is more important than Jacob He is powerful, sinless, pure, and holy.

Therefore, He can save you. Jacob was overthrown by sin. He is still dead and has not risen from the dead. But the Messiah can give you eternal life that never ends.

It is the word that helped the Messiah to overcome all sins. And the temptations came to Him at His most vulnerable moments. Very severe temptations that no man or woman had ever experienced in this world and will never face in the future, began to follow Him in great numbers after His baptism.

He shunned them as much as He could. But He came down into the world to face them on our behalf. So the Holy Spirit held Him in His arms and helped Him to go into the barren desert is outside the hubbub of human activities. "Then was Jesus led up of the Spirit into the wilderness to be tempted of the devil" (Matthew 4:1).

And who showed up but the old serpent who enticed Adam and Eve to sin way back at the beginning of the world. He began to throw gigantic rocks of temptations on the Messiah to kill Him.

The Brother was concluding forty days and nights of fasting on behalf of His brothers and sisters. "And when he had fasted forty days and forty nights, he was afterward an hungred" (Matthew 4:2).

He was very hungry, thirsty, fatigue, dirty, tired, etc. He had no good fortunes of health, success, etc. He was at the end of His life. He was dying.

As usual, the executioner of sin and death chose a very bad moment to try to kill the Messiah. "And when the tempter came to him, he said, If thou be the Son of God, command that these stones be made bread" (Matthew 4:3).

Satan tried to tempt the Messiah to change a stone in bread to satisfy His hunger

He enticed Him with the looks and smells of fresh bread. The brown rocks and stones around the Messiah seemed to almost jump out of their stony matter and turn into delicious and mouth-watering bread.

The serpent said, "If You are the everlasting Son

of God and equal to Him both as a Father and Son, command the truth that gives life and rest to this stones to turn into bread to give life to a hungry God who calls Himself the Brother of the people of this world."

But the Brother spoke to the devil with the authority of the Father of heaven and the earth. "But he answered and said, It is written, Man shall not live by bread alone, but by every word that proceedeth out of the mouth of God" (Matthew 4:4).

He told him, "The standing written word of the Father says, 'It is yet to be by bread that a brother or sister will grow into the image of the Father or be resurrected from the grave into His likeness. He or she will not be an eternal and all-wise person. But he or she will be like the Father by ever word of grace that comes out of the mouth of God.'" It is the word that will make you like Him.

Brothers and sisters, it is not acceptable in the sight of your God and Messiah that you have not yet come forward to receive your eternal life. The wonderful way He took care of the children of Israel was only a small taste of what He plans to accomplish in your life and especially in heaven. Those people were your fathers and mothers of the faith.

He covered all those multitudes with His cloud by day to protect them for the severe desert heart and by night from the wild animals and other enemies. He is your shade by day and by night even though you cannot see or hear Him.

He made them to pass the test at the Red Sea. He filled them with faith to trust in Him. And they crossed the Red Sea between two walls of water. He will give you the same faith to trust that He will make the impossible possible. He will help you to pass all the tests that are given to you to try your faith.

You will walk through two walls of water and cross to the other side. "Moreover, brethren, I would not that ye should be ignorant, how that all our fathers were under the cloud, and all passed through the sea;

And were all baptized unto Moses in the cloud and in the sea (1 Corinthians 10:1-4).

Just as the fathers and mothers of your faith walked between those two walls, so shall you wall through in the midst of trials. The clouds hanged over them like being immersed in the water of baptism.

You will be baptized by the power of the Holy Spirit in every trouble that has covered you up like water and is trying to drown you. You come out stronger and more righteous. You will cross over the other side and into greater height of righteousness and perfection.

They did not eat natural food. They ate celestial food. You are also feasting at the abundant table of God. Your bread and meat is the Body of the Savior. Your drink is His blood. The bread, meat, and blood are the Spirit of God. He is making you to grow into His likeness spiritually first.

Then at His Second Coming, He will give you new bodies. "And did all eat the same spiritual meat; And did all drink the same spiritual drink: for they drank of that spiritual Rock that followed them: and that Rock was Christ" (1 Corinthians 10:3, 4).

There is only one cup of blessings that all the saints of the world from the beginning of creation to the end of time drink from. He is the Messiah. All the prophets, holy patriarchs and matriarchs, the disciples drank from the same cup.

It has now been passed to you to drink your full fill. And that cup of all blessings is the Messiah. He is the Invisible Rock on whom you are standing. He is your Spirit Water of eternal life.

And He is your daily Manna that is making you grow into a holy person. He is creating divine culture in your mind and heart to make you think, talk, and act exactly like Him.

3. Spiritual bread

An imitation of the table of shewbread, Tabernacle Timna, Israel

During lunch time the following day, the 5,000 households, relatives, friends, and strangers gathered in the old place where the Messiah fed them to receive something to eat again. But He and His disciples were nowhere to be found.

All the boats of that they had used to come to shore and be with Him were still there tied to the quay. But the boat of the brothers who were the disciples of the Messiah was no longer among their boats. The brothers were missing.

They must have left for some other place. But they did not see the Messiah leaving with them. "The day following, when the people which stood on the other side of the sea saw that there was none other boat there, save that one whereunto his disciples were entered, and that Jesus went not with his disciples into the boat, but that his disciples were gone away alone;

(Howbeit there came other boats from Tiberias nigh unto the place where they did eat bread, after that the Lord had given thanks:)" (John 6:22, 23).

More and more people were coming from the town called Tiberias by boats to the Messiah. They wanted Him to get some few loaves of bread and little fishes, thank God for them, bless them, and give to them to eat like He did yesterday. He would create food for them to eat every day.

The people concluded that He might have found

some other way to be with the brothers that were following Him as the disciples. They guessed that He might be in Capernaum, a town that was located on the other side of the Sea of Galilee. So their boarded their boats and came looking for Him.

They commanded the people living in Capernaum to tell them where He was. "When the people therefore saw that Jesus was not there, neither his disciples, they also took shipping, and came to Capernaum, seeking for Jesus. And when they had found him on the other side of the sea, they said unto him, Rabbi, when camest thou hither?" (John 6:24, 25). When they found Him, they accused Him of leaving secretly without their notice.

He was sad that they did not remember all the beautiful messages from the mouth of God that He taught them. They wanted to satisfy only their immediate physical needs. They were ready to die for the King of Israel on earth but not for them Kingdom of God.

They did not care very much their spiritual needs. "Jesus answered them and said, Verily, verily, I say unto you, Ye seek me, not because ye saw the miracles, but because ye did eat of the loaves, and were filled.

Labour not for the meat which perisheth, but for that meat which endureth unto everlasting life, which the Son of man shall give unto you: for him hath God the Father sealed" (John 6:26, 27).

He is giving the same rebukes to Christians that He gave to those people who were more interested in having their physical rather than their spiritual needs met.

He is asking you to stop ordering Him to fulfill your immediate needs and instead focus your attention on the more important things that you really need. They are the love of God your Father, building a solid and eternal relationship with Him, and being saved to always live with Him forever.

He says, "Truth is life. If you follow nothing else but the truth, you will find life that is eternal, abundant, and awesome. You are always asking Me to satisfy your physical needs. But you have never taken interests or given ample time to consider how powerful and awesome those miracles are.

They were given to help you to discover how deep and great the love of God your Father for you is. It is very sad to see that you are all interested only in yourselves. You only want your physical needs to be met and nothing else.

Do not break yourselves trying to get things that are temporal in nature. You are wearing yourselves out if you are fighting to be full and complete like the holy angels by following your own ways.

You are dying to get perishable meats. That is no wise at all. However, if you are breaking yourselves and dying in order to get the real meats that have the eternal nature of God your Father in them, you will find fulfillments for yourselves. He will birth abundant and eternal lives into your bodies.

He sent the Messiah to be the Backbone on whom you can lean to receive endless eternities with all their overflowing provisions. They will meet all your needs and more besides.

God your Father has placed His seal of authority and powers as God, King, Lord and, therefore, the Supplier of all your needs on Him. He is wearing the engagement ring of the Bridegroom of the world on His finger."

He is inviting everyone saying, "Ho, every one that thirsteth, come ye to the waters, and he that hath no money; come ye, buy, and eat; yea, come, buy wine and milk without money and without price" (Isaiah 55:1).

He is inviting all the people of this earth to find true life by swimming in the water of love. And those who are yet to get money enough to buy a ticket to take them to heaven should not worry any more.

Salvation is free.

Come and buy this everlasting bread by giving Him all your hearts. Take all the salvation so freely offered to you and eat them until you are fully satisfied. Drink the wine and milk of eternal life. Fill your stomachs with them until the cups are empty.

Why are you behaving like mothers that are laboring and suffering intense pains trying to give births to their babies? Why are spending your life so painfully and sorrowfully like pregnant women birthing children trying to look for needs, wants, and accomplishments?

"Wherefore do ye spend money for that which is not bread? and your labour for that which satisfieth not? hearken diligently unto me, and eat ye that which is good, and let your soul delight itself in fatness" (Isaiah 55:2).

Do not spend your lives getting angry unless your needs are met and you are satisfied and happy. Find life by listening very carefully to the words of the Messiah and obeying them faithfully. Eat the fatness of God your Father.

You will grow up. You will look awesome. You will want nothing else but to excel yourself in seeking the best things from Him that will make you even more awesome.

The bread of this world does not give you lasting strength. You have to eat it several times in a day if you can get it in order to keep alive. But there is no fear of death in heaven due to starvation.

There is no lack of bread and water there. You will eat food and drink water plentifully.

They are some of the pleasures God has reserved for you. They will make your life very pleasant and enjoyable. Everything has been paid for you on the Cross of Calvary.

The people asked Him as to how they could kill everything in order to do the kind of works that God was doing. They were ready to kill them by bring them to total and complete accomplishments. "Then said they unto him, What shall we do, that we might work the works of God?" (John 6:28).

The Messiah told them that they missed the point. "Jesus answered and said unto them, This is the work of God, that ye believe on him whom he hath sent" (John 6:29).

God does not spend His life killing death in order to create things that are wonderful out of it for the sake of praises. He is not wasting His time in collecting trophies. He is spending His life in helping others. And this is what He wants everyone on this earth to do: They must faith in His Messenger. It is through Him that God the Father will create new people that will be eternal and awesome.

Remember and see to it that you are living your lives like that of your heavenly Father. Give yourselves to the works of faith. Suffer and die for the sake of the kind of His love.

It is gracious and eternal. Develop the strength of character and endurance by living by the truth. It will make you matured like Him.

Maturity is being patient, faithful, and loving even when you are under stress. "Remembering without ceasing your work of faith, and labour of love, and patience of hope in our Lord Jesus Christ, in the sight of God and our Father; Knowing, brethren beloved, your election of God" (1 Thessalonians 1:3, 4).

Return back to your Father by putting your faith in the Messiah and Lord God of heaven and the earth, and following Him only. God your heavenly Father is watching you following His Son.

Beloved brothers and sisters of the Messiah that are tenderly loved by God your Father, you have already been taught that He loves you. He has chosen you to be His sons and daughters. You are winners because the Messiah is your Brother. You have His life. See to it that you are living just like Him.

Do everything through love. "Above all things

have intense and unfailing love for one another, for love covers a multitude of sins [forgives and disregards the offenses of others]. [Prov. 10:12.]" (1 Peter 4:8, AMP).

Before you welcome any methods of living righteous lives into your hearts, welcome love first. Love is life. It is grace. So give it to one another without reserve and without limits. Give it with all your mind, heart, and strength. It is the greatest gift you have received from God.

Therefore, it is the greatest gift that you can give to anyone. It tramples all sins under its feet like a big and powerful bull that stomps its enemies under its feet.

They asked Him to prove Himself as the Messiah of God by killing Himself creating His life right before their eyes. "They said therefore unto him, What sign shewest thou then, that we may see, and believe thee? what dost thou work?" (John 6:30).

They wanted to see creation taking place right before their eyes. Then, they would place their face in Him that the nature and character of the heavenly Father were residing in Him. They asked Him not to wait but to go on and work some miracles and bring them to full accomplishments.

They pointed out that their fathers ate manna in the wilderness when they were on their way from Egypt to the Promised Land. God rained on them miracles bread from heaven from them to eat. That was a solid proof that He was supernatural.

But what proofs did the Messiah have to show that He was God in human flesh? "Our fathers did eat manna in the desert; as it is written, He gave them bread from heaven to eat" (John 6:31).

The people were giving more credits to Moses for the manna their ancestors ate in the desert than to God. "Then Jesus said unto them, Verily, verily, I say unto you, Moses gave you not that bread from heaven; but my Father giveth you the true bread from heaven. For the bread of God is he which cometh down from heaven, and giveth life unto the world" (John 6:32, 33).

The Messiah emphasized the importance of listening and obeying the truth. It is life and love. Moses was not the father or brother who created Israel. He does not have the supernatural power to give them strength to live day by day.

They cannot follow his footsteps in order to reach to heaven because he does not have supernatural powers that can save them. But God the Father is the one who created the people of the earth. He can give them both physical and spiritual bread to keep them living forever.

The true bread comes from heaven and not from the earth. It is Bread of God. It is the creative powers that can birth eternal life in people all over again.

The people asked the Messiah to give them the bread of heaven to help them feel the pangs of hunger no more. "Then said they unto him, Lord, evermore give us this bread" John 6:34). They wanted to feel full and satisfied all their lives.

He told them plainly that He is the eternal Bread of God. "And Jesus said unto them, I am the bread of life: he that cometh to me shall never hunger; and he that believeth on me shall never thirst. But I said unto you, That ye also have seen me, and believe not. All that the Father giveth me shall come to me; and him that cometh to me I will in no wise cast out.

For I came down from heaven, not to do mine own will, but the will of him that sent me. And this is the Father's will which hath sent me, that of all which he hath given me I should lose nothing, but should raise it up again at the last day.

And this is the will of him that sent me, that everyone which seeth the Son, and believeth on him, may have everlasting life: and I will raise him up at the last day" (John 6:35–40).

He says that He is the Brother that created all the

brothers and sisters He has placed in this world. He is the Creator of the lives. Therefore, He is their Bread of eternal life. He is their love.

Therefore, He is their life. If any brother or sister would welcome Him to live in his or her heart, he or she will never hunger again for the real things of life.

These things are God and His eternal life and unconditional love for them. Anyone who has faith in Him will never again thirst for the real things of life here on earth and in heaven.

There are people who have seen Him. They are swimming in the knowledge of knowing Him very well. But they have refused to place their faiths in His unlimited grace and mercy.

Everyone who is being placed into His hands by God the Father will welcome Him in his or her heart as the Father, who endures forever and, therefore, can save them. And anyone who embraces Him as the Father who stands forever will not be thrown out of His household.

He did not descend from heaven and forgot bringing the truth with Him. He is the truth that is in line with His Father's will for the world.

He has come to put into work the truth His Father has sent Him to carry out. This is truth is that everyone whom He has convinced to about his or her sins and wants to repent should come to His Son and will find salvation.

The Son will never turn His back on repentant sinners and walk away. He will do everything that is in His power to save that person. He will never lose him or her.

It is the command of God the Father that He must recreated repentant sinners on the day of resurrection. They will stand on their own two feet and walk this earth again. That will be the great of great fortunes when they receive eternally good health in their bodies again.

He repeated that the will of God your Father is

that you must have faith in His Messenger that He, too, is God the Almighty, Everlasting, All-Loving, and All-Knowing. If you have seen Him in your heart and believe in Him as your Creator and Messiah, you believe the same things about God your Father.

He is the exact replica of His Son. And if you have faith in the Messiah, your faith will turn for you into eternal life.

It will resurrect you from the dead. It will make you to stand on your own two feet on the day of resurrection when great fortunes will be poured into the bodies of the saints.

Unfortunately, the Jews shut their eyes to the spiritual teachings of the Messiah. They knew what He was talking about. But they were suffering from intellectual pride and arrogance. They picked up quarrels with them.

He accused Him of trying to make them cannibals. "The Jews then murmured at him, because he said, I am the bread which came down from heaven. And they said, Is not this Jesus, the son of Joseph, whose father and mother we know? how is it then that he saith, I came down from heaven?" (John 6:41, 42).

The Jews grew angry and bitter with the Messiah for not providing them with a good meal like He had done before. They refused to listen to spiritual food. They did not want to work anymore. They wanted God to rain them bread from heaven.

They tried to twist His words and use them against them. They declared that He was not the Bread of life.

They tried to prove that He was a mere human being just like themselves. They tried not to remember His miraculous birth and all the miracles and healings that He did.

They wanted free stuff but not the salvation of their own souls. They had no love for God but for themselves.

The Messiah told them that they were fighting Him because they were unconverted. "Jesus therefore answered and said unto them, Murmur not among yourselves. No man can come to me, except the Father which hath sent me draw him: and I will raise him up at the last day.

It is written in the prophets, And they shall be all taught of God. Every man therefore that hath heard, and hath learned of the Father, cometh unto me. Not that any man hath seen the Father, save he which is of God, he hath seen the Father" (John 6:43–46).

The Jews were not angry with the Messiah but they were fighting among themselves as to what He meant by saying that He was the Bread that came down from heaven.

No earthly being has the power to welcome God into his or her without Him first taking the initiative to woo him or her back to Him. It was not the powers of the Jews that were saving them from the flames of hell but the power of the Creator who provided them the way to come back to Him. Everyone is being wooed by Him to come back to Him.

It is God the Father who has provided salvation for the world through His beloved Son. He will promote people who listen to voice out of sin and into righteousness. The Son promises to raise them into eternal life on the day of His second return.

Just as predicted by the prophets, God Himself is the Teacher of all the people of this world. Anyone who listens to His voice and obeys His teachings as that of their Father will gladly come to His Son to receive salvation.

"But this shall be the covenant that I will make with the house of Israel; After those days, saith the LORD, I will put my law in their inward parts, and write it in their hearts; and will be their God, and they shall be my people" (Jeremiah 31:33).

He has cut the covenant of an eternal love for His children by cutting down His own Son on their behalf on the Cross of Calvary. And on the last day, He is wedding you to His Law.

You will love it more than you love yourself or anyone in this world. It will enter into your deepest as the greatest love you have ever discovered in your live.

The Law is all about supernatural love that has no beginning or end. You will know Him as your one and only God. And of course, you will always be His dearly beloved and eternal child.

Moreover His has forgiven and forgotten about your sins even His Son died to pay for them. "For I will be merciful to their unrighteousness, and their sins and their iniquities will I remember no more" (Hebrews 8:12). He is watching over you. He has taken care of the business of saving you from your sins, death, and hell.

He is the only Teacher you got on this earth. All the other good teachers who teach the truth are just agents. "And all thy children shall be taught of the LORD; and great shall be the peace of thy children" (Isaiah 54:13).

All of you are the disciples of God your Father. He will teach you until you have understood all His truths and are living by them. That is the time when you have deep and immovable peace and joy in your hearts.

The Lord has been watched over yourself from time immemorial. His love for you covers you from the everlasting to everlasting years without end. He loves you so much that in spite of your sins and hatred of Him, He took the necessary steps to bring you back to Him through the Cross of Calvary. His hands are outstretched.

They are embracing you. They are drawing ever closer to Him. "The LORD hath appeared of old unto me, saying, Yea, I have loved thee with an everlasting love: therefore with lovingkindness have I drawn thee" (Jeremiah 31:3).

The Son went on to explain what the bread of life means. "Verily, verily, I say unto you, He that believeth on me hath everlasting life. I am that bread of life. Your fathers did eat manna in the wilderness, and are dead.

This is the bread which cometh down from heaven, that a man may eat thereof, and not die. I am the living bread which came down from heaven: if any man eat of this bread, he shall live for ever: and the bread that I will give is my flesh, which I will give for the life of the world" (John 6:47–51).

He was saying, "The ultimate truth that I am telling you all is that anyone who has faith in Me as your Creator and Messiah has eternal life. I will live in such a soul as the God of love and life that will never end because I am everlasting.

I am He who is life. I am that part in your spirit or Brother that keeps you alive. Therefore, I am the Bread of life that supplies you with breaths and the strength to live not just in this world but especially in the one to come. I am also your Father who birthed His life into you to help you to exist in My world.

It is important, therefore, that you must follow My footsteps to help you enter into My eternal life and rejoice forever. Just as food gives you the strength and energy to keep alive, I will be the Bread that will supply you with eternal life if you accept Me to live in your soul.

Even miracle food like the one I provided for Israel will not keep you save you from getting tempted, tried, and put death because you have broken the Ten Commandments. So do not spend too much time begging Me for miracles.

Seek to know the deeper knowledge of God in order to grow more righteous like Him. That is the only way that will save you from your sin.

Miracles that will provide you food, water, wealth, politics, social life, security, etc. will not stop temptations, trials, and death from getting you. But if you will seek to eat the Miraculous Bread of heaven, you will not die in hell but live forever.

Life is your strong and loving brother that watches

of you and protects you from death. And there is no greater Brother in this world than I, your Messiah. And if you will eat Me as the Brother in order that I may in your soul, I will watch over and keep death far from you.

Moreover, I will add into you everlasting years. You will never see suffering and death again. I will enter into your genes and spirit like the nutrients that you consume to give you growth, body repair, and energy. I will recreate and make you to grow into a giant person with perfect righteousness.

I will recreate Myself into you just as I have put My Spirit into Adam and made the clay into a living and thoughtful person. I am the life that the world needs. I am a better deal than all the strengths and joys that your food and water can provide for you."

If your stomach is sinking and shrinking because of hunger and starvation, do not die. Jesus is the Living Bread of life. He says that He is the Bread that will give you wisdom, intelligence and strength to excel and to live forever. He came down from heaven to help you.

However, heaven is not a strange and distant place. It is your heaven, too. Anyone who will eat Him through the food and water He will provide will be filled with eternal life. It is like eating His body when you receive food and water from His hands. You will be immortal, beautiful and healthy just like Him.

The Jews closed their minds to listen to the beautiful and deep spiritual context of the words of the Messiah. They were acting like bad little children.

They clashed among themselves very fiercely. They were using words as weapons to fight each. The fighting was the fiercest among His seventy disciples. "The Jews therefore strove among themselves, saying, How can this man give us his flesh to eat?" (John 6:52).

They took the teachings literal on purpose in order to spite Him. They accused Him of trying to feed them with unclean meat. Moreover they were not cannibals. They would eat His flesh and drink His blood. They ate clean animals.

All that they wanted to do was fight Him because He was pointing to them the way to their Father. They did not like Him but for His miracles.

If God loved them, then He should rain meat and bread from heaven like He did for their ancestors for forty years in the wilderness. They hated the feast of only one day.

They wanted Him to feed them all their lives, kick out the Romans, and make them kings and queens of the world.

Since they did not want to learn anything about heavenly issues, He decided to speak their language also. It was not to be taken literally but spiritually.

"Then Jesus said unto them, Verily, verily, I say unto you, Except ye eat the flesh of the Son of man, and drink his blood, ye have no life in you.

Whoso eateth my flesh, and drinketh my blood, hath eternal life; and I will raise him up at the last day. For my flesh is meat indeed, and my blood is drink indeed. He that eateth my flesh, and drinketh my blood, dwelleth in me, and I in him.

As the living Father hath sent me, and I live by the Father: so he that eateth me, even he shall live by me. This is that bread which came down from heaven: not as your fathers did eat manna, and are dead: he that eateth of this bread shall live for ever" (John 6:53–58).

He is telling you that the real truth about salvation is that you must eat that lion of a body He has. Eat His body as the truth. His blood is the Law.

It will create eternal life. If you do not eat and drink truth as your food and water, you will have Spirit of God living in your soul. You are still dead in your iniquities and lawlessness.

If you eat the body and drink the blood of the Son of God as the word of truth from God your Father, you become one with Him in body and Spirit. He will get you out of the grave recreated and brand on the day of resurrection. He will make you stand on your own two feet again.

His lion of a body is supernatural. It is everlasting and powerful. If you accept Him into your soul, He can change your heart, mind, spirit, and body to be supernatural and holy just like His. His body and blood are the everlasting truths that created heaven and earth and still sustaining them.

But you must accept Him as body and blood into your heart by faith. He will fill you with His blood inside to wash away your sins. He will cover you with His blood like putting on wedding gowns.

The wedding gowns are symbols of brightly shinning powers that are burning inextinguishable fires. You will have the same thoughts and feelings with Him. They are righteous, holy, and eternal.

You will think, talk, and behave like Him. You will have one thought, word, and goal with Him. Thus, you will have the same divine culture. You will no longer follow your earthly traditions and cultures that are heavily influenced by lawlessness and all kinds of sins.

He ate the Spirit of God His Father. That was why He was able to live a perfect life without sinning at all. He was able to work miracles and resurrect from the dead.

So if you, too, would eat His body and drink His blood spiritually, you will achieve do the same thing He did. You will also resurrect from the dead with a supernatural body and spirit because you have Him living in your body and spirit.

He, the Messiah, is the Bread of heaven that provides food for the holy angels. He came down here to do the same thing for you.

Physical food gives strength for about four hours only. Miracle foods like the children of Israel acted just like ordinary food. They had to eat every day to keep alive. The bread and meat did not create new bodies and spirits in them.

When the time of deaths came, they died. The foods were only matter. They provided temporary energies.

They did not have eternal energies and strength to help the consumers to live eternally. They did not have the Spirit of God. God alone can create a new body and spirit in you.

So eat Him as if you are eating food and drink Him as if you are drinking water. And He will recreate you inside out.

As has been said before, He was in Capernaum when the crowds that were looking for food to eat found Him. He has about seventy disciples that time. The majority was deeply disappointed with Him for refusing to be crowned the King of Israel.

They had hoped to be the deputy kings, lords, and ministers in His kingdom. "These things said he in the synagogue, as he taught in Capernaum. Many therefore of his disciples, when they had heard this, said, This is an hard saying; who can hear it?" (John 6:59, 60).

They could not control their disappointments. To make matters worse, He refused to uplift them in the eyes of the people by providing them with daily bread and meat like their ancestors had in the desert.

They complained, "The truth of Father is too difficult to understand. Who can be able to lay his hand upon it and unpack it?

Who will understand this truth in order to become one with Him in knowledge? We will never receive His Spirit because His words are too difficult to understand."

The Lord could see strong reactions against His words from most of His disciples. He could feel their hate and anger against. "When Jesus knew in himself that his disciples murmured at it, he said unto them, Doth this offend you?

What and if ye shall see the Son of man ascend up where he was before? It is the spirit that quickeneth;

the flesh profiteth nothing: the words that I speak unto you, they are spirit, and they are life" (John 6:61–63).

He is telling some of you who are bitter with Him because you do not want to accept the truth and twist it to suit your own false teachings, "Are you abandoning Me?

Is that why you are flying away like birds from Me? You will see with your own eyes the Son of the Person, the Truth, help Himself to all His that He has just like He did before He became a Human Being.

The Spirit has eternal life. It is He who gives life to human beings. He will make them eternally alive from age to age.

My human body that had not died yet and resurrected from the grave was stronger than that of lion. However, it could not save anyone while still in its natural or earthly form. It is of no eternal benefit to anyone.

It cannot help believers lay hands on death, beat it, and conquer it. In fact, it cannot help them to defeat anything at all. But the words I am speaking to you on behalf as the Father who birthed you has My creative Spirit in them. They can birth eternal life in you."

He turned to His seventy disciples and laid their secret thoughts that were very hostile against in the open. "But there are some of you that believe not. For Jesus knew from the beginning who they were that believed not, and who should betray him" (John 6:64).

He said that they were opposing Him and turning the crowds against Him. They were misconstruing His words in revenge for not driving out the Romans and making them kings and lords of His kingdom.

They were atheists and agnostics right from the beginning before they were born. He knew they were faithless.

One of them was going to betray Him. He would be put to the because of Him. The betrayer was Judas Iscariot. He and his time-servers were only after power, wealth, riches, etc. They did not love God.

They did not want to be like Him and practice His righteousness of love, kindness, joy, peace, eternal life, etc.

He pointed out that no one can save himself or herself by his or her own intelligence and powers. The only Savior this world has is God. "And he said, Therefore said I unto you, that no man can come unto me, except it were given unto him of my Father" (John 6:65).

He is emphasizing that you have no power to change yourself into a holy, righteous, and eternal person. You cannot lay hand on heaven and rule it by your own personal efforts.

God the Father will choose when you have a willing heart to be saved. He will place you into His Son's hands to wash away your sins and fill you with the Holy Spirit.

He, in turn, will create a righteous character. Then, you will ready to be recreated and given an indestructible and eternal body and spirit on the day of the Messiah's Second Coming.

Fifty eight disciples from amongst the seventy men abandoned their discipleship. They were no longer counted amongst the twelve men from that day onward. "From that time many of his disciples went back, and walked no more with him" (John 6:66).

They claimed that His teachings were too hard to follow. But the real reason they left Him was that they wanted the Kingdom of God on the earth to be established in their lifetimes.

They did not want the rest of the world to be saved first before the purification of the earth with fire. Only twelve men followed Him.

He turned to the twelve men who were still standing around Him and gave them the option to leave Him too if they wanted. Then said Jesus unto the twelve, Will ye also go away?" (John 6:67).

He said, "God has set dishes filled with them with truth before the world. Have you also made the decision of rejecting it and going away?"

Some answered Him on behalf of eleven men. "Then Simon Peter answered him, Lord, to whom shall we go? thou hast the words of eternal life. And we believe and are sure that thou art that Christ, the Son of the living God" (John 6:68, 69).

He spoke on behalf of all the people who will be in the Messiah, saying, "Oh, our Lord, You are God. Where can we find gold apart from You?

You have the word that fills human beings up and makes them complete, fulfilled, righteous, and eternal like Yourself. We have faith in You. We know that you are the Messiah. You are the Son of the Ever Living God."

Not all twelve men loved Him. He knew that one of them was a betrayer. He loved the glories of the earth more than a good relationship with His Creator.

"Jesus answered them, Have not I chosen you twelve, and one of you is a devil? He spake of Judas Iscariot the son of Simon: for he it was that should betray him, being one of the twelve" (John 6:70, 71).

Do not be like Judas Iscariot but like the other good disciples. They suffered and were martyred because they believed and loved the truth that the Messiah.

He is the truth. He will save you if you live by the truth and not the lies of sin that the demons are spreading around the world to confuse people and kill them. Truth will save you. It is called the Messiah of Calvary.

3.   Their heart is far from me

No matter how holy and perfect a human being is, he or she is not your bread and water of eternal life. These people include Mary, Abraham, Mother (Saint) Teresa, etc. God alone is your Bread and water of life.

When religious leaders are spiritually blind, it makes matters worse for the Christians. The proud Pharisees who liked to advertise their righteousness in front of people gathered against the God of life and love. Some powerful scribes who wanted to be as loving as God the Father joined them. "Then came together unto him the Pharisees, and certain of the scribes, which came from Jerusalem" (Mark 7:1).

These powers that had risen against the Messiah came from Jerusalem. They were following Him everywhere trying to find some mistakes that He might do in order to nail Him on a Cross. They were watching the disciples of the Lord very closely. They almost fainted when they saw them not performing the ceremonial washing of hands. "They noticed that some of his disciples were eating their food with hands that were ritually unclean---that is, they had not washed them in the way the Pharisees said people should.

(For the Pharisees, as well as the rest of the Jews, follow the teaching they received from their ancestors: they do not eat unless they wash their hands in the proper way; nor do they eat anything that comes from the market unless they wash it first. And they follow many other rules which they have received, such as the proper way to wash cups, pots, copper bowls, and beds.)" (Mark 7:2–4, GNB).

These ceremonial washing was done in a special way. It was supposed to wash away the sins that irreligious people had rubbed on them when they had shaken hands with them. Some people wash not only their hands but they was them beginning from their elbows. The water was made to run from fingers towards the elbows instead of the usual washing that you do by allowing water to run from elbow to your fingers and let it drop off.

The Pharisees despised Jews who ate food with hands that were ceremonial unclean. It was not that they were unrighteous people but that their hands were made unrighteous through contact with Non-Jewish, and they ordered to wash the sin-infected hands with the righteousness of God, which was symbolized by water.

So they were very meticulous about hand washing. The righteous of God symbolized by the water washed away the sins that the Gentiles had deposited on them during business contacts in the market places. They would never eat unless they performed this ritual of hand washing.

They also washed their utensils, furniture, etc. in certain ways to make them holy and fit for them to use. They wanted to live very righteously just like their fathers who had lived before them who had formulated these laws about being righteous through these kinds of rituals.

The Pharisees were appalled to see the Messiah's disciples washing their hands in the normal way and not ritually. They went to the directly Messiah with their complaints. "Then the Pharisees and scribes asked him, Why walk not thy disciples according to the tradition of the elders, but eat bread with unwashen hands?"

God accused the Pharisees of being men and women who were full of themselves. "He answered and said unto them, Well hath Esaias prophesied of you hypocrites, as it is written, This people honoureth me with their lips, but their heart is far from me.

Howbeit in vain do they worship me, teaching for doctrines the commandments of men. For laying aside the commandment of God, ye hold the tradition of men, as the washing of pots and cups: and many other such like things ye do" (Mark 7:6–8).

They loved to show off that they were more spiritual than other people. He said that Prophet Isaiah was as sweet as honey to point out the sins of strong-headed Israel. The prophet said that Israel seemed to be flying very fast like birds to God to be close to Him. Though outwardly, they looked wise, intelligent, and strong people, they were hypocrites in their hearts.

They were celebrating Him as the Lord God of Israel with their lips only. But they were together with Him in their hands. They were taking censuses by head-counting.

They used the number of the physical of the Jews as belonging to Him. But they failed to count the true Jews by counting by those whose hearts were converted. True Jews are the born again believers.

The Pharisees, scribes, and all their followers who kept the traditions of their fathers had not surrendered their hearts to Him. They honor Him only for His miracles and healings. But they have refused to surrender their hearts Him.

They were very far from Him. The way they were worshipping and praising Him was very bad. It was awful. They were teaching people the laws of men.

The Law of love was like a strong rope that had bound to God. But they broke away from it. They tried to tie themselves to Him by using their own Messiah whom the claimed was righteous.

This Messiah was the human traditions or oral laws. The formulators claimed that the oral laws were birth by the Omnipotent God.

They were washing their utensils and many other things with the traditions that they inherited from their ancestors. That was the kind of love they were showing Him. They claimed that they doing the works of God and had become as righteous as He was.

He condemned their misuses of the Corban. And he said unto them, Full well ye reject the commandment of God, that ye may keep your own tradition.

For Moses said, Honour thy father and thy mother; and, Whoso curseth father or mother, let him die the death:

But ye say, If a man shall say to his father or mother, It is Corban, that is to say, a gift, by whatsoever thou mightest be profited by me; he shall be free" (Mark 7:11–13).

Corban is the love gift that is offered to God the Father. But it also includes seeking for His power in order to be like Him. The Law of love or the Ten Commandments that people must practice love towards God and other people such as their parents. But the priests found a way of getting rich by laying claims on Corbans on the Commandments of God.

They told the people to make wills that would give their money and other properties such as houses, farms, etc. the temple. Upon their deaths, these things would belong to the priests.

If they did that, they would not assist their parents who were in need because their properties were holy. The things they owned were now Corbans. They were dedicated to God.

He said it was sin to deny help to your parents on the ground you are serving God. "And ye suffer him no more to ought for his father or his mother; Making the word of God of none effect through your tradition, which ye have delivered: and many such like things do ye" (Mark 7:9–13).

He said the priests were not calling the people to give assistance to their fathers and mothers very lovingly and generously. A father is a symbol of the God the Father who gives births to life.

A mother is a symbol of God the Mother who gives births to love. So when you are assisting you parents, you are offering Corbans or love gifts to God.

But these leaders of the Jews were playing a dangerous game when they cast their responsibilities to their parents. They were demonstrating not just hatred to the Ten Commandments but against their Lawgiver

- God the Father.

The Messiah said that the teachings of the Pharisees were not from God. They were sinful. They came out of their evil hearts. "And when he had called all the people unto him, he said unto them, Hearken unto me every one of you, and understand" (Mark 7:14).

He accused the Pharisees, scribes, lawyers, Sadducees, etc. of making the beautiful Commandments of God appear evil as if they were laid down by the evil god of this world called Satan.

He asked all of you to listen to His passionate plea: "There is nothing from without a man, that entering into him can defile him: but the things which come out of him, those are they that defile the man. If any man have ears to hear, let him hear" (Mark 7:15, 16).

The disciples almost fainted when the God of love pointed out the sins of the powerful Pharisees. "Then came his disciples, and said unto him, Knowest thou that the Pharisees were offended, after they heard this saying?" (Matthew 15:12).

They told Him that the Pharisees were did not rejoice when they heard the words of the All-Powerful God.

The righteous plants that were not planted by God are not righteous all. They will be uprooted and burned because they are weeds. "But he answered and said, Every plant, which my heavenly Father hath not planted, shall be rooted up" (Matthew 15:13).

The Messiah asked His disciples not to look up to the Pharisees as their heroes and/or follow their teachings. They should break away from them. He said that the Pharisees were blind leaders.

If you follow somebody who is totally blind and you are blind too, both of you will end up in the ditch. A spiritual blind leader will lead people into hell. "Let them alone: they be blind leaders of the blind. And if the blind lead the blind, both shall fall into the ditch:

(Matthew 15:14).

Abel Grimmer (c.1570–c.1620), the blind leading the blid

The disciples did not understand what the Lord meant by this statement. "And when he was entered into the house from the people, his disciples asked him concerning the parable about the defilements by evil things that come from the heart" (Mark 7:17).

He explained to them what it meant. "Don't you understand either?" he asked. "Can't you see that the food you put into your body cannot defile you?

Food doesn't go into your heart, but only passes through the stomach and then goes into the sewer." (By saying this, he declared that every kind of food is acceptable in God's eyes.)

And then he added, "It is what comes from inside that defiles you. For from within, out of a person's heart, come evil thoughts, sexual immorality, theft, murder, adultery, greed, wickedness, deceit, lustful desires, envy, slander, pride, and foolishness. All these vile things come from within; they are what defile you" (Mark 7:18–23, NLT).

There are more corruptions in the Church of God than they have ever occurred before in the history of the human race. "This know also, that in the last days perilous times shall come.

For men shall be lovers of their own selves, covetous, boasters, proud, blasphemers, disobedient to parents, unthankful, unholy, Without natural affection, trucebreakers, false accusers, incontinent, fierce, despisers of those that are good, Traitors, heady, highminded, lovers of pleasures more than lovers of God;

Having a form of godliness, but denying the power thereof: from such turn away. For of this sort are they which creep into houses, and lead captive silly women laden with sins, led away with divers lusts, Ever learning, and never able to come to the knowledge of the truth.

Now as Jannes and Jambres withstood Moses, so do these also resist the truth: men of corrupt minds, reprobate concerning the faith. But they shall proceed no further: for their folly shall be manifest unto all men, as theirs also was" (2 Timothy 3:1–9).

4.   This know also, that in the last days perilous times shall come

These are the sins are in your heart and in the hearts of all the professed followers of the Lord. Please surrender yourself into the hand of God through prayers and fasting and He will change your heart to be as good as His own heart.

These are the last days when false Christians will try very desperately to shake you in order to lose faith in the Messiah. They are powerful in their arguments. They will claim that they know the truth. But the truth you can always follow safely is written in the Bible.

These are difficult and hard times to be a good Christian and at the same time be a friend of lost men and women who may pull you backwards. Many of Christians may not be strong and firm in the faith like you. But you must always keep your eyes on God. Do not be overwhelmed by the failings of mankind.

For men shall be lovers of their own selves

They love to listen only to the fallen spirits within themselves. They will claim that they are as righteous as God but they are lying.

Covetous

They love wealth more than God who is ready to give better and greater things in heaven and all the universes.

Boasters

They love beating their own chests and sounding their own self-importance.

Proud

They love to show off to each other that they are better than God and better than the next person.

Blasphemers

They steal the glory of God and put it on themselves and then curse and demean Him as of no importance to them whatsoever.

Disobedient to parents

They have changed their attitudes towards those who gave them birth from good to bad. It will worse as the end nears.

Unthankful

They feel that it is demeaning to say to the people who love them, "I love you." They would not admit their wrongs, mistakes, or sins. They feel that it is below their dignity to say, "I am sorry." Even when people have done good thing to them, they are too proud to say, "Thank you."

Unholy

They trampled on holiness and righteousness that could have changed them. They could have become holy and righteous like God. They exalt sin instead.

Without natural affection

Love, compassion, pity, gentleness, affection, etc. do not come to them naturally. They fake them.

Trucebreakers

They are unreliable. They do not return back to fulfill what they have promised to do to God or to anyone else. They have broken the covenant of love with their Messiah, and they break the promises they have made with each other.

False accusers

They are foxes. They are liars. They take oaths when they know that their statements are false.

Incontinent

They do not have self-control.

Fierce

Pride has made them to be cruel, revengeful and brutal. They are their own law.

Despisers of those that is good

They consider being good as weakness. So they despise good Christians as weak and cowardly people. They turn away from love that can build through prayers to God the Savior.

Traitors

They are cruel-hearted. This makes them to betray each other without fear or care in the world.

Heady

This is a person who gives what is in his mind to people he or she hates or despises. They do not even bother to hide their ill-feelings to each other.

Highminded

The Law describes the excellences of God in all of His dimensions: mind, heart, nature and Spirit. It is His divine and royal character. But pride has made sinners law-breakers. They do not want to be excellent and wonderful like the Creator.

Lovers of pleasures more than lovers of God

They are intoxicated with self-love. They feel that they are indebted to happy times regardless how they get it. Love for their God is very far from their minds.

Having a form of godliness but denying the power thereof from such turn away

They are the pictures of complete godliness and commitment to the Messiah but in their souls, they are at the bottom of all sinners. They do not accept the power of God as of any good to them. Walk aware from their colonies. Do not enter into them.

For of this sort are they which creep into houses, and lead captive silly women laden with sins, led away with divers lusts

People from the world of false Christians are the ones who worm their ways into the hearts of men and women who are trying to escape from sex addictions. They have no divine love for the morally weak people in the Church.

They act like sorcerers and take advantage of the weak, naive and trusting Church members. They use them to satisfy their own lusts.

Ever learning, and never able to come to the knowledge of the truth

They are learnt in everything that surrounds them just for the show. But they are never given the knowledge, understanding and absorption of divine truth in their minds, hearts and spirits.

Jannes and Jambres are said to be the two leading sorcerers who were confusing the Pharaoh of Egypt and turning them away from the true God. They flattered the king that they could help him to overcome the power of God against his kingdom.

When the Pharaoh wanted to listen to what God was telling him through Moses, they would raise such din that no one could understand what the prophet of God was saying. There such like people in the Church of God.

They are sorcerers and witches. Most of the people in the United States of America (USA) whether they know it or not are practicing Hinduism and/or Buddhism. But it is not the paganism of nature worship but of Satanism.

Converts from Hinduism and Buddhism, Zoroastrian, etc. who did not involve themselves with Satan or cut off themselves completely upon becoming Christians are some of the finest godly people in the Church.

"Now as Jannes and Jambres withstood Moses, so do these also resist the truth: men of corrupt minds, reprobate concerning the faith" (2 Timothy 3:8).

Unfortunately, USA has converted herself into the dark side of Far East pagan religions. They spend large sums of money to know about the New Age Region, which is another name for Hinduism, Buddhism, etc.

They come under many forms such as the Church of Scientology, etc. Scientology is the commitment to be a sorcerer (man) or witch (woman) for life. Almost all pastors, priests, rabbis, evangelists, laymen, laywomen, etc. are involved in it.

It has brought deep heart-aches in the church that are too numerous to count. Quarrels and fights for Church positions, discontents about how weird things are going on these days, etc. have multiplied in the Churches and so also have divorces. They use demons to break families apart, steal money, run politics, provide themselves with security, etc.

They read the mind of people in order to control them. The molest people through remote control that they only know how it operates. They want to control their environment so that they may be more successful than others.

They try to erase the picture of God from humanity. They teach pride and how to depend on one's own effort and not that of their Creator who knows what is best for them.

They are enemies of God their Messiah. That is why they hate Bible truths. It is shocking human beings could be so depraved of minds! They have perverted the simple and pure faith into heresies, legalism, hypocrisy, etc.

They are only interested in themselves. Their only interests in the Church are to ruin the faiths of many. "But they shall proceed no further: for their folly shall be manifest unto all men, as theirs also was" (2 Timothy 3:9).

But there is some bad news for them: They are not going to mislead the Church forever nor will they be given the chance to destroy her completely. Their foolishness is breeding in them terrible headaches.

They are failures in their spiritual pursuits. This fact is being noted by the faithful in the Church. The Lord will soon sweep them away.

10 CHAPTER

THE WATER OF LIFE

1. *My doctrine is not mine, but His that sent me*

The cup of water by Derek Jensen (Tysto), 2005-December-10, and the pot of water by someone else

The disciples came into the temple to worship the Lord during the Feast of the Tabernacles. But the Messiah was not amongst them. "Then the Jews sought him at the feast, and said, Where is he?" (John 7:11). The Jewish leaders asked them if their eyes had alighted on the Him, saying, "Have you seen Him?"

The people rose against the Lord God of heaven and the earth. They loved to oppose Him anything He said. They debated about all the things that He had taught. "And there was much murmuring among the people concerning him: for some said, He is a good man: others said, Nay; but he deceiveth the people" (John 7:12). They were two very strong opposing views to His teachings.

One group said, "He is the One who is called Love. He is the Most Excellent One. He is God of truth and love."

The other group, led by the Pharisees and Sadducees, opposed them very fiercely. They declared,

"No! He is driving people away us."

But none of the Jews who supported God stood up for Him. "Howbeit no man space openly of him for fear of the Jews" (John 7:13).

They did not want to show their faces when they were declaring their faith in the Messiah. Their love for Him was not very hot. They were afraid of their leaders. Their leaders had already made the decision to kill Him. His supporters were afraid of suffering the same fate like Him.

When half of the truths that the Feast of Tabernacle symbolized were taught, the Messiah appeared. He is the whole truth. "Now about the midst of the feast Jesus went up into the temple, and taught" (John 7:14).

The Feast of the Tabernacle pointed to Him. He is the Truth. He is the God of life on whom the temple was built. All the services of the temple pointed to Him. He entered into the temple to teach the worshipers how to meet with God when He has assumed His full glory.

The spirits of the fathers, mothers, and youth were thunder-strike by His teachings. They were shaken. They had built their lives of the false interpretations of the Word of God by their Pharisees and Sadducees.

But the Law-Giver was explaining to them the truth that He Himself had taught to their godly patriarchs, matriarchs, prophets, and prophetesses. "And the Jews marveled, saying, How knoweth this man letters, having never learned?" (John 7:15).

They exclaimed in shock and disbelief, "How did this Man surpass all knowledge? This is what love is all about. He knows what is written in the Book and exalts it highly when He has not even met God face to face yet."

Their loving Father taught them. "Jesus answered them, and said, My doctrine is not mine, but his that sent me. If any man will do his will, he shall know of the doctrine, whether it be of God, or whether I speak of myself. He that speaketh of himself seeketh his own glory: but he that seeketh his glory that sent him, the same is true, and no unrighteousness is in him" (John 7:16–18).

He said, "This doctrine that will get you to the God, your Mother, who gave births to you, is no Mine. God is not unrighteous when I am saying this. He is the God of life.

He is God the Father. He is the One who has sent Me to be the Righteous Head of His earthly family. He sent Me because I am very passionate about you.

Any breathing person who laid a loving hand on truth will know and exalt My doctrine. My doctrine will help you to meet God, the Mother of life. You will know whether My doctrine came from the loving God or from My own Righteous Spirit.

Whoever teaches doctrines to bring people to God that come from love with which he loves himself is commanding God the Father to glorify him. But whoever orders himself to always glorify the One who sent Me to the Righteous Head of human race; he has laid his hand on the truth.

The truth is powerful. God is not unrighteous. In Him is eternal life and love. He is not the god of darkness."

So far it was good. He spoke the truths that were all inclusive. The listeners were a part and parcel of His doctrines up to that point. He included them in the Gospel. It sounded good to them.

Then the Messiah turned to them and flashed out their secret thoughts. "Did not Moses give you the law, and yet none of you keepeth the law? Why go ye about to kill me?" (John 7:19).

He pointed out, "God is not unrighteous to give you the Law through Moses. And you are yet to be righteous like Him.

You are not doing the wealth of teachings that are written in the Law. Why are you ordering God the Father to give you the permission to kill Me?"

The crowds spoke as if they were wise fathers (and mothers). "The people answered and said, Thou hast a devil: who goeth about to kill thee?" (John 7:20).

They said, "You are the Satan, the chief of demons, to be able to know our secret thoughts. Who amongst us has commanded God the Father to allow us to kill You?"

God spoke with power and authority. "Jesus answered and said unto them, I have done one work, and ye all marvel. Moses therefore gave unto you circumcision; (not because it is of Moses, but of the fathers;) and ye on the Sabbath day circumcise a man.

If a man on the Sabbath day receive circumcision, that the law of Moses should not be broken; are ye angry at me, because I have made a man every whit whole on the Sabbath day? Judge not according to the appearance, but judge righteous judgment" (John 7:21–24).

He emphasized, "I did one wealth of a work of love. It filled the earth with the Presence of God, and all of you were shocked. Your hearts were towards Me, your Daddy.

The God of life gave you the rites of piercing the brothers through Moses. Moses is not He who is called Love. But the loving Daddy is the God of all. And because God the Father is love and All-Righteous, you pierce the brothers even on the Sabbath days.

You welcome the brothers into manhood with the welcome of God the Father by piercing them even on the Sabbath days so that powers of the laws of Moses may not be reduced.

Are you landing all your powers on Me to kill Me because I healed a man and made Him whole like God wants him to be on the Sabbath day?

Do not have a love for judging because of how you want righteous people to look like. Even the holiest people have not been authorized to judge sinners in this world. This kind of judgment is given by God the Father alone. He knows what is in human hearts. He judges lovingly and in the right way."

Some of the powerful people who lived in Jerusalem questioned the sincerity of their rulers in condemning the Messiah as a false Messiah. "Then said some of them of Jerusalem, Is not this he, whom they seek to kill? But, lo, he speaketh boldly, and they say nothing unto him.

Do the rulers know indeed that this is the very Christ? Howbeit we know this man whence he is: but when Christ cometh, no man knoweth whence he is" (John 7:25–27).

They said, "God is unrighteous if this is not He who is Love. Is not this He whom they are ordering God the Father to give them the chance to put to death?

He is here showing that He is the Life and the Love. He is preaching with a face that is burning with deep intensity.

God is not with these people. They are saying nothing to Him in the Name of the love of God. God is God. Do the heads of our nation know, of a truth, that this is the Love who is to come, the Righteous, Eternal, and Loving Messiah?

But God being with us, we know where this loving and lively Man is coming from. But when the Righteous, Eternal, and Loving Messiah appears, we will know not where He will come from."

The Messiah preached in a loud so that everyone could hear as He taught them the knowledge of God in the temple. He was preparing them to meet Him face to face and live with Him. "Then cried Jesus in the temple as he taught, saying, Ye both know me, and ye know whence I am: and I am not come of myself, but he that sent me is true, whom ye know not. But I know him: for I am from him, and he hath sent me" (John 7:28, 29).

He taught them that the people knew Him and where He came from them. But God was with Him. He came by the orders of God the Father to be the Righteous Head and God of the human family.

He is the Truth. The Jews had yet to know who He really is. But He, the Messiah, knew Him very well. He exalted Him very highly.

He came from Him. He was sent by Him because He had deep passions for the salvation of mankind.

The leaders knew that He spoke as God the Almighty. He was the equal of God the Father. They vowed to lay their hands on Him and kill Him that very moment. But they were powerless to carry out their threats.

God the Father did not give them the person to kill Him. "Then they sought to take him: but no man laid hands on him, because his hour was not yet come" (John 7:30).

Many people placed their faith in Him. He and they were one. "And many of the people believed on him, and said, When Christ cometh, will he do more miracles than these which this man hath done?" (John 7:31).

They exclaimed, "God is God. When the God the All-Righteous, Eternal, and Loving Messiah comes, will He do bigger bull of work than this One is creating so many and lovingly, too?"

The leaders of the Party of the Pharisees were composed of the members of the Sanhedrin (Council of Elders or Senators), and some priests heard about the heated debates that were going on between differing opinions amongst the people that had surrounded the Messiah as He was preaching in the outer court.

They sent temple guards to arrest Him for public disturbances and bring Him to court in order that they may execute Him. "The Pharisees heard that the people murmured such things concerning him; and the Pharisees and the chief priests sent officers to take him" (John 7:32).

The Messiah saw the soldiers surrounding Him.

He knew that they had come to arrest Him and kill Him. But He was not afraid to die. So He did not hide.

There were still some important truths that He had not preached that will help you to become holy and righteous and get you ready to meet Him during His Second Coming.

He also tried to reach to the hearts of the hardened soldiers and win them for heaven. "Then said Jesus unto them, Yet a little while am I with you, and then I go unto him that sent me. Ye shall seek me, and shall not find me: and where I am, thither ye cannot come" (John 7:33, 34).

He said that they must enjoy His Presence as much as they could while He was still with them. He will supply them with life and righteousness.

He would watch over them. But He would be going back to His eternal inheritances and the God of life who had sent Him to be the Messenger of Salvation or Righteous God or Head of the human life.

The unrepentant would be commanding Him as God their Daddy to do some miracles for them and heal them. But it would be too late. His Presence will not be readily acceptable as it was now.

They will not be ushered into His Presence that easily. He would be in the midst of stupendous love, awesome life, and everlasting inheritances. They will not have the powers to enter into His Presence or see His face.

The Jews debated amongst themselves as to what He made by these statements. "The Jewish authorities said among themselves, "Where is he about to go so that we shall not find him?

Will he go to the Greek cities where our people live, and teach the Greeks? He says that we will look for him but will not find him, and that we cannot go where he will be. What does he mean?" (John 7:35, 36, GNB).

The evidences that the Messiah was God Incarnate were before their eyes. But they would not accept them because they were not what they had pinned their hopes.

The wanted a Warrior-King like David who would fight the Romans and expel them from their land and restore Israel to her former glory of the Davidic times.

2. God made water His faithful witness to the whole world

Relocations began for all the people that Israel helped to build from the land that could not support called the wilderness of Sin. There were no extra blessings there except to be on the move. And at the sweet orders of the Lord, they descended on the land of Rephidim. But there were no springs or wells waiting for them there.

And the intelligent people lost their heads. "And all the congregation of the children of Israel journeyed from the wilderness of Sin, after their journeys, according to the commandment of the LORD, and pitched in Rephidim: and there was no water for the people to drink" (Exodus 17:1).

The mouths of the people spoke harsh words to Moses. They order him to create for them water in the desert to drink. Moses protested. He asked them as to why they were opening their mouths wide and poisoning him with their words.

Why were they stoning the Lord? "Wherefore the people did chide with Moses, and said, Give us water that we may drink. And Moses said unto them, Why chide ye with me? wherefore do ye tempt the LORD?" (Exodus 17:2).

They thirsted for life through water. They grew bitter and angry for fear that they might die of thirst. They loved life more than God their Creator of their very lives, water, and everything.

They spoke very angrily to Moses. They asked him as to why he helped them to get out of Egypt. They wanted to know if he had brought them, their children, and their livestock into the desert in order to massacre them by withholding water for them.

They picked up stones to throw at Moses and kill

him first before he killed them. "And Moses cried unto the LORD, saying, What shall I do unto this people? they be almost ready to stone me" (Exodus 17:4).

Moses cried to God with a loud and hoarse voice for fear of his life. "In what way can I work for this people? They have rejected me and are throwing stones at me."

The Lord told him to order all the elders to follow him. He should march ahead of them. He should take the rod of power and authority that had parted the Red Sea with him in his hand.

The Lord He Himself will also be standing on top of the rock facing them. He told Moses to whip the rock once and water would pour out of it for the people to drink. And Moses carried out the instructions perfectly.

The elders of Israel were the eye witnesses of Moses and of God.

The waterfall photo was by George Hodan, in public domain

"And the LORD said unto Moses, Go on before the people, and take with thee of the elders of Israel; and thy rod, wherewith thou smotest the river, take in thine hand, and go. Behold, I will stand before thee there upon the rock in Horeb; and thou shalt smite the rock, and there shall come water out of it, that the people may drink. And Moses did so in the sight of the elders of Israel" (Exodus 17:5, 6).

He shook the rock so much so that its foundation that was buried down deep in the bosom of the earth dissolved into liquid. Tremendous earthquakes took place down in the base of the rocky mountain.

Then out of the bosom of the rock water gushed out. It forms a gigantic and beautiful waterfall in the desert. The water formed a very big and deep river.

Water flowed through the camp of Israel and out into the desert to quench the thirst of other desert tribes. "He clave the rocks in the wilderness, and gave them drink as out of the great depths. He brought streams also out of the rock, and caused waters to run down like rivers" (Psalms 78:15, 16).

Water broke out from it and flowed like the River Nile. It flowed through the desert bringing life to the people, animals, birds, and plants. "He opened the rock, and the waters gushed out; they ran in the dry places like a river" (Psalms 105:41).

The desert folks were happy to find water at their door step. They drank and swam in the water. Their hearts rejoiced in the abundant provisions of the Lord their God.

He changed the hard rock into water. He is All-Powerful "Which turned the rock into a standing water, the flint into a fountain of waters" (Psalms 114:8). The hard rock that has no moisture content dissolved into a deep, roaring, and overflowing river. The people and their livestock drank the river of life. She flowed day and night for them as long as they were in Rephidim.

He made water His faithful witness to the whole world that He is the eternal Creator. Nothing is impossible for Him to create. He can bring water out of the hard rock. Though the people were faithless, they were very as important to Him.

He gave them in order to build up their faith in Him so that He could great things for them. "And did all drink the same spiritual drink: for they drank of that spiritual Rock that followed them: and that Rock was Christ" (1 Corinthians 10:4).

The real water is the one that comes from the

hands of the Rock of Ages. He is your Lord and Messiah. He is the Spiritual Water that will quench all your thirst and fill you with eternal life.

You will drink your troubles away. Water from the Spiritual Rock of Ages will never make you hunger and thirst against for love, peace, joy, security, eternities, etc. But Moses was displeased because of the shameful ways they treated their Savior. He had just rescued from the ironed hand of Egypt and made them cross the Red Sea on the dry ground.

But when they were thirsty, they wanted to crucify Him if they could get their hands on Him. "And he called the name of the place Massah, and Meribah, because of the chiding of the children of Israel, and because they tempted the LORD, saying, Is the LORD among us, or not?" (Exodus 17:7).

Moses called the Massah and Meribah. They were throwing stones on the Lord by asking, "Is the LORD among us, or not?" They asked if He was not sitting down very comfortably among them or not. But He did not retaliate. His love is unconditional.

Woe to God if your water is not forthcoming and is not plenty. If you ever thirst again even for a brief when there is no water, your mind will think very strange angry thoughts at Him who created water for you. If there is not water to drink and you do not know where to get it. It is war.

If there is no water for cooking, bathing, and doing all your domestic and commercial businesses, it is a war. If there is no house on the lake, sea or ocean, no boat, no chances of going on the ocean liner once a year, no chance of sporting on the water, it is always a war. You have an enemy who is against because He does not love you really. Etc. And that enemy is God.

Why? So and so is so blessed! You have nothing or the house is falling apart and there is no money to repair it. The boat is broken.

The car is not good. No scenic beauty around with water, it is God who prevented that. He should have put you somewhere near water like He has done others.

Water! Water! Water! You really do love water more than you love God. The enemy who does not place water near you is God. That was how you fought God at the Bitter Water of hate and anger when thirsted for water. Even if your throat is burning with thirst, please do not hate Him.

When you are still thirst for water, it brings out hatred and anger against God instead of humility and longing for that perfect heaven with Him where there is no thirst or lack of water. Whenever there is a problem, you like to repeat your behavior in the desert. You love to quarrel God all the time when you cannot solve a problem. "Give us water to drink."

You demand of the Great One shamelessly. "Give me this! Give me that! Give me! Give me!"

Your attitude towards your Maker is so selfish. Have you ever tried to listen to yourself as you pray to God? If all that you ask from Him is "Give me ...! Give me ...!"

Your prayers must be very nauseating even to a human being if he or she is able to listen to you. So where you are in trouble, you put God immediately to the test. You ask Him to prove His existence that He really does exist by doing this or that for you. He already knows that you are thirsty for something.

Why do you put Him to the test to prove His love for you? "Is the LORD among us or not?"

You keep demanding Him. It is because He loves you that He created you. He is always with you. You are the one who is not living abundantly.

You show yourself that you are immature spiritually and God still remains the All-Power, Holy and Loving Creator and Sustainer and, therefore, Father of heaven and earth. "But the LORD reprimanded Moses and Aaron.

He said, Because you did not have enough faith to acknowledge my holy power before the people of

Israel, you will not lead them into the land that I promised to give them."

This happened at Meribah, where the people of Israel complained against the LORD and where he showed them that he is holy" (Numbers 20:12, 13, GNB). He is always powerful, eternal, holy, perfect, kind, good and loving no matter what you accuse Him of.

It is because He loves you that He died for you through His only Son. Do not accuse Him of trying to murder you because your circumstances are unpleasant. "Why did you bring us up out of Egypt, to kill us and our children and our livestock with thirst?"

Even when you murdered Him on the cross, your Father still loved you so much that He, actually, prayed for your salvation while dying. "Then said Jesus, Father, forgive them; for they know not what they do. And they parted his raiment, and cast lots" (Luke 23:34).

He forgave you for murdering His Son. He is giving you the eternal life that is flowing like water from His Infinite Everlasting Being.

God strike the Rock of Ages. He was broken on the cross for you. So that out of Him healing water may flow to heal your of all your sins, weakness and death and give you everlasting life. "And did all drink the same spiritual drink: for they drank of that spiritual Rock that followed them: and that Rock was Christ" (1 Corinthians 10:4).

3. God will quench your thirst for eternal life

Look up to highest heaven where your rest is coming from and not to the universes. The stars may shine and glitter with the glories that are stupendous. But they are only created objects.

They can burn up. They will bellow smoke that rises high up as if incense is burning and releasing thick smoke that smells sweet. But God is eternal.

Look down on this earth and observe all her glories that shines and glitter like a beautiful woven wedding gown imbedded with jewels. Though wedding gowns are beautiful, they will grow old with age. They will be discarded.

This sinful earth may be the best and only inhabitable planet for you. Many of you appreciate her so much that you worship her planet, sun, moon, and stars as if she God your Creator. But she will wear and die out together with her solar system. Her life is almost spent.

She will die out just like candle that is all burnt out and gone. "Lift up your eyes to the heavens, and look upon the earth beneath: for the heavens shall vanish away like smoke, and the earth shall wax old like a garment, and they that dwell therein shall die in like manner: but my salvation shall be for ever, and my righteousness shall not be abolished" (Isaiah 51:6).

But the salvation through which the Messiah has made believers His brothers and sisters is eternal. Its righteousness will never be reduced but grow stronger and brighter every year.

Oh, you people who are being given troubles by thirsts, come to the Lord! The thirst for a loving relationship with God has no rights to kill you. He will fill all the people of the earth with the water of eternal life. They will never thirst for eternal life, love, and

298

relationships again.

Your Passover money that used to buy lambs to slaughter in worship can never buy you eternal life and love. Your tithes and offerings can never provide them. But praise be to the name of the Lord!

The Passover Lamb of God has bought you eternal life with all its glorious of unconditional love, forgiveness, peace, etc. on the Cross of Calvary. They are all free.

He is inviting you very kindly and lovingly to please come and have your fill of food and waters of life plenty. "Ho, every one that thirsteth, come ye to the waters, and he that hath no money; come ye, buy, and eat; yea, come, buy wine and milk without money and without price" (Isaiah 55:1).

Fill your stomachs up with life that will help you fly away into infinite glories. You do not need to sacrifice lambs to earn them. You will not need to even sacrifice yourself in any way to get God. You do not need to fulfill the full requirements of the Law to find Him. Drink the Brother's love that is more intoxicating than wine and sweeter than milk and be eternally satisfied.

Why are you crying over the money that you have spent with food that did not turn out to be good bread? You are suffering and trying to secure drinking water that is not water at all. You are not getting really satisfaction with what you are eating, drinking, wearing, loving, caring, and dying for.

If you want to truly live, then you must learn to listen to the voice of your Creator. Eat the bone marrow of the love of God. It is fat, juicy, and delicious.

Just as the bone marrow produces new blood cells to keep the individual alive, so will cells from the bone marrow of the Lord. It will supply you with red blood cells that will give you eternal life. You will love to eat His life like delicious foods. It is a good life.

Your soul will love it. "Wherefore do ye spend

money for that which is not bread? and your labour for that which satisfieth not? hearken diligently unto me, and eat ye that which is good, and let your soul delight itself in fatness" (Isaiah 55:2).

He will fill you with Himself so much so that you will never be selfish again. You will not worship yourself or others gods again. You will worship only the Lord your Creator. The word of life will satisfy your ears so much so that you will not hunger for other knowledge except for the divine one.

If you learn to be obedient, your will dead spirit will live again. It will receive the everlasting life of the Creator. He has provided the rights for you to be saved by the covenant of the blood of Calvary.

You are His eternal slave because you are receiving His breath and eternal life from Him. He said that you are very special to Him. Therefore, He has commanded from eternities past that you must be saved from your sins.

God taught the sages of ancient times the salvation of their souls. He taught them how to live right in order to have peace and joy at all times. He can help you, too, if you will invite Him to live your heart. "Behold, God is mine helper: the Lord is with them that uphold my soul" (Psalms 54:4).

He who has come down from heaven to live in your heart is Omnipotent or All-Powerful. He can save you. He is watching over you. He is moving you forward. He is increasing your knowledge and wisdom daily.

He is increasing your desire to live and to excel in your spiritual pursuit. Soon, He will give you that perfect and eternal health that can help you enjoy very abundant and joyous life.

He made Israel of old His witnesses to the goodness of the truth and how it can create a new and eternal life in the spirit of anyone. He blessed His Law and gave it creative powers to dispel darkness and build truth in human mind and hearts. He created truth in the hearts of the fathers and mothers of faith of ancient days.

He told them to pass on the message of good hope in the Messiah to their biological and adopted children of the faith. "For he established a testimony in Jacob, and appointed a law in Israel, which he commanded our fathers, that they should make them known to their children:

That the generation to come might know them, even the children which should be born; who should arise and declare them to their children: That they might set their hope in God, and not forget the works of God, but keep his commandments" (Psalms 78:5–7).

He wanted succeeding generations to know the truth. The Law was to be passed from the parents to their children throughout the succeeding generations of the human race. It will make them to stand righteous and holy forever. And they were to pass this Gospel around the world. Each generation was to pass it on the next one.

They were to come to God their Creator and choose Him as their one and only Divine Bridegroom. They were to place their hope of living a sinless, holy, and righteous life in Him. He would have approved the salvation of the whole world had they come to Him by faith and by obedience to the Ten Commandments.

All believers were to treat the Ten Commandments like persons with thoughts and feelings. They are the reflections of God's holy character. They were to see beyond the Law.

They would have seen a God that has thoughts and feelings of love, respect, joy, honor, peace, friendship, etc. He is asking the human race to keep the Law close to their hearts.

It is the truth that will lead them to better days. It will give them the rights to the recreate by God their Messiah on the day of His Second Coming.

Unfortunately, Israel did not obey the Ten

Commandments. Very few people among them took the initiative to preach them to other races. Spiritual pride and arrogance made Israel to stray from the knowledge of the spiritual context of the Law.

They were feelings of guilt, confusion, and loneliness. They knew they were lost. It made the very zealous in trying to keep the Law perfect by their own human efforts in order to please God.

They did not want other races to know Him for fear that the blessings may not be enough to be passed out around the world. "And might not be as their fathers, a stubborn and rebellious generation; a generation that set not their heart aright, and whose spirit was not stedfast with God" (Psalms 78:8).

Some people, especially, among the Gentiles did not even know that there exists an eternal Law for them to follow. They left building the Tower of Babel in Iraq and scattered around the world.

With time, they not only forgot God their Maker but also the Ten Commandments they were observe and follow to keep them holy, righteous, and intelligent.

4.   The Holy is the Water of life

Some soldiers were ambushed and surrounded by enemy soldiers. They fought for many days. Their food and water supplies ran out. Still, they continued to fight. They refused to surrender even though they were outnumbered. The government sent rescuers. They fought the enemies. The casualties on both sides were heavy.

Finally, they broke a way through the wall of enemy soldiers. They were stun at the courage and bravery of their fellow soldiers. The men were mere skeletons.

Their limbs were hanging long and thin. Their heads were bony with sunken eyes and dried parched lips. They were losing their voices. Their whispers could barely be heard.

They were dying of starvation and thirst. Yet, they refused to surrender to be mowed down like grass. Only sheer will power kept them working at their weapons in fighting their enemies.

The rescue team loaded them onto trucks and brought them into a safe place. The army doctors did not give them food to eat and water to drink immediately. Their throats were almost dried up.

They were constricted. Any mouthfuls of food and water could crack their esophagi and make them bleed. They were given intravenous fluids. Their dried, parched and cracked lips were wiped and moistened with water. A spoonful of water was dropped slowly into each mouth one at a time.

When they were strong enough to swallow something, they were given water to drink. When they were able to eat something, they were given soups for a few days. Then they were graduated to eating bolus of mashed food.

Finally, when they were strong enough to eat, they

were given food and plenty of water to drink. However, their amounts were increased slowly over a long time. They were all treated like newborn babies until their body systems became accustomed to receiving food and water by the mouthfuls.

Sinners are like those emaciated and starving soldiers. Ever since Adam and Eve sinned, we have been dying from hunger and thirst of spiritual food and water that flow from the life of the Creator. We are starving to death without God in our lives. Sin is killing us.

If you think that you are not under the curse of sin, just consider your life. Are you really invincible to pain, sorrow, and fear and death? You face the possibility of falling dead every minute of your life.

So you are dying because you are not in heaven with God. But as a loving and caring Father that the Holy Spirit is, He is calling very loudly to you to save yourself from starving to death by running to Him.

You do not have the power to save yourself from being destroyed in hell because of your sins. You do not have the strength to resurrect yourself from the grave.

Gold, silver or any other kind of currency cannot buy you a ticket to live near God in heaven forever. But the God of gods, the Sovereign Creator, King of kings and Lord of lords Himself came down from heaven to pay the price of setting you free from sin, and re-create and transport you to heaven.

The Holy Spirit has come down from heaven to change your heart from being sinful into being righteous, then recreate you physically and finally transport you to heaven.

The dove is a symbol of the Holy Spirit

He is calling out to you very loudly, saying, "Ho, every one that thirsteth, come ye to the waters, and he that hath no money; come ye, buy, and eat; yea, come, buy wine and milk without money and without price" (Isaiah 55:1).

Oh you, beloved! Are you thirsty for the true life that is found only in God? Come and drink the eternal, joyous, peaceful, and lovely life that is flowing from the Holy Spirit.

He freely gave you of Himself when He birthed you out of Himself. Come and refill yourself by drinking His life. You do not buy this special Daddy to father you and love you.

He is better than natural water, wine, milk, and honey. You will not spend all your fortunes in trying to find Him. He is already yours because He is Daddy.

Because He is your Father and Creator, the Holy Spirit is your spiritual food and water. He is giving you of Himself as your water of life. "In the last day, that great day of the feast, Jesus stood and cried, saying, If any man thirst, let him come unto me, and drink.

He that believeth on me, as the scripture hath said, out of his belly shall flow rivers of living water. (But this spake he of the Spirit, which they that believe on him should receive: for the Holy Ghost was not yet given; because that Jesus was not yet glorified.)" (John 7:37–39).

The Messiah promised, "If you are thirsting for eternal life to breathe, I will welcome you with the welcome of God the Father. Come to Me, the God of life, and drink the life of your Daddy.

Whoever has faith in Daddy's life, just as the Book says, from his (or her) womb will flow out boiling hot waters of eternal love and life. This Boiling Hot or Living Water is the Holy Spirit. With His life, flowing through your veins, He can help you live forever.

Just like the Messiah, the Holy Spirit is also giving Himself to you as your Bread of life. He said, "I am the Bread of life" (John 6:48).

All that you have to do is be like Peter when He was drowning. Cry out to Him, "Lord, save me" "But straightway Jesus spake unto them, saying, Be of good cheer; it is I; be not afraid.

And Peter answered him and said, Lord, if it be thou, bid me come unto thee on the water. And he said, Come. And when Peter was come down out of the ship, he walked on the water, to go to Jesus. But when he saw the wind boisterous, he was afraid; and beginning to sink, he cried, saying, Lord, save me.

And immediately Jesus stretched forth his hand, and caught him, and said unto him, O thou of little faith, wherefore didst thou doubt?" (John 14:27–31).

He will save you. For He is All-Powerful. And you will get God to be your Dad and Savior at no cost at all. You do not need to pay money to get Him to love you. He is your gold. He already loves you even before He decided to creator this universe as your home.

Everyone born of Adam and Eve has a place in God's heart. He loves everyone. Everyone can find Him. His power to help and save everyone is more than we all need. His home in heaven is enough for everyone. He is calling loudly, "Ho! You! Everyone! You need me. Come to me! I will save you."

This everyone is what He also says in John 3:16, "Whosoever believeth means that He has promised to save anyone and everyone who comes to Him by faith as He says in this wonderful scripture, "For God so loved the world, that he gave his only begotten Son, that WHOSOEVER believeth on him should not perish, but have eternal life" (ASV).

Are you thirsty for God? Do you need your soul to be saved from the purges of hell? Then come to the Creator of the World and the Sustainer of all life. Come to Jesus your Maker. He is the Alpha and Omega of all creation and all life. He is the Beginning and End of everything.

He has sent, God the Mighty Holy Spirit who is Himself also your Creator to so fill you with Himself that He will become an everlasting spring of water of life that will never run dry. For He is the Everlasting God.

The Lord and Savior, the Christ invites you to drink deep of the love, joy, peace and salvation of the Holy Spirit. "And he said unto me, It is done. I am Alpha and Omega, the beginning and the end. I will give unto him that is athirst of the fountain of the water of life freely" (Revelation 21:6).

You do not need to pay for the love of the Holy Spirit. He already loves you because He is your Dad. He only says, "Come!"

Do not spend your whole life chasing unfounded dreams. Do not spend your time, energy, gold, silver, money, etc. for a life that will end up in hell. But if you eat Jesus as your Bread and drink the Holy Spirit as your water, you will live. You will forever be of good health, strong in body and with shining skin.

The Lord will show you with His abundant goodness that has no limit. You will gaze at the over-abundant of fresh new grains, fresh new juices, olive oil, vegetarian milk, vegetarian meats, fresh fruits, vegetables, roots, nuts and edible stems of heaven before your eyes.

You will not buy them with silver, gold or money. You will not work for somebody in order to earn money to buy them.

You will not labor and sweat into exhaustion and fatigue in order to eke out a living like you do in this old world. You will not beg for food and search the dumping areas to look for something to eat. Everything in heaven will all be yours forever and ever to help you live eternally and joyfully.

The animals will be harmless, cute and very friendly. And every one of them from the largest to the smallest will be your pet to play with. You will occupy the mountain of the Lord. You will live in the Golden City of the Lord.

Your life will be very enjoyable like a river flowing merrily by. You will be full of fruitfulness and life like a garden that is well kept, planted and watered with intersected streams. You will not have any heart breaks of whatever kind again because the eyes of the Lord will forever watch over you.

The sufferings, death, evil and demons of this present world will never intrude again in His home to destroy His children as they are doing now. He will put a stop to all these heartaches and presence of evil by burning them up in hell.

He will see to it that you will not miss anything again that will make your life more enjoyable, peaceful, holy and happy. He will personally care for you. No evil will ever come between you and Him forever.

He has already given you the prove that He will both save and take care of you by His creation of the world and everything. "In the beginning God created the heaven and the earth.

And the earth was without form, and void; and darkness was upon the face of the deep. And the Spirit of God moved upon the face of the waters. And God said, Let there be light: and there was light" (Genesis 1:1–3).

This same God who made light out of darkness and went on to create the earth and the universes is your Dad. With the same power with which He created everything will He use it to love, protect, care and fill your table with good things to eat. He will surround you with more gifts that you will need.

You will be eternal, powerful and great. You are already famous among the holy angels and even among the demons because God died for you. You will be even more famous in heaven because you will be a king or queen sitting on your own throne next to the Almighty Everlasting God. Your fame as a baby of God, for whom He had to lower Himself into a mere inferior human being for a little while, suffer and die a very cruel death, will spread from star to star.

Those beings in other stars will be jealous of you just like the brother of the prodigal son was jealous because he was thrown a big welcome party by their dad. "Now his elder son was in the field: and as he came and drew nigh to the house, he heard musick and dancing. And he called one of the servants, and asked what these things meant.

And he said unto him, Thy brother is come; and thy father hath killed the fatted calf, because he hath received him safe and sound. And he was angry, and would not go in: therefore came his father out, and intreated him.

And he answering said to his father, Lo, these many years do I serve thee, neither transgressed I at any time thy commandment: and yet thou never gavest me a kid, that I might make merry with my friends: But as soon as this thy son was come, which hath devoured thy living with harlots, thou hast killed for him the fatted calf" (Luke 15:25–30).

They will ask God as to why He never promoted them to be sitting on thrones near Him when they have never even sinned, hated or murdered Him like we did. He will tell them to cheer up. He will tell them He loves them as much as He loves us.

And then they will join us in our singing, dancing and enjoyment. "And he said unto him, Son, thou art ever with me, and all that I have is thine. It was meet that we should make merry, and be glad: for this thy brother was dead, and is alive again; and was lost, and is found" (Luke 15:31, 32).

Because of the great happiness that will flood your soul, you will burst out into singing. For you will be a great musician then. The likes of which do not exist in our present world from the beginning of time to the end. You will compose sweet lyrics in praise of the Lord.

You will compose the tune and play it on your harp and other musical instruments. Everyone will love your songs. You will love the songs of other people and angels, too.

You will praise the Lord with music and dancing. He will smile indulgently at you, His baby, whom He has bought from hell with His own life and brought safely home at last.

Jesus promises that if you come to Him, you will win the victory of walking by faith and for trusting Him for your salvation. You will truly become His baby. "He that overcometh shall inherit all things; and I will be his God, and he shall be my son (or daughter)" (Revelation 21:7).

What are some of the inheritances you will get? He listed some of them in here: "And I saw a new heaven and a new earth: for the first heaven and the first earth were passed away; and there was no more sea.

And I John saw the holy city, New Jerusalem, coming down from God out of heaven, prepared as a bride adorned for her husband.

And I heard a great voice out of heaven saying, Behold, the tabernacle of God is with men, and he will dwell with them, and they shall be his people, and God himself shall be with them, and be their God.

And God shall wipe away all tears from their eyes; and there shall be no more death, neither sorrow, nor crying, neither shall there be any more pain: for the former things are passed away" (Revelation 21:1–4).

Listed below are a summary of some of the inheritances you will get according to the above scriptures:

1. A new heaven - He will give you a new universe. The sun, moon and stars will be recreated. They will never come under the afflictions of sin again. They will shine right and warm the earth right in order to sustain your life luxuriously and happily forever.

2. A new earth - no oceans or large seas will be there. The Lord will recreate the whole earth again. The whole of it will become one large Garden of Eden as He did in Genesis chapters 1 and 2.

3. New Jerusalem: It is a holy city. It is all golden and transparent and clear as glass, shining brightly and dazzling. It shines very beautifully like a bride who is bathed and perfumed and dressed with fine wedding gown and glittering jewels being led to meet her husband. That is how great and beautiful your new home is.

4. You will become a child of God.

5. God promises to be your God forever: To top the greatness of your inheritance, God the Father, God the Son and God the Holy Spirit will live with you there as your Daddy forever.

6. God will remove the pain of sorrowing. No more tears of sorrow or sadness. No more crying or weeping.

7. No more death - You will live forever like God.

8. No mourning or grieving because of pain, death, suffering, fears, shame, guilt, loss of anything, etc.

9.   No pain: Your spirit, mind, heart, feelings and body will be untouched by the pain of sin, shame, guilt, sicknesses, injuries, being hated, etc. For Satan, sin and death will not be there. Besides, you will be the conqueror with your God-given power over all evil so much so that they will not exist in your presence any more.

The Holy Spirit is inviting you so gently and so lovingly. He is saying, "Come!"

He is your spiritual water for your salvation. So drink deep of the water of love. Drink the eternal life of the Holy Spirit. Invite Him into your heart as your Permanent Guest. He is your ever flowing water in Jordan River of heaven.

When you drink that water of life whenever you are thirsty, it will keep you living forever. Christ is speaking through His church. His church is His bride. The Church is inviting you to come to God, be baptized and walk by faith. The Church is calling you, "Come!"

Do not delay! Come to your God and Dad. Are your hungry for spiritual food? Come and eat the Bread of heaven. He is the Christ. He tells you, "I am the Bread of life" (John 6:48).

Are you thirsty for something divine? Is it really good? Will it last forever? Is really awesome? If you are, you are searching for the Holy Spirit. You are thirsting for Him.

He is already in this world so that He can satisfy your thirsty for a life that is noble, perfect, awesome and everlasting. "And the Spirit and the bride say, Come. And let him that heareth say, Come. And let him that is athirst come. And whosoever will, let him take the water of life freely" (Revelation 22:17). You do pay any money to receive Him into your heart.

Allow the Holy Spirit to imbue you with His divine holy Presence. Let Him be your water. Let Him be your milk. Let Him be your food. Let Him be your life. He promises to satisfy your thirst for spiritual things.

He will make you holy and pure like clean, fresh and cool water. He wants to recreate your heart and make it completely new – with new thoughts, feelings, love, goals, aims, etc. Your spirit is dead because of sin.

When you die, you will not exist again unless He gives you His spirit. Then His spirit will make you live again.

So accept Him now so that you may have the opportunity to be resurrected from the grave or be changed into a new undying person when Jesus comes. "I will sprinkle clean water on you and make you clean from all your idols and everything else that has defiled you.

I will give you a new heart and a new mind. I will take away your stubborn heart of stone and give you an obedient heart. I will put my spirit in you and will see to it that you follow my laws and keep all the commands I have given you.

Then you will live in the land I gave your ancestors. You will be my people, and I will be your God. I will save you from everything that defiles you.

I will command the grain to be plentiful, so that you will not have any more famines. I will increase the yield of your fruit trees and your fields, so that there will be no more famines to disgrace you among the nations" (Ezekiel 36:30, GNB).

The Holy Spirit will come and live in your heart. He will make you a new person. Just confess your sins and He will take care of your salvation. "If we confess our sins, he is faithful and just to forgive us our sins, and to cleanse us from all unrighteousness" (1 John 1:9).

He has already forgiven you all your sins before you were even born. He wants not to make your completely new as if you have never sinned in your entire life.

Clean up your acts. The wonderful news of the gospel is that the Lord Jesus will clean up your sins for you since it is impossible for you to be holy and righteous by your own power. So rise up from that heap of rubbish where you willingly like in the mire of sin. Your freedom from sin and the fear of a never-ending gloom of the grave has come.

You will not end in the dirt or ashes of the earth forever. You will live again and that will be in the golden palace of God. For the righteous will arise from the dust as new everlasting beings. "And many of them that sleep in the dust of the earth shall awake, some to everlasting life, and some to shame and everlasting contempt" (Daniel 12:2).

Allow your spirit to be set on fire by the Holy Spirit. You are now set free from the prison of sin. You are no more the slave of sin.

That bondage to the Egypt of sin has been broken by the blood of the Lamb over the door of your heart just as Moses and Israel put the blood of the lambs over the door of their homes. "And it came to pass, that at midnight the LORD smote all the firstborn in the land of Egypt, from the firstborn of Pharaoh that sat on his throne unto the firstborn of the captive that was in the dungeon; and all the firstborn of cattle" (Exodus 12:29).

The Divine blood of Christ is splashed over your soul. When Satan wants to enter into your heart, He sees the blood of your Christ in your heart, and he runs away in fear of God. For your heart is the home of the Spirit of Christ.

He cries out in agony, and runs away. "Purge out therefore the old leaven, that ye may be a new lump, as ye are unleavened. For even Christ our Passover is sacrificed for us" (1 Corinthians 5:7). Give your sins over to your Savior so that He can wash you clean by His precious blood.

There is a hunger that comes because your body is

weak and is depleted of energy. So you feel hungry in your stomach. And you want something to eat. But there is also a hungry of your spirit. Just as people feel hungry when their stomachs are empty, they also feel hunger in their hearts for the spiritual.

They can be satisfied by God alone. Your inner man or inner person is hungry for his or her Creator. The bad thing is that most people are not going to the Creator so that He may satisfy the hunger of their souls.

They are buying highly perishable bread of the world that does not satisfy their souls. These breads they are buying with their lives may be in form of fame, riches, belonging, drugs that excite the senses needless such as alcohol, power, etc.

Even among Christians, many have not grasped the love and power of God. They are running after the frivolous excitements of this world.

They bother and afflict their bodies all their lives to work for the temporary achievements of this world. They afflict their minds unnecessarily in trying to find some things to satisfy the longing of their souls. But those longings are spiritual.

Nothing in this world can satisfy it except the Holy Spirit who created them. The Holy Spirit is inviting you to eat the true Bread of life. He is Jesus your Savior. He is the only one who can satisfy the hunger of your soul.

What make meat delicious are the fats that are imbedded in them. What makes egg yolk delicious is the fat.

The Holy Spirit is inviting you to enjoy the love and friendship of heaven. "Wherefore do ye spend money for that which is not bread? and your labour for that which satisfieth not? hearken diligently unto me, and eat ye that which is good, and let your soul delight itself in fatness" (Isaiah 55:2).

It is good, perfect, wonderful, enjoyable and eternal. God is the Best of the best love that can satisfy your soul forever.

Stand still and listen to the voice of your Holy Spirit. He is calling you to drink love and life that never ends like someone who is drinking milk or water until you will be satisfied.

His word is the seed that will create life in you. He will make you rich, powerful and famous just as He had make David, a poor shepherd boy, the most famous and beloved King of Israel.

During the reign of David, the Kingdom of Israel achieved its highest power and fame. The Holy Spirit promises to make you in heaven even more famous, more powerful and richer that King David.

This is your Father's solemn promise if you will listen to Him, "Incline your ear, and come unto me: hear, and your soul shall live; and I will make an everlasting covenant with you, even the sure mercies of David.

Behold, I have given him for a witness to the people, a leader and commander to the people. Behold, thou shalt call a nation that thou knowest not, and nations that knew not thee shall run unto thee because of the LORD thy God, and for the Holy One of Israel; for he hath glorified thee. Seek ye the LORD while he may be found, call ye upon him while he is near" (Isaiah 55:3–6).

This is the time of your salvation. The Holy Spirit is still in the business of calling people into His kingdom. Come before death snatches your life. Come before the time of probation ends. Come to Him and He will save you. He loves you very much.

As we discussed before, water is tasteless, colorless and odorless. You are like water that is not sweet. But when you accept the Lord Jesus Christ as your personal Savior, He will change you into a sweet and wonderful person.

He will change you as tasteless, colorless and odorless water into a sweet, tasty and sweet-smelling fresh appetizing wine.

This sweet wine is to encourage appetite. It does not make people drunk and/or unconscious. "And there were set there six waterpots of stone, after the manner of the purifying of the Jews, containing two or three firkins apiece. Jesus saith unto them, Fill the waterpots with water. And they filled them up to the brim.

And he saith unto them, Draw out now, and bear unto the governor of the feast. And they bare it. When the ruler of the feast had tasted the water that was made wine, and knew not whence it was: (but the servants which drew the water knew;) the governor of the feast called the bridegroom, And saith unto him,

Every man at the beginning doth set forth good wine; and when men have well drunk, then that which is worse: but thou hast kept the good wine until now" (John 2:6–10).

The Christ, our Mighty Lord, changed water into wine in a wedding in Cana. He wants to change your life into something of value to God. He will make you precious and desired by your Father.

Your Father will enjoy drinking your love like someone who enjoys drinking clean, fresh juice. Other people may find you desired and good to them also when the Spirit of Christ is in your heart.

The best of all rivers is the River Jordan of heaven. Its water will give you eternal life. Keep on struggling in your Christian walk. Soon, you will drink deep and long from the water of life. "And he shewed me a pure river of water of life, clear as crystal, proceeding out of the throne of God and of the Lamb.

In the midst of the street of it, and on either side of the river, was there the tree of life, which bare twelve manner of fruits, and yielded her fruit every month: and the leaves of the tree were for the healing of the nations.

And there shall be no more curse: but the throne of God and of the Lamb shall be in it; and his servants shall serve him: And they shall see his face; and his name shall be in their foreheads.

And there shall be no night there; and they need no candle, neither light of the sun; for the Lord God giveth them light: and they shall reign for ever and ever" (Revelation 22:1–5).

Thus, the Holy Spirit will continue to be our River flowing with the Water of Life even in heaven. He will give us a part of His spirit again like He did in the Garden of Eden. He will make us live forever like Himself.

So the best water is the Presence of the Holy Spirit in your life. Drink Him every day and every night.

Let Him spring up in your soul. He will make you complete and fully re-created and never to die or suffer again.

5. Never man spake like this man

Jesus teaching in the Temple, from the book Standard Bible Story Readers, Book Five, 1928, Authors O. A. Stemler and Bess Bruce Cleaveland

The sermons of the Messiah on the last day of the Feast of the Tabernacle won the hearts of most of the listeners. "Many of the people therefore, when they heard this saying, said, Of a truth this is the Prophet" (John 7:40).

They exclaimed, "Here comes Love! By the truth of the Almighty Father, He is He who is Love. He is the Prophet who is to parent us like God does."

Some went even further. They placed their faiths in Him. "Others said, This is the Christ. But some said, Shall Christ come out of Galilee?" (John 7:41).

They declared, "Here comes Love! He is He who is Love: the Eternal, Righteous, and Loving God the Messiah."

The story of the three Maggi or wise men that came from the East and visited King Herod to inquire him about the birth place of the Messiah was well known by all the Jews. "When Herod the king had heard these things, he was troubled, and all Jerusalem with him. And when he had gathered all the chief priests and scribes of the people together, he demanded of them where Christ should be born.

And they said unto him, In Bethlehem of Judaea:

for thus it is written by the prophet, And thou Bethlehem, in the land of Juda, art not the least among the princes of Juda: for out of thee shall come a Governor, that shall rule my people Israel" (Matthew 2:3–6).

They also knew how they lost their children to the sword of Herod in his mad search for the King of Israel. They were denying facts just to spite at the Messiah. They claimed, "Hath not the scripture said, That Christ cometh of the seed of David, and out of the town of Bethlehem, where David was?" (John 7:42).

The story of the rebellious Jews against the Messiah is well-known in heaven and all over the world. They were warring against the believers who were their own family members and relatives.

They were falling away from the truth like seeds of corn that are being forcefully removed from its cob. "So there was a division among the people because of him" (John 7:43).

They were not really fighting their own families and relatives but the Righteous Daddy. Whenever a daddy speaks, his rebellious children will disobey him but the righteous ones will obey him.

The Jewish leaders had sent their soldiers to arrest the Messiah. But His kind, gentle, and loving words broke the hard hearts of the soldiers. They were sorry for their sins.

They had burning desires in their hearts to meet with their loving God and live with Him forever. They refused to lay their rough hands on Him.

They went back to their powerful generals and captains empty-handed. They brave the risks of being killed or thrown to jail for refusing to arrest the Messiah. "And some of them would have taken him; but no man laid hands on him.

Then came the officers to the chief priests and Pharisees; and they said unto them, Why have ye not brought him?" (John 7:44, 45).

The enemies of God questioned their soldiers as to

why they did not bring the Messiah to them by force if possible. The soldiers were witnesses to the Messiah's Divinity. "The officers answered, Never man spake like this man" (John 7:46).

They declared very firmly, "God is with Him. The words of God that this Man is saying are so loving and tender that no other man can say them just like Him."

The Pharisees questions their soldiers if they were also drawn away the appearance of the Supernatural seen on the face of the Messiah. "God is God, "they declared, "None of us has been deceived by Him even though He had the appearance of the Divine and is a Miracle Worker."

They accused the laity of not knowing the scriptures. They claimed that the commoners were under the curse of God because they did not know the scriptures. "Then answered them the Pharisees, Are ye also deceived? Have any of the rulers or of the Pharisees believed on him? But this people who knoweth not the law are cursed" (John 7:47–49).

One of the members of the Sanhedrin called them to reason. "Nicodemus saith unto them, (he that came to Jesus by night, being one of them,) Doth our law judge any man, before it hear him, and know what he doeth?" (John 7:50, 51).

Nicodemus thwarted their plans to have the Messiah executed. They wanted to condemn Him on false accusations. But the Messiah's friends were in the council, too.

They were Nicodemus and Joseph of Arimathea. His enemies could not proceed with the court in His absentia.

It was against the Law of God to condemn someone without giving him (or her) an opportunity to defend himself. "They answered and said unto him, Art thou also of Galilee? Search, and look: for out of Galilee ariseth no prophet. And every man went unto his own house" (John 7:52, 53).

11 CHAPTER

THE SON OF GOD WAS HOMELESS FOR YOUR SAKE

The Son of man hath not where to lay his head

The people surround the Messiah very thick. They were draining the life out of Him. He needed time alone to recuperate and regain His strength. But the unsympathetic refused to acknowledge the humanity that He had put on. He needed rest, too, just like they did.

So He was forced to ask His disciples to take Him into one of their boats and row to opposite of Lake Galilee where few families lived. "Now when Jesus saw great multitudes about him, he gave commandment to depart unto the other side" (Matthew 8:18).

As they were getting into the boat, "And a certain scribe came, and said unto him, Master, I will follow thee whithersoever thou goest" (Matthew 8:19). He asked to join the disciples of the famous Teacher. He knew that His eyes will lead to them into a very glorious life on this earth.

To the shock of everyone and especially the disciples, the Messiah was cold towards this scribe. Many people have suspected him to be no one else but Judas Iscariot. He was a learned man. He was well-versed in the scriptures. He was a copyist, too.

He was copying the Old Testament and made it available for the people to read. "And Jesus saith unto him, The foxes have holes, and the birds of the air have nests; but the Son of man hath not where to lay his head" (Matthew 8:20).

The loving God, the Messiah, spoke him very authoritatively. He said that animals and birds have residences but He, though a superior Human Being than these lower creatures, was not faring better than them. He had house to rest His weary head.

The dead to bury their own dead. Do not look back

The Messiah asked someone to follow Him and be His disciple. He replied and said that God wanted him to return home and bury his father before he could take up the discipleship of the Messiah. "And another of his disciples said unto him, Lord, suffer me first to go and bury my father" (Matthew 8:21).

It was God calling him to follow him. But he had his own doctrine that he thought would get him to heaven faster. But it was leading his mind backwards. He was looking at death instead onto the face of the Lord and the eternal life He was ready to give him. "But Jesus said unto him, Follow me; and let the dead bury their dead" (Matthew 8:22).

The God of love spoke to Him with authority and ordered him, "Follow the passions of My Fatherhood that gave birth to you. Give over death into the hands death. Let it kill itself and bury itself, too."

The Messiah came to give life. He did not come to glorify death or dead people. He came to give the dead life. And His disciples must not fear death. He will deal with it and bury it, too.

No one who is looking back is fit for the kingdom of God

One of His told Him that he would like to return home and discuss the cost of being a disciple first with his parents, wife, and children before he could make his final decision. He knew that he would never see them again. He was on his way to the grave for choosing to be the disciple of the Messiah. "And another also said, Lord, I will follow thee; but let me first go bid them farewell, which are at home at my house" (Luke 9:61).

The Messiah had the rights to tell him that indecisiveness will be the undoing of the weak-minded. It will send them to hell. "And Jesus said unto him, No man, having put his hand to the plough, and looking back, is fit for the kingdom of God" (Luke 9:62).

You are either the disciple of the Messiah or of the devil. You cannot serve the two masters at the same time.

They do not have the same agenda. Therefore, there is no way that they can cooperate to achieve the same results. The distinction between them is like comparing the bright light of the noonday to the darkness of midnight when no artificial or natural lights like the moon or stars are shining.

God is still righteous even if everyone on this earth is unrighteous. A man may spread out his hands and grab his plow but if he looks behind him instead of keep his eyes in front of him as he plows, will not see where wants to plow.

It is the same with the kingdom of God. You must keep looking on the Cross of Calvary and pray at the same time in order to arrive into the Kingdom of God. He who looks behind is looking at the god of this world.

12 CHAPTER

ASK, AND IT SHALL BE GIVEN YOU

1. Ask, and it shall be given you

One day, the Messiah was engrossed in a prayer. He was oblivious to His surrounding as He communicated with His Father. He did not even know that His disciples were eavesdropping on His prayer.

It was sounded very beautiful and moving to them. When He finished praying, the disciples asked Him to teach them to pray. "And it came to pass, that, as he was praying in a certain place, when he ceased, one of his disciples said unto him, Lord, teach us to pray, as John also taught his disciples" (Luke 11:1).

He had taught them how to pray the same prayer three years earlier on the Mount of Blessing. They had apparently not paid attention to the method of praying that He had taught them. They forgot it.

Very patiently, He repeated it again to them. "And he said unto them, When ye pray, say, Our Father which art in heaven, Hallowed be thy name. Thy kingdom come. Thy will be done, as in heaven, so in earth. Give us day by day our daily bread. And forgive us our sins; for we also forgive every one that is indebted to us. And lead us not into temptation; but deliver us from evil" (Luke 11:2–4).

He said that He answers prayers very faithfully. He is not too busy to answer your prayers.

He is your Friend. You must not be afraid to ask Him for anything just like earthly friends who feel no shame when they are begging for help.

They know that their friends love them too much to despise them for being needy. "And he said unto them, Which of you shall have a friend, and shall go unto him at midnight, and say unto him,

Friend, lend me three loaves; For a friend of mine in his journey is come to me, and I have nothing to set before him?

And he from within shall answer and say, Trouble me not: the door is now shut, and my children are with me in bed;

I cannot rise and give thee. I say unto you, Though he will not rise and give him, because he is his friend, yet because of his importunity he will rise and give him as many as he needeth" (Luke 11:5–8).

The compassionate Messiah went everywhere on foot and spread the word of God. He always seized any available opportunity to preach wherever the people congregated for prayers and worshipped.

He invited the whole world to celebrate the greatness of the Kingdom of God where all your needs will be met.

He is asking men, women, and children to register their names as her citizens. He is watching very tenderly over the people whose lives have been made bitter by sicknesses, diseases, hunger, thirst, homelessness, etc.

He will heal them. He invites, And I say unto you, Ask, and it shall be given you; seek, and ye shall find; knock, and it shall be opened unto you. For every one that asketh receiveth; and he that seeketh findeth; and to him that knocketh it shall be opened" (Luke 11:9, 10).

He is still relieving the suffering of the people who are hard pressed. He is making them strong, powerful, and intelligent. He is teaching them the truth in order to make them the fathers and mothers of righteousness.

When He sees people repenting and coming back to Him, His compassion goes out to them. He sees Himself in them. He counts Himself as one of them.

They are in much pain. They are dying. They are outcasts.

They were driven away from the Garden of Eden by their sins like a farmer that is driving away birds from eating his crops. Sin has driven them away from the blessed Presence of God their Father. But He wants to resurrect their eternal lives to be just like His.

They are like sheep that are wandering all alone among predators. They have no shepherd to watch over them. "But when he saw the multitudes, he was moved with compassion on them, because they fainted, and were scattered abroad, as sheep having no shepherd" (Matthew 9:36).

He saw you in those people. And He was and is still very compassionate about your needs. He will fulfill every one of them if not now; it will be at His Second Coming.

He said that though you are bad parents, you do not give poisonous snakes, stones, etc. for your children to eat. He is holier than you.

He will give you far better than earthly parents give to their children. "If a son shall ask bread of any of you that is a father, will he give him a stone?

Or if he ask a fish, will he for a fish give him a serpent? Or if he shall ask an egg, will he offer him a scorpion?

If ye then, being evil, know how to give good gifts unto your children: how much more shall your heavenly Father give the Holy Spirit to them that ask him?" (Luke 11:11–13).

He is complaining that there is no one to create truth in their hearts once again that will definitely give them peace, security, and eternal life. So He offered Himself to be their Good Shepherd.

But He needs assistants while He is still taking care of their businesses in heaven. "Then saith he unto his disciples,

The harvest truly is plenteous, but the labourers are few; Pray ye therefore the Lord of the harvest, that he will send forth labourers into his harvest" (Matthew 9:37, 38).

The people of the world are good crops. They have hearts that need to be tutored to bear fruits of righteousness.

And most of them will come back to God their Creator if there are harvesters who will go out, reap them from the fields of sin, and bring the Father's harvests back home to Him.

The Messiah is complaining that many Christians are abandoning the joyous works of harvesting His good crops. Instead, they are harvesting worthless fruits that cannot breathe, think, love, and live forever.

He is asking every one of you to order God the Father in His capacity as the Person who gave births to them to send out workers among them and bring them back to Him.

2. God will take care of you in your storms

Men and women have seen the powers of the Creator on the high seas. Those who descend down into the ships to make a living on the high seas have met with the powerful of God. "They that go down to the sea in ships, that do business in great waters; These see the works of the LORD, and his wonders in the deep" (Psalms 107:23, 24).

The merchants thought that they were powerful seamen. But their works cannot be compared to that of the Creator. His works are attractive to people. They are awed into speechlessness when they see and hear the howling of the winds and rising of the waves.

They cannot imitate the astounding works of the Lord in the oceans, seas, lakes, etc. when He lashes the waters into the furious storms lambasting both sea and land.

They are terrified when they hear His majestic voice speaking whipping the storms and waves of the oceans, seas, lakes, rivers, etc. He gives the orders. The winds rise from their repose.

There is no denial to their presence when they raise their voices. They come down in full force on the seas and land.

Everything bows to their full forces. Men and women go into hiding from the terror of the storms. Even the bravest of all hearts submit to the power of the winds. Natural can rule supreme over human beings whenever it chooses to.

The water answers the call of the powers of heaven to also show human beings that they, too, are powerful. The winds and the waves cooperate with each other better than human friends do.

The waves rise and try to mountain up to God's throne but He forces them back to the earth as if they were heavy mud.

They could not cross the boundaries between

heaven and earth that He set for them. They obey His orders to the letter. Unfortunately, the ships are not so lucky when the storms hit the waves of the seas. The waves just keep rolling towards the ships without stopping to rest.

They try to swamp the ships on the high seas. "For he commandeth, and raiseth the stormy wind, which lifteth up the waves thereof.

They mount up to the heaven, they go down again to the depths: their soul is melted because of trouble. They reel to and fro, and stagger like a drunken man, and are at their wits' end" (Psalms 107:25–27).

The spirits of the men and women traveling in those ships, ocean liners, boats, canoes, etc. are fearful. They feel like animals that are being led to be slaughtered on the burn offerings to pay for their sins. Nature is trouble when it is angry. It is destructive. Human beings are too weak to overpower it.

When the storms are in full control of the vessels, the seafarers are shaken and are afraid. They run forward like helpless little children and at another the shaking of the winds and the waves, they fall backward together as if they were complete intoxicated and drunk.

They have lost all intelligence, wisdom, and physical powers to deal with nature gone wild. They are the mercy of the elements.

People cry out to God with loud voice. They are afraid of the watery graves that are staring them on their faces menacingly.

Death is hard pressed on them. They begged the Lord to have mercy on them.

They know that He is their only Savior if they want to live. "Then they cry unto the LORD in their trouble, and he bringeth them out of their distresses. He maketh the storm calm, so that the waves thereof are still" (Psalms 107:28, 29).

Human beings have seen His powers in the storms. They beg Him to spare their lives. He answers their prayers.

He steps on the heads of the stormy winds and heads of the gigantic winds. He orders them to keep quiet.

When they hear His All-Powerful voice, they become as humble as lambs. They all lie down at His feet and keep quiet.

The people thank God for saving their lives. There is also joy among them because God has given them another chance to live. "Then are they glad because they be quiet; so he brunet them unto their desired haven" (Psalms 107:30).

The elements that rose up against them have been tamed by the powers of the Almighty. They are at peace, once again, with the rulers of the earth who had just cowered before them.

The Creator guides His children to safe harbors. They are ever grateful to Him for saving their lives from water graves.

Pagans should get baptized immediately when they know that the Lord has saved them from the hands of nature gone wild. He is merciful to both believers and pagans.

His love is very attractive to the sons and daughters that He built out Himself put in warm blooded flesh. "Oh that men would praise the LORD for his goodness, and for his wonderful works to the children of men!

Let them exalt him also in the congregation of the people, and praise him in the assembly of the elders" (Psalms 107:31, 32).

God will take care of you in your storms. Let the whole earth will praise Him for all the wonderful things He has done for them.

He has made them strong and intelligent people to choose Him as their everlasting Friend and Companion above anyone or anything else on this world. He is the eternal Friend because He is their God, King, and Lord.

3. The unjust judge

The unjust judge and the persistent widow

All the parables of the Lord are your inheritances. They are worth more than all the diamonds and gold in this world.

If you listen to His sayings and follow them closely, they will lead you to your abundant up in glory land. He said that you must never reduce yourself into nothingness.

You belong to Him. Irrespective of all the adversities you are meeting, you are still the men and women He wanted so much that He fathered you into existence. He loves you very much.

He is asking you to pray all the time to the God of truth and life. Ask Him to have His stamp on you and everything you are doing and own. Let His compassion rest on you.

You must never be emptied of His Spirit which can cause you to faint or lose heart. "And he spake a parable unto them to this end, that men ought always to pray, and not to faint; Saying, There was in a city a judge, which feared not God, neither regarded man: And there was a widow in that city; and she came unto him, saying, Avenge me of mine adversary" (Luke 18:1–3).

He said, "There was a certain city that was full of life and love except for her judge. He did not recognize the loving God as his own Brother. In fact, he did not like Him at all. He hated Him. He had no love for his fellow human beings either even though they were very righteous people.

And in that same town did God put a certain widow to live. She had no one look after her except her Maker alone.

She would come to this cruel and heartless judge and ask for his help on behalf of the God of life and love who made them all.

She would beg, 'Please have a passion to look into the truth that I am presenting you. My enemy is fighting me. His mouth is poisoning me. He will kill me.'

He never took notice of her from the day she came begging for his intervention. Her case grew ancient. He never looked at her even once.

But she trusted in the Lord. She came on coming and crying to him every day.

Finally, he could not take it anymore. He was worn out with her lamentations. "And he would not for a while: but afterward he said within himself, Though I fear not God, nor regard man; Yet because this widow troubled me, I will avenge her, lest by her continual coming she weary me" (Luke 18:4, 5).

He mourned about his own mental breakdown because of the insistent begging of this poor widow for justice. He said that even though he was an agnostic and hated God, he would at least obey Him this once and give justice to this widow or she would kill him by her constant crying for justice.

The Messiah decried this evil man. And the Lord said, "Then the Lord said, Listen to what the unjust judge says!

And will not [our just] God defend and protect and avenge His elect (His chosen ones), who cry to Him day and night? Will He defer them and delay help on their behalf?

I tell you, He will defend and protect and avenge

them speedily. However, when the Son of Man comes, will He find [persistence in] faith on the earth?" (Luke 18:6–8, AMP).

The crooked judge was a worshipper of the cruel god of darkness called Satan. That was why he had no heart for people who were in suffering. But God is the God of truth.

He has Brains to see to it that you are saved from the cruelties of the god of darkness. His ears are wide open. They are listening to your constant cries that have made your voices very coarse and faint.

He has not forgotten you. He is full of your pains. He is eternally loving and compassionate.

He will rescue you because He is the God of truth. He is presenting Himself to you as your Dad and best Friend.

He is asking you to have faith in Him whether you have received what you have asked from Him or not. The most important thing He wants to do for you are to find you ready on the day of His Second Coming.

He is knocking at your door. If you open that door to Him, He will always live in your house. He will share the same table of love and friendship with you.

He says, "Behold, I stand at the door, and knock: if any man hear my voice, and open the door, I will come in to him, and will sup with him, and he with me.

To him that overcometh will I grant to sit with me in my throne, even as I also overcame, and am set down with my Father in his throne" (Revelation 3:20, 21).

Better listen to Him. It is to your own benefits when He is calling you to go to Him.

This All-Powerful God from whose Being thunders and electric lightning explodes continually has come to fill you with His Spirit so that you may have His mind and heart.

He rebukes us of our sins especially to those who are of His family. He walks before us to dry up deep oceans, seas, lakes, rivers, etc. to help us walk towards heaven.

He scolds us for forgetting to be good Christians. He urges us not to leave Him. Otherwise, our foolhardy will land us into problems. The worst thing to come upon us is hell.

He comes to make us strong and courageous to be able to face enemies that are after the destruction of our salvation. He encourages us to trust in Him. He tells us that with His power, we can do anything as well as help people who are in need such as safety issues, salvation of their souls, food, shelter, etc.

Then He fills us with His power. He makes us to rise up and begin to move forward in saving people who are in of His help.

Sometimes, we may not have the brains or the means to help people but He takes us as we are and strengthens us to help us do what is impossible according to the world.

When we are in the midst of our battles and struggles, He gives us the strength to overcome our adversaries. He helps us to shock our enemies by the great things we will achieve. They had thought that we were helpless and at their mercy.

Then the Lord shocks them because He made us wiser, more intelligent and stronger than them. Many people will know that it was the Lord who was working through you. And He gets all the credit. He gives you the honor before people and the holy angels.

He loves calling each and every one of His children by name. He has assigned each person a special task to do.

He is calling everyone to work for Him and especially to be good fathers, mothers, siblings, etc. He works miracles through us to help relieve the suffering of His children around us.

We anoint them with the Gospel of people. They are filled with the Holy Spirit.

We bring people from nowhere and make them become noble, dignified and special. We make them princes and princesses of the Lord.

He teaches us not to use Him as a source of an income but to love Him truly for who He is. He is God, and therefore, can do anything but He is also our Father. As our Father, He also wants to be loved unconditionally, that is, we love Him because He is our Dad and not because of the miracles He can do in our lives.

When we begin to despise our fellow Christians whom we think are weaker than us, He rebukes us. Sometimes, we give wrong advice to people. When they try to do what we have asked them to do, they suffer.

Other times, we mislead people intentionally or unintentionally. The Lord tells us to apologize to them and help them live safer and happier lives.

As our Loving but very authoritative Dad, He tells us when we have sinned against ourselves. He tells us what we have done and how to do right. He afflicts us with remorse and guilt so that we would not sin again.

Then He cheers us up when we repent. He tells us that He has already forgiven us our sins.

He promises us great rewards if we would choose to be good children and not follow the devil and our own inclinations to sin. He will make us princes and princesses of heaven.

He will recreate us all over again. He will make us eternal and resistant to decay and dying. Etc.

Sometimes, the people who become our enemies are well known to us. But when we carefully listen to His Spirit speaking through our consciences, He helps to detect when we are being lured into sin or are in harm's way. Then we cry to Him for help. He helps us escape.

If we could not escape because we were foolish like sheep and got enticed or forced into sin or crimes, when we cry out to Him, He will heal our broken hearts, hurt feelings, disturbed minds and broken bodies. He will help us live as a whole being again.

He sends us to preach. He makes us talk tough to sinners even if it is breaking our hurts to make them cry.

Sometimes, our message fans the flame of wrath from guilty consciences. But we continue to take our stand for Him and give His message to the dying world with courage and humility.

Sometimes, the people's sins land them into trouble. They have wars within their consciences, in their families, neighborhood, etc. They sins have resulted into droughts, famine, hunger, diseases, death, etc.

The Lord asks us to tell them exactly how sin began and how they can save themselves. He tells us to tell them about the Holy Spirit – how He wants to sanctify them and make them holy again.

There is a new heaven and a new world waiting for them, and they should not miss them.

While the world is chaffing under the load of sin and dehumanization of Satan, the Lord has safely brought us out. He shows us the way to heaven. He convinces our hearts how to keep the Ten Commandments holy.

Even though we break them by the hour because we have fallen short of the glory of God (Romans 3:23), there is a peace which comes only from Him if we repent. He will make use good people. He will take us to heaven.

13 CHAPTER

THE TRUTH SHALL MAKE YOU FREE

1. *I proceeded forth and came from God*

James Shaw Crompton (1853-1916), the Messiah appeared
to John on the Island of Patmos. He is back in heaven surrounded
great glories and powers eternal

The Messiah warned all unbelievers, "I am
leaving and going back to heaven. You will order Me
to take you there because you think that you are good
enough for heaven based on your own self-
righteousness.

I am warning you that you will die in hell because
of your sin of pride and arrogance. You are
committing suicides in which there is no hope of
resurrection into celestial beings.

You cannot enter into heaven through salvation of
works based on human ideologies, philosophies, etc. of
who God is and how to get to Him. Human theories
will not take you to the place where I am going.

No matter how much you may try to enter into the

Presence of God on your own efforts, you will fail. You cannot get into heaven. You do not have the supernatural power of saving yourself from this hell.

You cannot come where I am going." "Then said Jesus again unto them, I go my way, and ye shall seek me, and shall die in your sins: whither I go, ye cannot come" (John 8:21).

The Bible scholars who were deceived by their own interpretations of God's word could not understand what the teachings of the Messiah. "Then said the Jews, Will he kill himself? because he saith, Whither I go, ye cannot come" (John 8:22).

They swore in the name of God that He was going to commit suicide. They accused Him of avoiding trouble by committing suicide. But there would be no mass suicides in Israel.

They would not follow His example of short-cuts to lives problems by committing suicide. He knew that they loved life and would not follow Him to the grave. They were not cowards like Him.

He told them they were speaking nonsense that can only come from the mouths of sinful human beings like themselves.

They had fallen nature. That was why they were suspecting Him of trying to commit suicide when such a thought was far from His mind. "And he said unto them, Ye are from beneath; I am from above: ye are of this world; I am not of this world.

I said therefore unto you, that ye shall die in your sins: for if ye believe not that I am he, ye shall die in your sins." (John 8:23, 24).

He said that the Jews and all the people of the earth were earth bound creatures because of their sins. Just He told the Jews He is also telling you that He came from the real and highest heaven where God His Father lives. All the people from the beginning of the world to the end live in sin and death.

He was not a member of your sinful human race. There are simply no sinners found anywhere else in all the universes and in heaven except on this world.

He only adopted human flesh in order to save you from sin. But your created nature is not His eternal nature. He has never been and will never be from this world.

He warned the Jews and you, too, that you will all die in your sins without any hope of resurrection into eternal life if you resist living by faith and not by works.

You need to have faith in Him that He is your Messiah and can, therefore, save you. He had gone through all this trouble of telling them who He really was.

He was God the Almighty Creator. And yet they refused to believe that He was telling the truth. "Then said they unto him, Who art thou?

And Jesus saith unto them, Even the same that I said unto you from the beginning. I have many things to say and to judge of you: but he that sent me is true; and I speak to the world those things which I have heard of him" (John 8:25, 26).

He told them that the proof that He is supernatural will come when after they had murdered Him, He would rise from the dead and give salvation to the whole world.

He said, "I have been trying to explain to you that I am the beginning and the end. As your Messiah, I will I have the power to create life in you that is eternal, abundant, and joyous.

I will change you based on your thoughts, words, and actions. And I can begin it right now and send you to hell. But because God your Father loves you and I love you, He has sent Me to save you.

I am now giving you the chance to repent from all your sins, and I will save you. God your Father is nothing else but the whole truth.

Legalists and hypocrites all claim to know Him very well and to love Him very much. But they have never seen His face or heard His voice. But I know

Him in a very personal way.

He and I are Members of the Triune God. And I am passing to the whole world His messages of love and hope that He told Me to tell you."

The cobwebs of human theories, false Bible interpretations, etc. covered the minds of the listeners. They could not understand what He was telling them.

He was speaking about the awesome love of God their Father and how was now sacrificing His Son in order that they may live in a wonderful and eternal world where they will never suffer again. "They understood not that he spake to them of the Father" (John 8:27).

He speaks deep truths concerning the mission of His coming into the world as her Messiah. "Then said Jesus unto them, When ye have lifted up the Son of man, then shall ye know that I am he, and that I do nothing of myself; but as my Father hath taught me, I speak these things.

And he that sent me is with me: the Father hath not left me alone; for I do always those things that please him" (John 8:28, 29).

He was saying, "When you have hanged the Person of the Godhead who is also the person of humanity on the Cross, then you will understand very clearly all the truths that I told you that I AM WHO I AM. I am God.

I do not run things without consultations from the other two Members of the Godhead—God our Father and God the Holy Spirit. I am preaching the messages of hope, love, resurrection, eternal life, etc. of the Trinity.

He who has sent Me to be the Head of the human race or the Second Adam is with Me. He has never quarreled with Me.

He has never found an unpleasant occasion to stop loving Me and from cooperating with Me in everything that I do. He has not broken off His loving relationship with Me.

He is the one and only Daddy I have. He is also your Daddy. I love Him very much. Everything that I do and all the words that I speak are for His exaltation on this earth.

And one day, He will be your only God, King and Lord down here on this earth. He is happy with Me that I am working on His behalf to save you from sin. He is very pleased with Me that I am bringing the world back into His gentle and loving arms."

When the people heard the messages of love and hope, they believed that the Messiah was speaking the truth. He was both their Messiah and God. "As he spake these words, many believed on him" (John 8:30).

He started to encourage them and strengthen their faith in God their Father. "Then said Jesus to those Jews which believed on him, If ye continue in my word, then are ye my disciples indeed; And ye shall know the truth, and the truth shall make you free" (John 8:31, 32).

He is saying, "All men and women who have faith in Me should always walk in the Way. I am now your culture and tradition.

I am covering you with my glorious and brightly shinning veil of righteousness because you are receiving My word of truth and life into your hearts.

If you continue to obey My word of truth very faithfully, you are truly My disciples. You will learn the truth in depth and in its broadness.

The truth will drive out errors and sins from your minds and hearts. It will create salvation in you. It will make you free, independent, and celestial beings."

Some of the proud Jews declared that they are already freed from sin and death. Even the Greeks and Romans could not dominate their independent spirits.

The blood of the free and independent Abraham was running through their veins. "They answered him, We be Abraham's seed, and were never in bondage to any man: how sayest thou, Ye shall be made free?"

(John 8:33).

They said that even to the end of the world, they will always be an independent race. In what way was God going to give them more freedom that they already did not have?

Jesus pointed out that there is no one on earth who is an island and lives by himself or for himself. Sad to say, they are slaves of sin.

They are being bludgeoned into the dust by their sins and by the demons. "Jesus answered them, Verily, verily, I say unto you, Whosoever committeth sin is the servant of sin.

And the servant abideth not in the house for ever: but the Son abideth ever" (John 8:34, 35).

He looked at the stubborn and spiritually arrogant Pharisees and Sadducees with pity and said that He is the truth. God the Father is truth.

It is impossible for all the people who live in the world of sin to suddenly stand up and claim, "I am holy and perfect!"

They cannot be holy on their own personal efforts through obeying laws such as the tradition of the fathers or the oral laws. They are born in sin, and they are living sin.

Sin has cut their righteousness out when Adam ate the fruits from the Tree of Good and Evil. He and his descendants are the slaves of sin.

A slave is not allowed to take charge of the family affairs and running them under his name. He cannot inherit anything.

All the people of this world are slaves of God the Father. This world and everything in her does not belong to them. Even their very lives are owned by God the Father.

They cannot extricate themselves from demons, sin, and death because they are the slaves of Satan. They all need supernatural help.

This world is the house of God the Father. He has given her to His Son, the Messiah, to inherit as His own kingdom. The Son is the eternal inheritor of His Father's infinite kingdom.

He lives from everlasting to everlasting. Now, any sinner who wants to be free from sin and the fear of death can ask the Son for help. If the Son therefore shall make you free, ye shall be free indeed" (John 8:36).

If the Son stands up in His hot and fiery glory on your behalf, He will burn sin, death, and demons to death. He will liberate you from them all. You will be true liberated. The liberation of the Son of God is what the world really needs.

As God, He knew everything about each individual Jew or Gentile from the everlasting past. He knew that they could trace their roots to Abraham. And He also knew that the Jewish leaders had put themselves under oath to murder Him.

They had ordered spies to follow Him around to catch any politically or religiously incorrect word He spoke to He and use it against in order to execute Him.

They are desperately longing to murder because Him because they do not want His word to enter into their hearts and bring changes in them. But every word that came out of His mouth was the word of God His Father. He and His Father always spoke the same thoughts and the same language.

They both had the same mind, heart, and goal in life. "I know that ye are Abraham's seed; but ye seek to kill me, because my word hath no place in you. I speak that which I have seen with my Father: and ye do that which ye have seen with your father" (John 8:37, 38).

But the people of this world are different. They are not the children of God the Father. They only obey the father of this world.

The Jewish leaders insisted that Abraham was the only father they had. They did not have any other father beside him. "They answered and said unto him, Abraham is our father.

Jesus saith unto them, If ye were Abraham's

children, ye would do the works of Abraham. But now ye seek to kill me, a man that hath told you the truth, which I have heard of God: this did not Abraham" (John 8:39, 40).

The Lord told them plainly that it is not blood that counts but the spirit. Yes, they had the blood of Abraham but they do not have his spirit of searching for God by faith and of depending only on him. Abraham crossed many countries looking for God.

He lived by truth. He died in faith that he would see Him in the land of the living.

But the ecclesiastical leaders of Israel were not following his footsteps. They were not the descendants of this great man of faith. Their father was not Abraham but someone very evil. "Ye do the deeds of your father.

Then said they to him, We be not born of fornication; we have one Father, even God." (John 8:41).

By now the Jewish leaders were galled to the spirit. They were really mad. They became abusive in their language.

They said that they were not bastards. Their mothers were not adulterating around. They all had one Father. He was God the Father who made them to be conceived in their mothers' wombs. He was a bastard. Joseph was no His father.

The Messiah said that He was astounded by the claims of the Jews who were trying to kill Him. "Jesus said unto them, If God were your Father, ye would love me: for I proceeded forth and came from God; neither came I of myself, but he sent me" (John 8:42).

He said, "Is this God the Father whom I know very well right from the everlasting that you are claiming to be the Father who seeded you on the earth? You are very wrong.

You do not know Him at all. If this God whom I know very well is your Father, you would have loved and worshipped Me from the day I was born as a

Human Being amongst you.

I was came out of His glorious Supernatural tribe of the Triune God and descended down here on earth. I am not representing only one Member of Godhead but the whole Family. I am not a Stand Alone Supernatural Spirit.

I stand together with God the Father and God the Holy Spirit. I am representing the Triune God as the Head of the families of this earth. I am representing you as God and King of this world this world in the meetings of the Triune Godhead.

2. You are of your father the devil

He asked the Jews as to why they could not understand what He was telling them. He had simplified the truth down to the very basics but they too dull to grasp it. Somebody was blocking their minds from accepting the truth. "Why do ye not understand my speech? even because ye cannot hear my word.

Ye are of your father the devil, and the lusts of your father ye will do. He was a murderer from the beginning, and abode not in the truth, because there is no truth in him. When he speaketh a lie, he speaketh of his own: for he is a liar, and the father of it" (John 8:43, 44).

The Messiah pointed out to them that they were born of someone who loved to parade himself as the one and only father on this earth. Their father was the serpent. They inherited the sins of their father. They were full of the lusts of pride, arrogance, selfishness, adulteries, lying, stealing, etc.

Their father, the serpent, was a murderer right from the days of the Garden of Eden when he deceived the world to eat the fruits from the Tree of the Knowledge of Good and Evil. He told them that if they ate the fruits they would not die but they did.

The people of this world have never been the same ever since. They are dying day and night. They are being murdered by the serpent. It is his tradition to never speak or live by the truth. He is yet to understand what truth really is. It is not a part of his nature. Whenever he opens his mouth to speak, he speaks lies and more lies. Lying comes naturally to him. He is the king of lies and falsehoods. All unbelievers are liars just like the serpent who fathered them.

He continued to give His scathing rebukes to the Jewish leaders and all unbelievers of the world, saying, "And because I tell you the truth, ye believe me not.

Which of you convinceth me of sin? And if I say the truth, why do ye not believe me?" (John 8:45, 46).

He said that He never lied to anyone. He is the Truth. But the world has rejected Him, the Truth. Who among them can put Him to death because of any sin He had committed?

Even in the judgment hall of God He would be found to be holy, pure, and sinless. He would pass the judgment with flying colors. He would be saved because of His purity and holiness.

He had lived His life based on nothing else but the truth. He spoke and lived the truth that He preached based on the Bible as written in the Old Testament.

These are glaring facts but most of the people of the world have refused to come to Him to receive salvation. When will they begin to have faith in Him? When will they start to come back to their own Creator?

But He said, "He that is of God heareth God's words: ye therefore hear them not, because ye are not of God" (John 8:47).

Honest people who believe in the word of the Messiah are proving that they are truly the children of God the Father. The actions of unbelievers show that they are not the child of the Most High.

The Jews were cut to the heart. He spoke the truth. But instead of accepting their errors, they tried to stifle their consciences by accusing Him of an ignorant pagan who did not know the Torah. They claimed that they were always excellent in their judgments.

He was Satan himself. "Then answered the Jews, and said unto him, Say we not well that thou art a Samaritan, and hast a devil?" (John 8:48).

He said that the spirit pride, murder, hatred, selfishness, immoralities, etc. of Satan are yet to enter into the Spirit of God. He has lived from everlasting to everlasting as the holy and righteous God. He said that His only goal in life throughout all eternities was to please His heavenly Father. But the Jews and all the people of this world are disrespectful and unloving to Him, their own God and Messiah.

They dishonor Him day and night without shame. "Jesus answered, I have not a devil; but I honour my Father, and ye do dishonour me" (John 8:49).

"Anyway," He said, "And I seek not mine own glory: there is one that seeketh and judgeth" (John 8:50).

He said that He does not command glory to come to Him. It is exists naturally in the Spirit of God His Father. He is the One who will lift Him up from this earth and reinstate Him back into His former glory. But the people of the earth are ready to die for recognition.

God the Father will judge them for their wrongdoings against Him. But He will glorify Him and exalt Him very highly.

He appealed them to them once again, saying, "Verily, verily, I say unto you, If a man keep my saying, he shall never see death" (John 8:51).

He said that the Truth was visible and standing before their eyes. He was speaking to them.

If they would obey Him and treasure His words in their hearts, they will be saved. They will eternally happy and blessed. They will not face death in hell.

The Jews tried to resist the appeals of the Holy Spirit by shifting blames on the Lord's holy Messiah. "Then said the Jews unto him, Now we know that thou hast a devil.

Abraham is dead, and the prophets; and thou sayest, If a man keep my saying, he shall never taste of death. Art thou greater than our father Abraham, which is dead? and the prophets are dead: whom makest thou thyself?" (John 8:52, 53).

The consciences of the debaters were singed when they told God, "We have just found out that you are Satan. Abraham and the prophets have all died like the rest of our ancestors. They did not from death to life.

Now here you are saying, 'If anyone keeps My

word in his heart, he will pass from death to life.' Only God can speak with confidence and power.

He had already explained to the about the resurrection from the dead. Still, the Sadducees refused to believe that other worlds and universes exist and that heaven rules over them. How plainer can the explanation about the existence of extraterrestrial life get when it given by God Himself?

The Sadducees were downright disrespectful to God by refusing to believe in His existence, the existence of angels and other extraterrestrial lives. "Jesus answered, If I honour myself, my honour is nothing: it is my Father that honoureth me; of whom ye say, that he is your God:

Yet ye have not known him; but I know him: and if I should say, I know him not, I shall be a liar like unto you: but I know him, and keep his saying" John 8:54, 55).

Your father Abraham rejoiced to see my day: and he saw it, and was glad" (John 8:54–56).

He said that if He came down to the earth to glorify Himself before them as God, His love would not carry much weight. But He came because He loved His Father and the people of this world.

Because of that, His Father is glorifying His Name throughout heaven and the universes as Someone who is very awesome and can be trusted by them all. He was the very One they were claiming to be their Father.

They had no idea about He really was. But as for Him, He knew who God was. To deny His existence and His loving nature would show that He was a liar just like the unbelieving Jews such as the Sadducees.

But He as the Son knew who His Father's nature and character. He was a very obedient and loving Son. He obeyed all His Father's commandments.

He made a profound statement as to who He really was. He said, "Your father Abraham rejoiced to see my day: and he saw it, and was glad" (John 8:56).

He said Abraham shook and danced with joy when He saw Him in person.

The Jews knew very well that He was God in their midst. But they were so full of themselves they refused to surrender their lives to Him.

They were jealous of Him. They wanted to be God and not like God. "Then said the Jews unto him, Thou art not yet fifty years old, and hast thou seen Abraham?" (John 8:57).

They denied the undeniable truth that was revealed to them from the Creator's own mouth. Sin is the greatest and deadliest enemy of fallen mankind.

The Messiah knew that it was the same jealousies of Satan that made him rebel against him in heaven. Now, the people of the earth are his slaves.

They are rebelling against the God of heaven out of envy and jealous because they are not the almighty and everlasting. "Jesus said unto them, Verily, verily, I say unto you, Before Abraham was, I am" (John 8:58).

He spoke the truth when He said the awesome words, "I AM WHO I AM. Before Abraham was I AM." He and His two angels were visitors in his house. They ate dinner with him. (Genesis 18:1–15).

Many times, the Jewish ecclesiastical leadership had persecuted the prophets and even murdered some of them. Now, they wanted to murder the Messiah who created them.

He came down to the earth to save them from sin and eternal loss. "Then took they up stones to cast at him: but Jesus hid himself, and went out of the temple, going through the midst of them, and so passed by" (John 8:59).

He escaped from their hands and left the temple. They claimed that He was pretending to be God and must die. But they were the ones blaspheming the Everlasting One as a mere creature like themselves. They will face Him one day. They will all bow before Him.

He is God the Almighty and Everlasting God and

Messiah. "Wherefore God also hath highly exalted him, and given him a name which is above every name: That at the name of Jesus every knee should bow, of things in heaven, and things in earth, and things under the earth;

And that every tongue should confess that Jesus Christ is Lord, to the glory of God the Father" (Philippians 2:9–11).

3. The soldier of Christ

God said, "You are involved in a life and death struggle. But it is not a physical war. It is a war between Me and the devil and, unfortunately, you are also caught up in it. "God is a spirit" (John 4:24).

Since I am a Spirit, I live in the spiritual world, which cannot be seen, heard or touched by all sinful beings all the time. However, when I created your genes in the body of Adam, I made you both a spirit and physical being.

Unfortunately, you have been contaminated by sin. So you cannot fly up to heaven to see Me. You can see Me standing right before your ears.

You cannot hear My voice that is roaring over your head more than the roars of many thunders. Angels are also spirits. "Who maketh his angels spirits; his ministers a flaming fire" (Psalms 104:4).

Unfortunately, some of them have fallen into sin. These are the spirits of the air or the space that surrounds the fallen world. Sin is the order of their government. "Wherein in time past you walked according to the course of this world, according to the prince of the power of this air, of the spirit that now worketh on the children of unbelief:

In which also we all conversed in time past, in the desires of our flesh, fulfilling the will of the flesh and of our thoughts, and were by nature children of wrath, even as the rest" (Ephesians 2:2, 3, DRB).

I talk to you through your mind and heart. Unfortunately, Satan and his evil spirits are also trying to do that. Adam and Eve gave them the permission to tempt you constantly and put you to death.

There is this spiritual world I want you to focus your attention to. I am the Supreme God and Ruler of the holy spiritual world in which you have a part.

Although your spirit died in the Garden of Eden, it is going to come back into your body at the Second Coming of Christ. So fight for the opportunity to join

Me in my spiritual world again. It is even more real than your physical world.

Your world is dark with sin and death. My world is full of blazing light, eternal life, perfectly delightful joy, unconditional love, endless peace, riches that this world cannot contain even one percent of it, etc. My territory covers heaven and all the numberless universes. Your world is really nothing.

Since you are a dual-purpose person, having both the spirit and the body, you must begin to relate very seriously to your spiritual self even more than the physical self. That is your opportunity to regain your full stature of being both a spiritual as well as a physical person. I will empower your spirit to destroy Satan."

Even if you are the seed of Adam that has been infected with sin, you also have the seed of God in you. It is His Spirit that He breathed in you when He created Adam. "And the LORD God formed man of the dust of the ground, and breathed into his nostrils the breath of life; and man became a living soul" (Genesis 2:7).

He is working in your soul by refilling you with His Spirit. He has placed Daddy's own spear in your hand to kill those dragons that are called Satan, sin, death, and hell that are trying to destroy you.

He has given you the power to bring break off the teeth of the dragon and to destroy all his powers. You can destroy his powers over you through prayers and fasting.

He is empowering you with His own strength to fight sin in your body. So sin is not your master. The Spirit of God is your Master. So your war is throwing spears into your own flesh and bones to injure or kill yourself.

You are fighting against your unholy passions, desires, urges, will weakened by sin. They are encouraged to rebel against God and against you by the devil. You are at a head on collisions with Satan and your sins.

You will not die but they will because you hate and despise them. "For though we walk in the flesh, we do not war after the flesh: (For the weapons of our warfare are not carnal, but mighty through God to the pulling down of strong holds;)

Casting down imaginations, and every high thing that exalteth itself against the knowledge of God, and bringing into captivity every thought to the obedience of Christ; And having in a readiness to revenge all disobedience, when your obedience is fulfilled" (2 Corinthians 10:3–6).

You have laid hold of the spear of God, that is His Spirit, firmly in hand and are fighting sin with all your strength. You are angry with it for enticing you and pulling you away from righteousness.

You are angry at the image of self that is in your mind that has exalted itself higher than your Maker and Messiah. You are bringing all your self-promoting thoughts under His control.

Walk now in the path of the righteousness of God called sanctification. Feast only on His holy and no more the dishes of sin. You are standing up strong together with the Maker of your life to take over your life and repay all the sins that have been eating your spirit and body by killing them all.

You are killing the falsehoods and flatteries of sin with which it has been driving your life with the weapons of truth. After you have killed or completed your victory and become like God, you will always obey Him faithfully and eternally.

The Lord says, "I am empowering to destroy arsenals of Satan that he delights in. He is proud, selfish, egoistic and arrogant. He arrogantly boasted about His power to do whatever he wanted, which was to seize my throne by force.

He boasted, "And thou saidst in thy heart: I will ascend into heaven, I will exalt my throne above the stars of God, I will sit in the mountain of the covenant, in the sides of the north. I will ascend above the height of the clouds, I will be like the most High" (Isaiah 14:13, 14, DRB).

Destroy Satan by being humble like the Messiah. Your Savior is the Second Godhead. It has not even crossed His mind to be the First Godhead or also take the position of the Third Godhead.

He, actually, became an inferior mortal creature in order to say you. He was born filthy. He depended on His earthly parents for His bath, food, shelter and love.

He got injuries learning how to walk, hitting his thumb in the carpentry workshop with a hammer, etc. He knew being thirsty and hungry. He depended on food, water and air for His physical survival. He knew sadness and loneliness. He was denial and betrayed by his inner circle of friends.

The feudal, ecclesiastical, military, and political powers that were ruling His land executed Him without illegally without any criminal charges. "For let this mind be in you, which was also in Christ Jesus:

Who being in the form of God, thought it not robbery to be equal with God: But emptied himself, taking the form of a servant, being made in the likeness of men, and in habit found as a man. He humbled himself, becoming obedient unto death, even to the death of the cross" Philippians 2:5–8, DRB).

God continued to say, "He did it all for you. That is a friend worth living and dying for. If you become humble and Christ-like, I will give you the same treatment I have given Him. I will resurrect you from the dead or change your body to become immortal like His during His Second Coming.

I am going to reveal myself to you visibly too. I will crown you as a king or queen to serve as a royal power in my kingdom and enjoy its honors, respect, and everything.

The Holy Spirit and I are of the same in mind and heart like Jesus. Fight Satan by being like the Trinity. I was humble enough to give my Son to die for you with the possibility that He might not resurrect from the dead. After the ascension of Christ to heaven, the Holy Spirit moved His capital to your earth. That took humility born out of intense love for you."

Be a Soldier of Christ and break down the citadels of demons. "Thou therefore endure hardness, as a good soldier of Jesus Christ" (2 Timothy 2:3).

Inhale the power of the Lord and breathe it always to keep your spiritually fit soldier. You are fighting all kinds of sins and demons.

Show them that you are a powerful soldier by not surrendering yourself into the hands of your deadly enemy called sin. You are warring for the true wealth.

This wealth is the Spirit of God your Maker and Messiah. So act up like a good soldier. No more surrendering of your will to the control of sin. You are powerful. Let your hands be strong and steady holding on your weapons as you fight sin like soldier hammering on their enemies with their arsenals.

The Most Excellent is the King of kings is the Commander-in-Chief. He is the All-Righteous and All-Loving Messiah. He will help you win the war.

Tirzah used to be the royal residence of the Kings of Israel. They were surrounded with their royal soldiers and looked awesome and magnificent. There is nothing that looks more magnificent, awesome and fearful like waves of military marching off to war.

When you are angry at sin and/or the devil, you have the magnificence and terrifying appearance of the military. The Messiah is completely delighted with you when you are fighting demons and sins in order to be holy and righteous like Him.

He says, "Thou art beautiful, O my love, sweet and comely as Jerusalem terrible as an army set in array" (Song of Solomon 6:4, DRB).

4. Fight Sin like an Eagle attacking its prey

The Lord promises, "It has large pupils that have little diffraction or spreading of incoming light. I will give you sharp, keen and alert spiritual eyesight that can see through temptations and know where they are leading. I will give you the courage to fight sin. You will stop temptations and weaknesses before they make inroads in your mind, heart, body and spirit.

I will also give you the wisdom and intellect to observe your surrounding where ever you are and the courage to run away from sin."

Adrian Pingstone, 2004, Bald Eagle

"From thence she looketh for the prey, and her eyes behold afar off" (Job 39:29, DRB). The eagle has keen and sharp eyesight that can see a snake or rat two miles way up in the sky.

The eagles have powerful and strong beaks. They are shaped like hooks in order to tear off flesh from their preys. "Her young ones shall suck up blood: and wheresoever the carcass shall be, she is immediately there" (Job 39:30, DRB). Eagles have strong legs and claws for holding their prey. They have long claws that hurt their prey.

The Lord asks you, "Be My eagle. When that monsters called sin or Satan come near kick them out of your life by your powerful spiritual legs that are stronger and more dangerous than the claws of eagles. Be a ferocious fighter for righteousness like an eagle."

Eagles live on high trees and high mountains where they build their nests. "She abideth among the rocks, and dwelleth among cragged flints, and stony hills, where there is no access" (Job 39:28, DRB).

Especially of bald eagles, it has been observed that they are monogamous. They remain faithful until death. If inferior creatures can be faithful to their mates, you can do a better job than they.

You are a virgin who is engaged to be married soon to Christ when you were baptized. Keep your vows to be faithful to Him and Him only. "For I have espoused you to one husband, that I may present you as a chaste virgin to Christ" (2 Corinthians 11:2, DRB).

You can also be faithful to Jesus until death or until you meet with Him face to face and live together forever. Temptations and trials come because you are living in this world. They will come whether you are a Christian or not. But it is to your advantage to fight sin and be liberated from its consequences by the Lord.

Even if fighting sin or standing up for God may mean death, be brave and do the right thing. Love the Lord to death. No matter how much you may try to dodge death, you will, one day, die.

Many people are willing to die for causes that have nothing to do with God. If you are required to die for the Messiah, be courageous and go on and witness for Him by your death. You will be a glorious victor on the day of resurrection.

As a martyr, you will stand closer to the Lord than those people whose lives were much more peaceful than yours. "Fear none of those things which thou shalt suffer. Behold, the devil will cast some of you into prison, that you may be tried: and you shall have tribulation ten days. Be thou faithful unto death: and I will give thee the crown of life" (Revelation 2:10, DRB).

Eagles have powerful wings that make them fly very fast. The Lord is ever present in this world. He uses our human expression about how He comes to our rescue.

He says that He flied from heaven to help us as fast as the blowing of a mighty storm. "And he rode upon the cherubims, and flew: and slid upon the wings of the wind" (2 Samuel 22:11, DRB).

He gave this capability of the eagles with wings to fly away from danger to the church during the times of her severe persecutions. "And there were given to the woman two wings of a great eagle, that she might fly into the desert, unto her place, where she is nourished for a time and times, and half a time, from the face of the serpent" (Revelation 12:14, DRB).

The Messiah will give you this capability again when He comes again. He will make you over-comer gravity and all nature that hinder your activities. You will not be earth-bound like most animals.

You will have the ability to fly through space faster than an eagle. You will fly cover billions of miles within only a period of seven days and reach in heaven.

You could have covered that distance within a shorter time but the Lord is going to introduce you to other beings living in other worlds. You are the wonderful baby He loves and for whom He died. So it will take you and all the saved ones seven days to reach there.

Besides, there will be millions of babies and children that angels will be carrying whose parents were not saved. Family reunions and meetings of friends will also take a lot of time. And best of all, you will hold onto Jesus, the Holy Spirit and myself so tightly and wouldn't wont to let go of the Lord and it will take a while to get going.

Unlike many other creatures, eagles do not shed their feathers all at once. They shed them in patches starting from the head. This helps them to still have some feathers in their wings even during molting. They need the wings to enable them to fly to their homes on top of tall trees and high mountains and also to hunt.

The Lord promises, "I am the All-Powerful Supernatural Eagle. I fought Satan. I destroyed that evil power that held you fast as its helpless slave of born in sin, suffering and death.

I broke the teeth of the dragon and rescued you from his evil clutches. I have brought you into my kingdom of love and everlasting.

I have sent you patriarchs, prophets and my beloved Son, Jesus Christ, and the Holy Spirit to help you and bring you to Him. "You have seen what I have done to the Egyptians, how I have carried you upon the wings of eagles, and have taken you to myself.

If therefore you will hear my voice, and keep my covenant, you shall be my peculiar possession above all people: for all the earth is mine. And you shall be to me a priestly kingdom, and a holy nation. These are the words thou shalt speak to the children of Israel" (Exodus 19:4–6).

There is a rush of energy and strength even in the weakest of a father or mother to carry his or her child especially when the child is tired or in danger. Parents carry their children on their shoulders, backs, arms, heads, etc. and run for long distances when there is fire, war has erupted, road is rough, etc. which they would ordinarily not have the strength to do when things are good and peaceful. Eagles have that fit, too. They carry their young on their wings.

The Lord says, "As you journey through the wilderness of this life, you have met and will continue to meet ferocious giants who would love to hate you, poisonous snakes, thirst, starvation, etc. on the way.

Do not faint of fear. I am with you. I will bring you safe to my home. I am the strongest and best of all Parents. I am able to carry you on my wings safely through this hell.

Hunters who shoot at the flying eagles may kill the parent but the young is safe because it is lying on top of its parent. Nothing can get to you except through Me. And I am the Everlasting One. I do not get injured, sick or die.

You will be forever safe. My arms are all around you. I convicted you of you sins. I brought you into tears.

You felt guilty and ashamed of your sins. You repented. You make Me awesomely happy when you are humble. That same power and wisdom will guide you to heaven. You are my baby. I am carrying you in my arms.

We are going to heaven together. "The Lord God, who is your leader, himself will fight for you, as he did in Egypt in the sight of all. And in the wilderness (as thou hast seen) the Lord thy God hath carried thee, as a man is wont to carry his little son, all the way that you have come, until you came to this place" (Deuteronomy 1:30, 31, DRB).

Obey Me as a faithful son or daughter. Do not run wild. Listen to my voice careful and pay attention to my words I spoke through the Bible.

Listen to the voice of the Holy Spirit in your heart to help you do what is right all the time. "You shall obey me, the LORD, who brought you out of Egypt (of sin) with great power and strength; you are to bow down to me and offer sacrifices to me" (2 Kings 17:36, GNB).

Live for Me. Show to the world how loving I am and how much I want to save them. By your words and actions, lead them to Me. You are my prophet/prophetess even though you are not inspired like the prophets of old. "And I make a covenant with you:

I have given you my power and my teachings to be yours forever, and from now on you are to obey me and teach your children and your descendants to obey me for all time to come" (Isaiah 59:21, GNB). I have put my word in your mouth. Speak them for Me.

When you obey Me, I will heal your sin-sick soul and genes that began to die on the day of birth due to bad effects of sin. "But unto you that fear my name, the Sun of justice shall arise, and health in his wings: and you shall go forth, and shall leap like calves of the herd" (Malachi 4:2, DRB). I will give you eternal life.

You will be my eternal son or daughter. Love, reverent, respect, honor and worship only Me as your only God and Father.

If you give Me all your heart, I will transfer you from this world to live in my home permanent. "Jesus said to him: Thou shalt love the Lord thy God with thy whole heart and with thy whole soul and with thy whole mind" (Matthew 22:37, DRB).

Let your love be sincere and total. "If you obey me completely, live by my laws, and win my approval by doing what I command, as my servant David did, I will always be with you. I will make you king of Israel (in heaven)" (1 Kings 11:38, GNB).

I will save you. I will present you in front of all the angels as my beloved son or daughter who loves Me. I give you honor before all the inhabitants of all the universes as child who loves Me so much so that he or she hated the world and even the useless clothes of the world you are wearing. I have better things in heaven for you.

I want to give you complete protection and Peace. I am rescuing you from the devil. I will, soon, drown Satan and his hordes in the Red Sea of hell. He will and his supporters will burn up. They will never pose as a threat to you again.

As a dutiful and All-Loving Father, I want to personally tend to your table. I will supply you with the goodness of heaven. It is a land of plenty of bread and water which will satisfy your soul. Her food and water are extraordinary. They will make your body a superpower of energy and good health.

They will make you to live forever. I will give intellect to your mind, wisdom and understanding of all divine matters to your heart. I will make your heart into supernatural steel that is unbreakable by fire or floods of hell.

You will lean only on Me very happily and trustfully like vines hanging on the stem of a tree for support. "I will make my people strong; they will worship and obey me" The LORD has spoken" (Zechariah 10:12, GNB).

You will love and worship Me willingly and joyfully throughout all eternities of eternities. "And you shall be my people: and I will be your God" (Jeremiah 30:22, DRB).

I will bequeath on you a kingdom that never ends. You will serve Me in my royal court as king or queen to oversee my affairs. You will delegate angels to serve and worship Me.

It is a powerful and rich kingdom that will owns heaven and all the universes and their inhabitants. Everything will be so perfect and wonderful for you.

I chose to have you as My son or daughter. So I willed you to be born out of my spirit. I put my spirit into flesh and fathered you. I own you. But you fell into sin through the Adam. It hurt very terribly to watch a part of my suffering under the load of sin and dying.

You are living in the desert of sin. Your life was empty. It had no meaning. You were dying of thirst and starvation for my love and eternal life. So I came as an eagle and lifted you up. I put you on my wings and flew away with you. I brought you into my spiritual kingdom through repentance and baptism.

Day and night, I protect you from death very tenderly the same way I take care of my own life. You became the love of my heart. You are the apple of eye. You became my passion and, therefore, my life. I want to reveal my glorious Presence to you.

I want you to draw closer to Me every waking moments of your life. "But the Lord's portion is his people: Jacob the lot of his inheritance. He found him in a desert land, in a place of horror, and of vast wilderness: he led him about, and taught him: and he kept him as the apple of his eye.

As the eagle enticing her young to fly, and hovering over them, he spread his wings, and hath taken him and carried him on his shoulders. The Lord alone was his leader: and there was no strange god with him" (Deuteronomy 32:9–12, DRB).

I am like eagle that trains its young how to fly. So every day, I come to you to teach you how to obey and follow my footsteps. You are young, helpless and fragile like an eaglet.

I have to raise you gently and lovingly you up from your pigsty of sin with my hands like an eagle lifting up its young in its powerful beaks but with great care and tenderness.

I stand above you with great excitement because I love you very much. I wish you can hear my booming voice like the sound of many thunders as I tell you that I love you. I am extremely excited about you like an eagle fluttering over its young with its wings.

An eagle lifts and drops its young on its wing and flies with it up into the sky and then drops it. The young one will hurl towards the earth and certain death. But just as it is near the ground, the parent eagle flies under its young and the eaglet falls on its back. It will fly with it back into high up, and then drops it again.

Over and over again, it will show its young one how to fly. Then, one day, as its sees its parents spreading its wings and fly, it will stretch out its wings and begin to fly, too. I have shown you in the Bible how to live a godly life through my Son.

Now, I am walking you through it. I lift you up from your pigsty of sin and make you to stand on holy grounds. I am giving your spiritual feet so that you stand up straight and be strong.

I am teaching you how to walk straight towards Me. "Wherefore, lift up the hands which hang down and the feeble knees: And make straight steps with your feet: that no one, halting, may go out of the way; but rather be healed. Follow peace with all men and

holiness: without which no man shall see God"
(Hebrews 12:12–14, DRB).

I am showing you what is sin and what is the right
thing to do. I am empowering you to do right and leave
sinning.

I am the Almighty and Everlasting Eagle of
heaven and the earth. I fathered you by my power. As
a Dad, I made provisions for you. I created the world
as your shelter, food and water sources.

When Satan, sin and death tried to annihilate you,
I pass death sentences on them instead. I condemned
them on the cross and acquitted you. I am powerful
enough to give you all the support you.

I have all the intellect and wisdom you to take
care of you and fill you with eternal life. "Knowest
thou not, or hast thou not heard? the Lord is the
everlasting God, who hath created the ends of the
earth: he shall not faint, nor labour, neither is there any
searching out of his wisdom. It is he that giveth
strength to the weary, and increaseth force and might
to them that are not.

You shall faint, and labour, and young men shall
fall by infirmity. But they that hope in the Lord shall
renew their strength, they shall take wings as eagles,
they shall run and not be weary, they shall walk and
not faint" (Isaiah 40:28–31, DRB).

Sin has caused every aspect of your being to be
confused, disoriented at times and just plain sick and
dizzy from all the bombardments of temptations and
trials. As the Almighty One, I will make you strong
and sturdy like oak trees. You will withstand all the
storms of life and heat of all problems and, actually,
thrive in spite of them all.

I know that your physical body is tired, exhausted
and fatigued every day from trying to live but I have
given you the Holy Spirit to fill you with power. He
has the power also to give you everlasting energy.

Hold on to Him and you will, soon, become a new
person. You have fallen from the angelic wisdom,

intellect and wisdom which I had placed in Adam before he ruined your life. But I am giving you my life again. You will be strong, robust and shining with eternal good health.

I am coming to get you out of this world. You will fly away like an eagle to heavenly realms where God lives. You will be an everlasting youth with the new blood of Jesus running through your veins. "Who forgiveth all thy iniquities: who healeth all thy diseases.

Who redeemeth thy life from destruction: who crowneth thee with mercy and compassion? Who satisfieth thy desire with good things: thy youth shall be renewed like the eagle's. The Lord doth mercies, and judgment for all that suffer wrong" (Psalms 103:3–6, DRB).

I am writing My Ten Commandments in your heart. You will not be a perpetual sinner but an everlasting sin. "But this shall be the covenant that I will make with the house of Israel, after those days, saith the LORD, I will put my law in their inward parts, and write it in their hearts; and will be their God, and they shall be my people.

And they shall teach no more every man his neighbour, and every man his brother, saying, Know the LORD: for they shall all know me, from the least of them unto the greatest of them, saith the LORD: for I will forgive their iniquity, and I will remember their sin no more" (Jeremiah 31:33, 34).

I will run and meet you with much love and forgiving kindness even before you make the decision to leave your life and sin and come to Me. "And he arose, and came to his father. But when he was yet a great way off, his father saw him, and had compassion, and ran, and fell on his neck, and kissed him" (Luke 15:20).

You are my prodigal child. But I love you more than you can ever know or understand. I am telling you nothing else but the truth.

I place my love into your hands. I am kindly asking you to please accept it. It is yours and free of charge. Take Me as your God and Dad and I will forever be your refuge and Protector. I do not change like the wind.

My love never ends because I do not sin or die. I am the Everlasting Love that created and holds the world together.

I will wipe out sin from your heart so that you may peace and grow intellectually and with wisdom to be able to enjoy my love fully. I will always take care of you and make sure that you are enjoying my tender love every day. Love will be uplifting to your spirit to also love Me back.

It will regenerate your genes and spirit with energy to go out and accomplish impossible dreams in this world and in the world to come because you want to make Me happy. My love is good and honest. It gives life.

It is endearing and loyal. "The LORD hath appeared of old unto me, saying, Yea, I have loved thee with an everlasting love: therefore with lovingkindness have I drawn thee" (Jeremiah 31:3).

My love gives joy and peace that never ends. And so when you learn to love like Me, you have peace and joy that no evil can destroy from this time forth and forever. My love will increase in stages as you are able to absorb it. The increase of my love will never end because I am infinitely All-Love, great and Almighty God of heaven and end who lives forever.

5. Fight demons, sin, and all evil like a wild horse

wpclipart, jumping horse, in public domain

God says, "I have made the bones of horses strong and filled their muscles with energy. He leaps like a locust over bushes, streams and rocks easily as if he has wings."

In some parts of the world, soldiers still use horses as vehicles for fighting in a war. When a horse hears the battle cry, it becomes completely frenzied. It loves action and rushes like the wind into the middle of a fighting without any fear. "Was it you, Job, who made horses so strong and gave them their flowing manes? Did you make them leap like locusts and frighten people with their snorting?

They eagerly paw the ground in the valley; they rush into battle with all their strength. They do not know the meaning of fear, and no sword can turn them back. The weapons which their riders carry rattle and flash in the sun.

Trembling with excitement, the horses race ahead; when the trumpet blows, they can't stand still. At each blast of the trumpet they snort; they can smell a battle before they get near, and they hear the officers shouting commands" (Job 39:19–25, GNB).

Through the power of the Holy Spirit residing in your heart, you are a conqueror of demons, sins and all weaknesses of the flesh. I will give you the strength of the wild horse to paw the ground very swiftly and leap over obstacles smoothly and easily.

Just as I have given horses strength in their bones and flesh, I have filled your spirit with my power and strength to subdue and eliminate transgressions and

369

iniquities from out your flesh. I will make you fearless and strong against the rolling waves of the oceans of sin.

They will not sweep you away. You will not drown. Even in the midst of the oceans, you will stand up straight and undefeated. You will not go under the sea of sin but walk on top of it, a conqueror.

Like arrows that are shot at the horse but it remains fearless, I will make you fearless before this wicked world. The arrows, spears, bullets, missiles, etc. of temptations and trials may heat you like the strikes of lightning but they will not kill you. They will make you stronger in spirit. You are becoming strong like your Heavenly Dad. "And I saw: and behold a white horse, and he that sat on him had a bow, and there was a crown given him, and he went forth conquering that he might conquer" (Revelation 6:2, DRB).

As you battle on against sin, demons and all-wrongs, you will be a white horse that the Master Horseman rides on. He will use you to conquer the world and destroy the power of sin and of the devil.

He will make you to bring peace in the hearts of hurting and suffering people. "And his eyes were as a flame of fire: and on his head were many diadems. And he had a name written, which no man knoweth but himself. And out of his mouth proceedeth a sharp two-edged sword, that with it he may strike the nations.

And he shall rule them with a rod of iron: and he treadeth the winepress of the fierceness of the wrath of God the Almighty. And he hath on his garment and on his thigh written: KING OF KINGS AND LORD OF LORDS" (Revelation 19:12, 15, 16).

When the Lord has brought peace in the world, He will let you loose. You will graze on the rich hillsides of the new earth peacefully and contently like a horse grazing in green pasture.

14 CHAPTER

I AM THE GOOD SHEPHERD

1. The Divine Shepherd is God the Father

"The LORD is my shepherd; I shall not want" (Psalms 23:1). The Lord your God is your Good Shepherd. If He is living in your heart, you will never go around searching for anything that you need. He will supply all your needs.

Bernhard Plockhorst, 1825–1907, The Good Shepherd, in public domain.

A shepherd is a leader. He leads by example, word, and actions. He leads and the sheep follows him whenever he was them to go. God is God because He is the Creator. He creates things in order to lead them as their Shepherd.

The statement of "I shall not want" is not necessary about earthly needs being met by the Shepherd but that you do not need another God when He lives in your heart. He will meet your passion to live and to excel.

He will satisfy your drives for the perfect feelings. He will fulfill your desires for the most blissful moments. He will supply perfect joys that last eternity. He will give you better joys than this world can.

A sheep means the last one that knows or that listens and follows. The humble sheep will always listen and follows the Divine Sheep. He will always be calling for His sheep because it is the last side of Him. He is the Head and the sheep is the body.

The Head belongs to the body or church and the body belongs to the Head. "Giving thanks unto the Father, which hath made us meet to be partakers of the inheritance of the saints in light" (Colossians 1:12).

\The flock follows the owner with happy noises when they are being taken out to graze and to drink water. These are the kinds of followers that are appreciative of the care of the Shepherd for them. They offer Him continual praises because He is loving and caring.

They treat God the Father with respect and love because He has made them a part of His divine and royal family. They give Him all honors and praises because he had made them His holy, perfect, and awesome inheritance from this earth.

He is, now, leading them to walk in the light of His wisdom and intelligence so that they can bond together.

The holy Shepherd is also a Pastor. The definition of the word pastor is "to put to pasture."

In short, it means the shepherd. There is only one Pastor in heaven and on the earth. He is the Messiah of God. He employs men and women to work for Him.

Some of them these pastors are called disciples, apostles, prophets, teachers, rabbits, priests, bishops, elders, etc. Some pastors are good but some are bad.

God the Father Himself is the Pastor of this world. He is assisted by the Messiah and the Holy Spirit.

When He sent the Messiah and the Holy Spirit into the world, He said, "And I will give you pastors according to mine heart, which shall feed you with knowledge and understanding" (Jeremiah 3:15).

He said that He has given the world Pastors that have met or fulfilled all the Laws of His heart. They will lead you into green pastures that will feed your minds, hearts, bodies, and spirits eternally well. They will take His knowledge and impart it to you to make you holy and righteous.

They will take His wisdom and understanding of matters and teach you to be intelligent and wise like Himself. They will appoint some of you as pastors to look after His earthly flock.

Human beings are foolish like sheep. They can walk over a cliff and fall into the bottomless pit of sin with their wide eyes open.

They are not only falling into the pit but are pushing others along with them to die in the same way like them. "All we like sheep have gone astray; we have turned every one to his own way; and the LORD hath laid on him the iniquity of us all" (Isaiah 53:6).

But since God the Father knows that human beings are just sheep, He sent the Good Shepherd to take care of them. He is the God and King of heaven and the earth. And the Good Shepherd died so that His sheep can live again on a higher and eternal level.

He is assuring them of His undying love for them, saying, "I am the good shepherd: the good shepherd giveth his life for the sheep" (John 10:11).

The true and most excellent Shepherd has died for your sins. He will make you good and excellent like Himself. He is putting His excellent Spirit into you. You will no longer be a foolish sheep but a wise one.

Because the Messiah suffered and died for the salvation of the lost children of God the Father, He has been promoted by Him as His equal in power and glory. He is carrying the name of the First Godhead as the God the Father of all.

He has decreed that everyone in heaven, on the earth and all the universes worship the Second Godhead, the Messiah, as much as they do worship Him. "Wherefore God also hath highly exalted him, and given him a name which is above every name:

That at the name of Jesus every knee should bow, of things in heaven, and things in earth, and things under the earth; And that every tongue should confess that Jesus Christ is Lord, to the glory of God the Father" (Philippians 2:9–11).

God the Father says that whatever good all His children in heaven and all the universes do to Jesus will be as if they are doing to Him. All the love and praises they give to the Messiah are being given to Him, too. So they should all look to Jesus as God and Daddy.

The Shepherd and His sheep are always moving together because He was kind enough to get into the dirt, blood, and sweat of the hard work of rescuing the sheep from the mouths of the dragon. He beat Satan and shook him really bad until he dropped the sheep from his mouth.

He rescued His flock from the hands of the chief of darkness. "Who hath delivered us from the power of darkness, and hath translated us into the kingdom of his dear Son" (Colossians 1:13).

God the Father has now handed over the kingdom of light into the hands of His Beloved Son. He has asked Him to get His sheep out of this dark world of sin and death and resettle them up there.

The Beloved Son has now taken your mind, heart and spirit out of this world of sin. He has made you to live in Him.

If anybody wants to look for you, he or she will find you living together in the Messiah. That is the only place where you can be found.

You have and Him are one. "In whom we have redemption through his blood, even the forgiveness of sins" (Colossians 1:14).

He forgave your sins because He loves you. He untied the power of sin from your mind, heart, spirit, and flesh and threw it away. He not only has washed away all your sins but has transfused His blood throughout your veins and arteries so much so that you now look like Him.

You and the Messiah are now one Person. But it does not stop there. "Who is the image of the invisible

God, the firstborn of every creature" (Colossians 1:15).

The Son is the exact image and form of God His Father. He looks, talks, and acts just like His Father. So now, you are not only looking like the Messiah but like God the Father also.

The Messiah is His firstborn Son and you are the baby of the family. You came out of His Spirit.

He is the very One from whom proceeded all creations. He spat all the universes out of His mouth. And this earth, too, is the production of His All-Powerful Spirit. There are creations human beings know about but there are many more that the Creator has not yet revealed to them.

They are all made by Him and Him alone. "For by him were all things created, that are in heaven, and that are in earth, visible and invisible, whether they be thrones, or dominions, or principalities, or powers: all things were created by him, and for him" (Colossians 1:16).

He made kings and queens who live all over the universes in order to replica Him as the King of kings. He made them helpers of His endless dominions.

He made some people the presidents and chiefs of His territories. Everything exists by His power. And, of course, they were created by Him.

He is God the Everlasting, All-Powerful, and All-Knowing. Everything stands by the power of the Creator. "And he is before all things, and by him all things consist. And he is the head of the body, the church: who is the beginning, the firstborn from the dead; that in all things he might have the preeminence" (Colossians 1:17, 18).

He is the Head and the sheep is Body because He lives from everlasting to everlasting. He is greater and more powerful than death. That was why He conquered it and rose out of the grave as an Almighty Victor. He is giving help to everyone who wants to live again after death. Everything and everyone presents themselves before to beg for life. He supplies

His life and energy to all with royal liberality.

II. The Desires of Ages

Even the throats of the young and powerful lions can burn with thirst when they find no water. His stomach can gnaw terrible with hunger which can kill him if he finds no prey.

But those who have made the King of kings the Commander of their lives will be protected from dangers that kill love, faith, hope, and trust. "The young lions do lack, and suffer hunger: but they that seek the LORD shall not want any good thing" (Psalms 34:10).

All the temporal needs of the saints may not all be fulfilled but He will give you the basics of life such as love, belonging, shelter, food, water, etc. "But my God shall supply all your need according to his riches in glory by Christ Jesus" (Philippians 4:19).

God the Father will fulfill all your needs because He is your Daddy. He will draw you ever closer to from now on and through all eternities so that you can enjoy His abundances to the full.

He wants you to enjoy the glories of His love, power, peace, joy, etc. which He has already stored for you through His Messiah and your Messiah.

The Great Shepherd is more desirable than the things of the earth. And at the end of time when earthquakes will shake the foundation of the earth and all the security, safety, joy, and peace of mankind have collapsed, One Man will remain standing after the dust has settled down.

He is Desire of all Nations. He will meet the desires of all the people who have placed their hope and faith in Him. "And I will shake all nations, and the desire of all nations shall come: and I will fill this house with glory, saith the LORD of hosts" (Haggai 2:7). The Desire of all Nations will give them new life.

III. The valley of death

Ezekiel is in the valley of dried bones

You can fall into the deep valley of death accidentally. You can fall into it through troubles not of your own making. You can also fall down there because of some bad choices you made in your life.

However, you are never alone when you fallen into the deep valley of death. The Shepherd is not going to blame the sheep for its fall.

He just wants to get His sheep out of that deep hole or it will die. "Yea, though I walk through the valley of the shadow of death, I will fear no evil: for thou art with me; thy rod and thy staff they comfort me." (Psalms 23:4).

God is walking down there in the valley of death with. He is always beside you whether you are a good child or not. He just wants to help His little lamb.

He will hold up your courage. He will give you plenty of strength to get out of that deep hole. Never think that you are alone especially when things get really bad.

Do not faint and die because demons and troubles have surrounded you thick like bees. The goodness and Sabbath rest of God is always with you. You will not desire or need anything other than Him alone who made you and has saved you.

He promises you, "Fear thou not; for I am with thee: be not dismayed; for I am thy God: I will strengthen thee; yea, I will help thee; yea, I will uphold thee with the right hand of my righteousness" (Isaiah 41:10). Your Creator promises to always be with you come sunshine or rain.

He asks you not to allow your head turn around and around in confusion as to the strange and evil things taking place in your life. "The LORD is my light and my salvation; whom shall I fear? the LORD is the strength of my life; of whom shall I be afraid?" (Psalms 27:1).

The everlasting light of God has already been shinning on you before you were born. It is the light of creative energy. It will give you love, joy, peace, eternal life, wisdom, intelligent, and strength from eternity to eternity.

It is your salvation from wrong into right, from sin into righteousness, and from death into eternal life. There is nothing to be afraid of you.

You have the full power of God working in you to hold you steady and make you immortal. You say, "I have set the LORD always before me: because he is at my right hand, I shall not be moved" (Psalms 16:8).

You have chosen to be married to God so that He may save, protect, and provide for you. Continue to look up to Him like a sweet wife who adores her husband and thinks that he is able to do anything to make her happy. He is your refuge in good and in bad times.

 He is holding you with His right hand of love and tenderness because you are on an eternal date with Him. So stop fear when you see the luminaries running around crazing and the storms are blowing really badly. Do not fear when the bottom has fallen out and surface of the earth is sinking into her own bosom.

You are in God's hands. In spite of all these temptations and tragedies of life, good things are coming out of your spirit.

The Lord is making something excellent out of you. He is making you as sweet as honey and as strong as a lion. You must live in fear anymore. Everything is going to be alright.

God is still with you even when things are bad. He who gave you life will protect you from harm. He is watching over you.

He will empower you by holding His right hand of power. He will lead you in the way of holiness, righteousness, faith, hope, love, and peace.

He will hold you up above the storms of this life. "O give thanks unto the LORD, for he is good: for his mercy endureth for ever" (Psalms 107:1). Praise the Lord for His excellent sweetness is everlasting. His rest and grace will follow you wherever you because He is your everlasting strength.

He is your Shepherd and you are His little sweet lamb. He will feed you with green, nutritious, and grass. He will protect you with His rod that gave Satan a fatal wound on the head. He is guiding with His royal staff to provide for all your needs.

He blessed the men and women of yester year's faith as an example of how He is going to take care of you. "But made his own people to go forth like sheep, and guided them in the wilderness like a flock" (Psalms 78:52).

He was their Shepherd. They were His beloved sheep. He cared for them very tenderly. He was compassionate with their weaknesses. He empathized with their sorrows, pain and sickness.

He was their cool shade when it was very hot. He was their warmth when it was very cold.

He was their shield when wolves, hyenas, lions, bears, etc. were lurking nearby. He was their shelter. He was the provider of their food, water, and clothes.

He gave them intelligence, wisdom, and strength. In summary, He was their love.

The Lord is your Shepherd. He will keep you safe from the traps of demons who are trying to destroy your faith all the time. "O fear the LORD, ye his saints: for there is no want to them that fear him" (Psalms 34:9).

You will see great powers when you are walking with the Lord. He will put holiness in your body because there has never been and will never be a righteous and holy God like Him.

You have no other desire but to be just like Him in every way. He will stabilize your life. He will make you strong and able to face any challenge and conquer.

IV. Little foxes that are ruining the Lord's vineyard

The Messiah words are always true. He told all of you to be careful of lions, lionesses, hyenas, wolves, robbers, etc. who find their ways into the house throw crags, holes, etc. to steal the sheep.

Demons entered into the hearts of the human race to persecute and murder them. "Verily, verily, I say unto you, He that entereth not by the door into the sheepfold, but climbeth up some other way, the same is a thief and a robber" (John 10:1).

Thieves and robbers never come to rob or steal when the owner of the sheep is wide awake. They do not try to break into the house through the door when the guard is fully armed and is standing at the door.

Robbers are violent people. They can kill the owner of the sheep in order to rob him of his sheep. That is how demons sneak into the minds and hearts of human beings to make them sin and then murder them.

The Messiah came in open view of heaven and earth as prophesied in the Bible. He fulfilled every prophecy about His birth, life, death, resurrection and ascension to heaven.

No one on earth has fulfilled all the prophecies to the letter like the He did. "But he that entereth in by the door is the shepherd of the sheep. And a stranger will they not follow, but will flee from him: for they know not the voice of strangers" (John 10:4, 5).

There were men who rose up as the Christ before the Messiah started His mission. But none of them have received world acclaimed like the true Savior. Many recognize the voice of God in Him, and they followed Him. There will arise many false Christs before His Second Coming. They will all die out when He takes His place on the earth again.

The true Messiah is everlasting in nature. "Then said Jesus unto them again, Verily, verily, I say unto you, I am the door of the sheep. All that ever came before me are thieves and robbers: but the sheep did not hear them. I am the door: by me if any man enter in, he shall be saved, and shall go in and out, and find pasture.

The thief cometh not, but for to steal, and to kill, and to destroy: I am come that they might have life, and that they might have it more abundantly" (John 10:7–10).

The demons and false Messiahs are like predation to the sheep. There is a heavy loss of sheep to predators. Sheep are constantly being attacked by them because they usually do not defend themselves. They do not try to run away like goats. Even if they survive the attacks, they can die from the injuries.

They were the first animals to be domesticated because of their docility and almost kind faces. But they do suffer from many parasites, viruses, and infectious diseases. They are forms of sin that have infected the flock of God beginning from the Garden of Eden when Adam and Eve sinned.

Sin is a thief, robber, and murderer. It is making the lives of the people on the earth very miserable and killing them. But the Messiah is inviting the sheep to come back to Him to receive good health that will last beyond eternity.

The doorkeeper is the Holy Spirit. He knows both the sheep and the Shepherd. When the Owner of the sheep comes, the Holy Spirit opens for Him the door.

He comes in and washes away the sins of the sinner. "To him the porter openeth; and the sheep hear his voice: and he calleth his own sheep by name, and leadeth them out. And when he putteth forth his own sheep, he goeth before them, and the sheep follow him: for they know his voice" (John 10:3, 4).

The Messiah builds His righteous character in him or her. He opens the door of the heart and they walk out together to explore life. The sheep is no longer proud and self-centered. He or she shares his or her life together with the Messiah. They know each other.

God said that He came among the people of the world. He walked among them on this earth. He prepared for them both physical and spiritual foods. He planted foods for them that produced plenty of fruits.

He gave them the Holy Spirit who has plenty of good fruits. "But the fruit of the Spirit is love, joy, peace, longsuffering, gentleness, goodness, faith, Meekness, temperance: against such there is no law (Galatians 5:22, 23). He provided for them plenty of fortunes that are enough for everyone on earth.

But when He handed the earth to mankind, troubles started. "And I brought you into a plentiful country, to eat the fruit thereof and the goodness thereof; but when ye entered, ye defiled my land, and made mine heritage an abomination" (Jeremiah 2:7, 8).

The people He had appointed to pastor them in the churches, governments, business sectors, etc. have done a very poor job. Bad pastors are savages. They do not have personal relationships with God.

The Lord your God says that He has provided means for the church to be supported by kind and generous believers. They are paying tithes and offerings to finance His mission of saving the world.

They are building schools, universities, hospitals, nursing homes, farms, and do many other businesses to spread the Gospel and to train men and women to be spiritual.

wpclipart, Corsac fox
Vulpes, in public domain

God has His people among the pastors. Satan also has sent his agents as pastors in the church. They are the foxes who are ruining the Lord's vineyard. "Take us the foxes, the little foxes, that spoil the vines: for our vines have tender grapes" (Song of Solomon 2:15).

The vineyard is the Lord's church. But demons have invaded her through their stooges. They masquerade as pastors sent by the Lord. Some are plain demoniacs, sorcerers, witches, etc.

Some pastors in the West practice Buddhism or Hinduism that involved in Satanism to get demoniac powers to steal sermons from other preachers and/or Bible students to help them excel in preaching in televisions, radios, internets, etc.

Many priests in both the Catholics and Protestant are heavily involved in sorceries to help them preach or read the minds of the flocks in order to mind control them. Some of them even steal, murder, cheat, commit adulteries, etc. These are not pastors who meet temptations and may fall but they repent from their sins and follow God once again. To err is human.

The savage pastors are the habitual sinners who take pride in breaking the law of God. They look holy outside by inwardly, they are demons. "Beware of false prophets, which come to you in sheep's clothing, but inwardly they are ravening wolves" (Matthew 7:15).

Some pastors are not striving for holiness like the Messiah did. He was a devote worshipper and student of the scriptures.

He was shepherded His church on earth better than anyone has ever shepherded a church. They are savages.

Among them are the Anti-Christs, false prophets, false miracle workers, false healers, lazy pastors who do not enjoy personal devotions, etc. "For the pastors are become brutish, and have not sought the LORD: therefore they shall not prosper, and all their flocks shall be scattered" (Jeremiah 10:21).

They invited themselves to the pulpits when the Lord had not commanded them to shepherd His flock. They are not giving glory to God but to themselves. They will not produce generations of faithful followers who will live to honor the Lord and not themselves. The flock tends to imitate their leaders.

If a leader is spiritually weak, the flock will tend to be generally weak, too. They will not follow God wisely and passionately.

They have handed the sheep of the Lord over to evil spirits by the way they live or preach. It all started with Adam and Eve. They invited demons in the world. But these demons are their enemies.

They have brought transgressions and sorrow into the beautiful heritage that He had given to mankind. They are destroying not only human lives but their habitation as well.

There are greedy people among the leadership of the church who are using force or tricks to empower themselves by using church. They are pushing out conscientious Christians out of the church because they have refused to use corrupt methods to forge ahead.

They feast on the good things of the church but care less about the spiritual health of the members. They are abusing the blessings the Messiah has poured on the church.

They use the flock as stepping stones to greater glories for themselves and/or for personal indulgences in unholy passions. "Seemeth it a small thing unto you to have eaten up the good pasture, but ye must tread down with your feet the residue of your pastures?

And to have drunk of the deep waters, but ye must foul the residue with your feet? And as for my flock, they eat that which ye have trodden with your feet; and they drink that which ye have fouled with your feet" (Ezekiel 34:18, 19).

They have crushed the faith of many believers by their bold rebellion against the King of kings. They have once drunk of the fountain of life.

They have once met God. But they keep these heavenly experiences to themselves.

They refuse to share their experiences with the church so that they, too, may have a hunger for their Maker. They make the church look like a polluted dirty river that is not worth drinking water from.

Some of them are downright selfish. They will not preach for fear that sinners become decent people and take their places in the churches. There are whole races that have been ignored systematically for fear that if they become Christians, they will take over the leadership of the church.

They use name of Jesus to fight them. They claim that these people hate Christians and Jews. They turn good Christians against who could have reached out to them and brought them into the church.

There are tribalism and nepotism taking place in every race under the sun because of Jesus. They are the Whites, Blacks, Semites, Indians, American Indians, Yellow, and the in-betweens. One tribe wants to enjoy the blessings of Jesus alone and keep the other tribes out. These are savage pastors.

They are brutal in the sermons and comments on purpose to keep others out of the church or from aiming high to work for God. "Therefore thus saith the Lord GOD unto them; Behold, I, even I, will judge between the fat cattle and between the lean cattle. Because ye have thrust with side and with shoulder, and pushed all the diseased with your horns, till ye have scattered them abroad" (Ezekiel 34:20, 21).

The Messiah and Helper of the world said that He will come after the people who use His name wrongly to throw or keep people out of the church. He will punish them. He will throw out the pastors, evangelists, and other church workers who are fattening or empowering themselves by using the church.

Since you are still in the world of sin, do not be surprised to find that spiritual pastors are getting fewer and fewer as time draws to a close. The majority of them are upholding the causes of demons.

They are destroying the Church of God instead of building her. "Many pastors have destroyed my vineyard, they have trodden my portion under foot, they have made my pleasant portion a desolate wilderness" (Jeremiah 12:10). They are stepping on the heads of the flock and grinding them into the dust with their ironed feet.

The bad pastors have driven many people out of the Church by their sinful lifestyles which they have found it impossible to hide from the scrutiny of the world. Their lukewarm sermons and, sometimes, downright Satanic ones deny the existence of God.

They promote homosexual activities. They fight states and nations that do not legalize support homosexuality.

Once the Law of God is out of the door, in come immoralities, stealing, Sabbath breaking, racism, political jabs, tribalism, support for ethnic discriminations or violence, pride, jealousies, envy, etc. through the windows. They have driven many people from the churches.

Some of them have sent their politicians overseas to fight promising them swift victories from Jesus Christ. But war is war.

It takes victims from both sides of the opposing forces. Without shame, these pastors damp the politicians and look for the next to control.

The wicked shepherds have also destroyed the church. "They have made it desolate, and being desolate it mourneth unto me; the whole land is made desolate, because no man layeth it to heart" (Jeremiah 12:11).

She is crying out to her Maker for help. In fact, the whole earth is crying out to God their Good Shepherd for help. Most people on earth are pagans because the leadership of the church have failed to live up to the divine standard set for them by the Messiah Himself. Had all of them been as holy and righteous as the Messiah, most of the population of the people on the earth would have been deeply spiritually. There is time for change.

Many of them would have come to the Messiah by now. But the pastors do not really care. They only worry about personal issues and not demonstrating divinity by word, deed, and lifestyle to the world.

V.   Savage pastors will be punished

Crooked shepherds are foolish men and women who are driven by their own greed for power, fame or wealth. They lack vision that will multiply the glory of God on earth.

They have not grasped the deep spiritual context of the Bible that could have created deep longing for the Lord their Messiah. They could have yearned for Him more deeply than words can express instead of promoting themselves on the expense of the Church. Since they lack vision, they tend to make bad judgments.

When troubles come, they abandon the flock and try to save only themselves. "Woe be unto the pastors that destroy and scatter the sheep of my pasture! saith the LORD. Therefore thus saith the LORD God of Israel against the pastors that feed my people; Ye have scattered my flock, and driven them away, and have not visited them: behold, I will visit upon you the evil of your doings, saith the LORD" (Jeremiah 23:1, 2).

Bad priests or pastors are a curse not only to themselves but the church. They are the leaders of the church but they are not leading her right. They are the persecutors of the Holy Spirit. They counteract whatever He is doing with bad influences that make the church to crawl instead of running in full speed into the arms of the Lord.

Wicked shepherds do not have the wisdom of God to know that the times are bad and that they are contributing to the disasters that have come and/or are coming into the world. The flocks are scattering right under their noses but they feel no shame that they are the causes of the troubles in the Church.

They are accruing punishments on themselves by their sinful acts against the Church. They will not escape punishments on the Day of Judgment.

On that day, the Lord will not tolerate their presence in His sight any more. He will chase them away. He will cut off His life from flowing into them.

Unfortunately, the downfalls of many Christians are caused by thoughtless pastors. They drive out believers from the churches only to fall headlong into the valley of death.

Their evil words and/or actions against the holy flock of the Lord will get them into real trouble with the Great Shepherd of all. "Woe be unto the pastors that destroy and scatter the sheep of my pasture! saith the LORD" (Jeremiah 23:1).

He orders pastors not to give the flock their minds when they are disappointed or angry. "Recompense to no man evil for evil. Provide things honest in the sight of all men" (Romans 12:17). They must in no way take personal revenge on those who do not like or love them.

They must never practice the policy of pay backs. You know that as a shepherd you are supposed to be spiritually stronger than the weak sheep you are shepherding. So why all these hatred and revenges against them even though they had angered or disappointed you?

You are not their leader but God. You, too, are His follower. So you have not right to scatter the flock because of personal issues against them.

Do not commit the same sins the priests of Israel of days gone but did against God and the people by involving themselves idol worship, sorceries, alcoholism, adulteries, lying, stealing, Sabbath-breaking, etc. They made the people to stop coming to pray in the temple.

It was a matter of time when they, too, fell into disgrace before the Lord. The wicked influences of the priests led them astray. Israel did not escape punishment.

They have been driven out to live among the nations. They have suffered greatly because of their unfaithfulness to God. Do not think that wicked Christian pastors will escape punishment. If anything, they will suffer worse than the Twelve Tribes of Israel who used to be as strong as a young lion when they were faithful to God.

They know about the unconditional love of God yet they are abusing it every day. But you are taking advantage of Him by destroying His church thinking that He is too loving to punish you. You are accusing Him of being immoral just like.

But He will show you who is glorious and not to be fooled. "Therefore thus smith the LORD God of Israel against the pastors that feed my people; Ye have scattered my flock, and driven them away, and have not visited them: behold, I will visit upon you the evil of your doings, saith the LORD" (Jeremiah 23:2).

You have cause the fall of many Christians by your lukewarm attitude towards spiritual things. They do not have any good example to follow in how to live like God.

Go out and bring them back into the church.

Confess your sins to those you have hurt by your bad example.

Promise to them that you will try to follow God from now on. And do not run after them to glorify yourself but their Maker and Savior. If you do not set things right, the promised that He will make you to be swept sweep away with the floods of destruction that will swamp the earth that will take place very soon.

Savage, uncouth, and unrighteous pastors would ululate not with joy but with pain on the Day of Judgment when the Lord will rise up to punish them. "Howl, ye shepherds, and cry; and wallow yourselves in the ashes, ye principal of the flock: for the days of your slaughter and of your dispersions are accomplished; and ye shall fall like a pleasant vessel" (Jeremiah 25:35).

The presidents of the flock who mismanaged their positions will cry out at the top of their voices on the day when each of them will be ordered to give an account of all the evil he or she had done to the people. They had cause great pain to the people. But now the tables are turned.

They will receive great pains from which there will be no escape. They had thrown the flock into the ashes and dirt.

There will they also end on the day when the time of probation will be over. They had led the Lamb of God and his flock to the slaughter. He will also lead them to the slaughter unless they repent and turn away from worshipping demons.

They will end as nothing like Cain who murdered Abel, his brother, over how to worship the Lord. He was cursed. And today, he has no descendant living among the people of the earth.

The shepherds were supposed to be the slaves of the Lord's flock. "And the shepherds shall have no way to flee, nor the principal of the flock to escape" (Jeremiah 25:35).

Instead, they lord it over them and mistreated

horribly. They did not present a loving and caring God to them. But they took advantage of the Lord to empower and enrich themselves over the people.

They appointed themselves as presidents of the church for gain. And they will not escape punishment for their greed in trying to steal the power of God over His people.

Out of their mouths will come out loud lamentations and mourning on the day of revenge. Leaders of the churches will scream with pain like women ululating at wedding parties. "A voice of the cry of the shepherds, and an howling of the principal of the flock, shall be heard: for the LORD hath spoiled their pasture" (Jeremiah 25:36).

They will weep without loud cries because the Lord has rejected them. He will abandon unfaithful men and women who used to pasture His flock.

Since the salvation of the Church has come, she must not waste any more time mourning about bad pastors, priests, rabbis, deacons, deaconesses, etc. She must stop giving power to these bad people to boast that they have the power to make the lives of believers miserable and send them to hell if they want.

Instead, she should look up into the compassionate eyes of the Lord all the time and rejoice always in His abundant love and care. She should be taking her Messiah every day for giving her a second chance to be eternally happy and healthy again.

Jesus Christ is your Savior and not angels or human beings. He has lambs that are terribly mistreated in the Church.

Their pride is injured. Their livelihood has been taken away from them.

Their good names are destroyed. But in spite of all their sufferings, they have refused to abandon God their Savior, they still cling to that hope that He will rescue them one day.

The Lord has promised, "And I will gather the remnant of my flock out of all countries whither I have driven them, and will bring them again to their folds; and they shall be fruitful and increase.

And I will set up shepherds over them which shall feed them: and they shall fear no more, nor be dismayed, neither shall they be lacking, saith the LORD" (Jeremiah 23:3, 4).

The Lord has promised to gather all of them in His tender arms. He will bandage the broken bonds. He will pour healing oil on their sores.

He will carry the wounded and sick in His tender arms. He will bring back into His fold those who have been abused and driven out to find pasture in the wild. He still loves them. He needs them to be in His flock. They will bear fruits of righteousness. They will grow into big, healthy, powerful, and eternal sheep.

VI. Repentant pastors will be saved

Do the priests, rabbis, pastors, etc. really know the Lord they purport to love and serve? They need to take time to search for Him with all their minds, hearts, feelings, strength, etc.

All keepers of God's Law must learn that the Law is their relative. It is their friend. It is not condemning them for their sins in order to send them to hell.

It is their family. It is guiding them in good thoughts, words, and actions in order to bring joy and contentment in their hearts.

Bad pastors are redeemable. Instead of having God only in their heads, they need to invite Him into their hearts also. They should have a passion for Him and not just doctrines and theories.

It is not weakness to have strong feelings for Him. It is not weakness to cry, mourn, and pine for Him openly as well as privately. It is good to be called paranoia, fool, emotional, etc. for His sake.

Though they may badmouth you, most people are more comfortable around people who have strong feelings for God than the strong and emotionless theologians.

Loving, warm, intelligent, and deeply spiritual sermons that go deep into human souls come out of men and women who had very deep passions during the times when they were preparing the sermons.

The Messiah was not strong as steel in His emotions. He was warm, loving, passionate as well as wise, intelligent, strong, and powerful.

If there is no strong commitment and passion for God in your life, it means that you do not know Him. "The priests said not, Where is the LORD? and they that handle the law knew me not: the pastors also transgressed against me, and the prophets prophesied by Baal, and walked after things that do not profit" (Jeremiah 2:8).

You are a pastor who is like a flea or bug. You are a blood sucker both on God and the flock. You are killing them. You are sucking out their strength instead of feeding them with good spiritual food so that they can build good spiritual health in their souls.

The false Christs, false prophets, false miracle workers, false healers, etc. are disciples of Baal or Satan. They are chasing after a person who was defeated right from heaven when he rebelled against God before he came down here and deceived Adam and Eve.

As shepherds, you are supposed to walk ahead of the flock and show them how to be holy and righteous. Instead, your pet sins have confused them. They do not know whether to pursue holiness seriously or keep some pet sins like you.

The whole church has become lukewarm because of you. "And unto the angel of the church of the Laodiceans write; These things saith the Amen, the faithful and true witness, the beginning of the creation of God." (Revelation 3:14).

A message has gone out from the Messiah to all the pastors whose weak spiritual influences have made the last day churches as lukewarm as the old church of Laodicea in the days of the first apostles of the Messiah. They and their churches love to show off that they love the Lord.

They carry out worship services when they did not mean a word they are telling Him. He in whom you have placed your faith is talking to you.

You call Him the Amen or the Answer to all your needs. He will hold you up with both of His hands. He is the Faith that draws all believers to Himself.

He is true Friend and Helper of all. He was already in existence before the beginning of all creations.

He says that He knows everything that is in your heart, mind, spirit and genes. He knows everything you have done and the ones you are up to. You have never been too cold or dead.

You have never been a fire that burns all sins and demons around you. "I know thy works, that thou art neither cold nor hot: I would thou wert cold or hot. So then because thou art lukewarm, and neither cold nor hot, I will spue thee out of my mouth" (Revelation 3:15, 16).

He said that if you only would show yourself to Him as dead cold or a burning fire, He would have decided long ago what to do with you. But you are like beer that is still brewing in the pot.

It is lukewarm. And like it you are neither very cold and nor boiling hot with the fire of the Holy Spirit. He said that He does not have a thirst for your lukewarm reception and love.

He is shifting you around in His mouth with His tongue and because you are unpalatable, He is about to spew you out.

You have no reason to complain if He spews you out. "Because thou sayest, I am rich, and increased with goods, and have need of nothing; and knowest not that thou art wretched, and miserable, and poor, and blind, and naked" (Revelation 3:17).

You all claim that you are the total sum of what is called wealth. Everyone should look at you to see what true riches mean. You have already excelled in riches than everyone around you.

You never go around to anyone or even to God to beg for anything. But you have not learned that you are a broken up man or woman who does not have any clothes on and even an underwear. You are completely messed up and sinful in your thoughts.

You were born spiritually blind, deaf, and dumb. You are soiling yourself with your filthy sins.

He is asking you to come to Him. He wants you to take Him as your way of life. Look up to Him for everything.

He will show you how to buy true riches from Him. Yes, buy real gold that died in the fire and came out crystal clean, pure, holy and eternal.

This gold or Messiah will make you truly rich and wealthy for His own glory. You will live in Him and will expound His glories throughout all the universes. He will dress you up with beautiful white veils that glitter and shine brighter than the stars because they are shinning with His divine beauty.

His kinds of clothes are the ones you will put on. "I counsel thee to buy of me gold tried in the fire, that thou mayest be rich; and white raiment, that thou mayest be clothed, and that the shame of thy nakedness do not appear; and anoint thine eyes with eyesalve, that thou mayest see" (Revelation 3:18).

No one will ever notice or observe that you were once brought down low by sin. They will not even make mentions of it. They will not remind you that you used to be a sinner. He will make your eyes like of His own relatives who are called God the Father and God the Holy Spirit.

They will be intelligent and wise eyes because they will be filled with His Spirit. He will be looking at the world through your eyes because He is your brother. You will share the same eyes, mouth, and ears.

He says that as for Himself, He loves each and every one of you from time immemorial. He has placed His love on you, and He will go on loving you from eternity to eternity.

Since His brotherly love has placed you into His hands, it is imperative that He gives you the necessary rebukes and painful disciplines because you are His beloved brother or sister. "As many as I love, I rebuke and chasten: be zealous therefore, and repent" (Revelation 3:19).

He loves you very much. That is why He is asking to change by mourning for all your sins and turning away from them completely.

He is talking on behalf of God the Father, God the Holy and on His own behalf, too, when He said, "Behold, I stand at the door, and knock: if any man hear my voice, and open the door, I will come in to him, and will sup with him, and he with me" (Revelation 3:20).

He said that He has shown up in front of your heart's door. He said that it is not only Him but God the Father and God the Holy Spirit who have all been standing, waiting for a very long time, and knocking at your heart's door. He said that your heart is actually His own heart that He lent you for a little while.

He is knocking at His own door when He is knocking at your heart's door. He has been knocking so long, loud, and loud that His hand is hurting as if set on fire. His hand has all but got burned knocking at your door.

He is waiting very patiently for the slightest chance that you may, one day, hear the knock at your door and hear His voice asking you to let Him come in.

If you will open that door that belongs to both of you, He will enter in as your Trinity God. He has come so that you will all enjoy everlasting dinner together.

God describes His throne to that of the

bridegroom when he sits down beside his bride. The bridegroom is the center of attention because of his love for his bride. Everyone who comes into the wedding looks up for the bridegroom and congratulates him.

The Lord said that His throne is very honorable like that of bridegroom who is wedding his wife. The party revolves around him.

He is the center of attention. But the party that goes around the Creator is happier than of the best weddings on earth. His throne is the throne of everlasting love, compassion, joy, and peace. He is the Spirit to whom all honors, respect, love, etc. are accord in heaven and all the universes.

He says that He will share the throne of the center of attention with you on one condition. You must leave your life of sin.

You must conquer it by His blood and the power of the Holy Spirit. "To him that overcometh will I grant to sit with me in my throne, even as I also overcame, and am set down with my Father in his throne" (Revelation 3:21).

You must slaughter those sins. You must punish them for making you sin. You must give them the full force of your strength and power.

You must cut off their heads and remove their roots from your blood. They must never enter into you again.

He overthrew the kingdom of darkness. You can overthrow them, too, by His everlasting powers.

Then, you will belong to the Messiah alone. He is sitting on His throne beside that of God His Father. They are the thrones of full honor and respect being offered by countless of animate and inanimate creations. He will offer you a seat beside His own. It is the high exalted throne of love, honor, and respect showered by holy angels and all the creations at large.

Anyone who has been created with a mind has ears to listen. They were created to listen to the voice of God the Holy and to follow Him only. So use your brains and senses to listen, obey, and follow Him from now on and throughout all eternities upon eternities without end. "He that hath an ear, let him hear what the Spirit saith unto the churches" (Revelation 3:22).

The Lord compared the vineyard to a man or woman who married into a family that owned a vineyard. The vineyard would one day be passed onto him or her, thanks to the generosity of the in-laws.

God said that bad pastors are like people who are not treating the vineyard of His in-laws well. They are ruining it.

What will He inherit if they are going destroying the inheritance which was supposed to be passed on to Him by His in-laws? They are driving the flocks out of the churches. The sheep will not survive life in the wilderness of sin.

The in-laws are the good pastors. They are taking care of the Messiah's bride. They will hand her to Him on their wedding day in heaven. The bad pastors are also destroying God's in-laws or the good pastors.

VI. The pastors are responsible for the security of the places of worship

It is the responsibilities of the pastors to see that their flocks are worshipping in structures that are safe, dry, and healthy. If they do not have decent church buildings, then they need to mobilize the worshippers and resources to erect the churches.

It is their responsibilities to see that church buildings are maintained and kept in good order. If they are left unrepaired, it will eventually fall apart. They are to organize the flocks into deacons, deaconesses, etc.

They should various groups of volunteers to repair the church, wash and keep curtains, utensils, etc. clean. Some should have to repair furniture, dust them, etc. on regular basis. The flock will scatter if the church builds fall apart. That will bring a huge disgrace to the name of the Lord.

The sacredness of the place of worship is more important than its grandeur, costs, etc. Men and woman have worshipped in tents, caves, seashores, permanent buildings, semi-permanent buildings, temporary ones, under trees, etc. and have met with God.

But if there are opportunities of erecting permanent structures, the duties of carrying them out fall squarely on the pastors. They can mobilize the worshippers locally and/or internationally to help them build churches for God. "My tabernacle is spoiled, and all my cords are broken: my children are gone forth of me, and they are not: there is none to stretch forth my tent any more, and to set up my curtains" (Jeremiah 10:20).

VIII.   Bring the backsliders back into the church

Most of the people who attend church are broken in spirit and/or body. Many of them have lost faith and/or hope in the God of heaven and earth. The Messiah is asking the shepherds to bring these discouraged people close to Him with words of the Bible.

The word of God has His Spirit. It will tell that the Messiah loves them.

He will fill them with the spirit of love, courage, power, etc. "The diseased have ye not strengthened, neither have ye healed that which was sick, neither have ye bound up that which was broken, neither have ye brought again that which was driven away, neither have ye sought that which was lost; but with force and with cruelty have ye ruled them" (Ezekiel 34:4).

The faiths of most pastors are so weak few if any miracles and healings take place these days when they pray. Because most of them have only head knowledge about what is written in the Bible, few receive visions and dreams God to help them guide the church.

The worst thing in the sight of God is that few pastors are practicing their calling of being sympathetic friends of the sick, poor, discouraged, lonely, the dying, etc.

Never involve yourself in the gossip of the church whether it is true or not. Sooner or later, the victim will hear about.

It will discourage them from attending church. Sick the weak ones, pray for them, and counsel them. You must always discipline your mouth and the mouths of your family members to never the pass the news to other people.

Most of the so-called news is not worth putting into your mind, anyway. Personal sins of other people are dirty. Do not cloak your mind with them. Treat them as a doctor would treat sick people.

You are their spiritual doctor. But do not enjoy listening to them and passing them on. It can drive the victims as well as people who are looking for decent pastors out of the church.

Administration is a two way street. Do not give all the talking. Learn to listen to receive a feedback if your message is getting through.

If you hand down orders from above without allowing them to participate and discuss how to run the church affairs, you are being a dictator. You do not love them. You are cruel.

Lead them a step at a time. School them slowly and patiently if you see that the church is not ready for change. When your big plan finally comes up, they will be ready for it.

They are people who are being thrown out of the churches on daily basis by racism, tribalism, social rejections, insults, sex abuses, stealing, political differences, hypocrites, legalists, etc.

The Lord has appointed shepherds to go out and look for these lost sheep and bring them home.

There are church members who have backslidden into sin because of their poor choices. "And they were scattered, because there is no shepherd: and they became meat to all the beasts of the field, when they were scattered.

My sheep wandered through all the mountains, and upon every high hill: yea, my flock was scattered upon all the face of the earth, and none did search or seek after them" (Ezekiel 34:5, 6).

And many of them did not have a spiritual figure in the church to emulate. They are among the wild beasts called demons and people who are worse than formal Christians.

Demons are driving them on a wild ride and there are helpless. They are falling down into the abyss of hell. The wild lives of sin kill them any time. Their Savior has ordered you to go and search for them.

Therefore, it is important that you must repent from your sin of lukewarm Christianity immediately and go out and search for them before it is too late.

They can die any time and you must bring them to the Lord fast. Bring them back home to their Messiah for love and protection.

The Lord has these words to say to the pastors who are satisfied with what they are doing. They wonder why the Lord is fusses so much about backsliders when there are so many other things to do in the church. "Therefore, ye shepherds, hear the word of the LORD; As I live, saith the Lord GOD, surely because my flock became a prey, and my flock became meat to every beast of the field, because there was no shepherd, neither did my shepherds search for my flock, but the shepherds fed themselves, and fed not my flock" (Ezekiel 34:7, 8).

He said He cannot enjoy living as an eternal God while His children are suffering and being murdered by demons out there in the wild world of sin. They are scatter everywhere in the world.

They are food for demons. They have no shepherd

to lead them back into the fold. They are crying out for help. No shepherd is asking for their welfare or paying them visits.

They are too busy glorifying themselves in the church doing what they want instead of what the Lord wants. Sinners come first and not the pastors. They were ordained for the sake of sinners and not because they are holier or better specimen of guys than the flock.

Many backslidden Christians feel too sinful or inadequate to approach the Presence of God. It is the duty of the pastors to encourage them to come back to Him.

It is the Lord who is ordering you to ask where the former Christians have gone and to search them, befriend them, love them, and win their hearts back to the Lord.

The Messiah is offended when you are making yourself comfortable doing your safe and respectable jobs in the Church. He wants you to go out there to do the hard work of bringing backslidden Christians back into the church.

They may be living in unsafe areas. They may not be respectable people any more. But they are still the beloved and beautiful flock of the Lord. He has ordained you as a priest to get them back into the church on His behalf.

But if you insist in living a safe and comfortable life behind the locked gates of the church, sooner or later you will crush against the Messiah. He is a Rock Block and will put sense back into your mind. He will order you not to run forever on your own energy.

The Lord is not giving you support in playing it safe by locking yourself up in the church. "Therefore, O ye shepherds, hear the word of the LORD; Thus saith the Lord GOD; Behold, I am against the shepherds; and I will require my flock at their hand, and cause them to cease from feeding the flock; neither shall the shepherds feed themselves anymore; for I will deliver my flock from their mouth, that they may not be meat for them" (Ezekiel 34:9, 10).

God has placed the blood of every backslidden Christians that has never been invited back into the church on the pastors and elders.

He threatened to allow His unfaithful messengers to die if they continue to ignore backslidden Christians to prevent them from continue to feed off the church while doing nothing for the spiritual needs of the flock. He will save the church out of the pastors who have turned into devouring beasts.

There are not going to be so many shepherds in the churches are they are now. Many are going a great job. Each of them has unique ways of handling issues.

These special talents, gifts, educations and experiences are of great benefits to the church. However, when their human weaknesses take over, they result in abuses of their church offices. Their sins are curses on the church and on her followers. Because of these human weaknesses, the Lord Himself will step in one day.

He will take over the leadership of the church. He will feed them with the correct love, words and example. "And I will set up one shepherd over them, and he shall feed them, even my servant David; he shall feed them, and he shall be their shepherd.

And I the LORD will be their God, and my servant David a prince among them; I the LORD have spoken it" (Ezekiel 34:23, 24).

The Lord God who is the over-all Shepherd is God the Father. David the Prince is Jesus Christ the King of kings. The Triune Godhead is the Seeker of the lost. He is the Father of all. He must search for His children that are lost.

He is the King of His everlasting kingdom that will never decay, falter and disintegrate like the kingdoms and nations of the earth. He has called all soul-winners to co-labor with Him in winning the souls of His children.

The work of the pastors is a never-ending work. Day and night, they must watch over the flock the Good Shepherd has place under their care. He will come back soon. That is the time when He will give peace to the pastors and ask them to take their rest and enjoy themselves.

He will be the Shepherd of His flock in person and not through pastors again. "Behold, the days come, saith the LORD, that I will raise unto David a righteous Branch, and a King shall reign and prosper, and shall execute judgment and justice in the earth.

In his days Judah shall be saved, and Israel shall dwell safely: and this is his name whereby he shall be called, THE LORD OUR RIGHTEOUSNESS" (Jeremiah 23:5, 6).

The Messiah has risen from the family of King David as the King of Israel and of the whole world.

IX.   I am the Good Shepherd

The Shepherd is the Elder Brother. He is caring and loving. He knows how to shepherd His brothers and sisters.

Jan Luyken (April 16, 1649 - April 5, 1712), the Good Shepherd

They are His very adorable and lovely lambs. The sheep can recognize the loving voice of their excellent Brother-Shepherd.

They rushed out of house together to have fun in the pastures, meadows, and rivers with the oldest Brother leading the way. They follow Him fearless because they know that their All-Powerful and All-Benevolent Brother is ready to die to protect them from any harm. "I am the good shepherd: the good shepherd giveth his life for the sheep" (John 10:11).

He said that He is the Sweetheart of the world. If people would learn to know Him, they would love Him with all of their hearts. Love shook Him like an earthquake and drove Him out of His throne.

It threw Him down here among sinners. He suffered for them. In fact, it was love that murdered Him on the Cross of Calvary. He has already paid for the sins of all the people of the earth because He loves them very much.

He is the true Shepherd of beautiful and darling flock. The Messiah is the Most Excellent Shepherd in heaven and on the earth. No sheep or lamb goes missing, gets sick or injured, stolen or eaten by wild animals when the flock is under His watchful eyes and tender care of His hands.

This Most Excellent of all Shepherds died for a mere lamb like you so that you may become an eternal, unconquerable and joyful person. He has promised not to abandon His beloved children into the hands of evil leaders.

But those shepherds who were not invited to care for the flock but welcomed themselves into the church and took offices are not a part of the flock of the Lord. That is why when they see troubles coming into the Church through the doors, they escape through the windows.

Wolves from the world of darkness are flocking into the Church. They are eating and scattering the flock to the four winds of the world.

It does not hurt the false leaders because they do not love the people. They cared nothing about the eternal destinies of the flock under their care. They are more dangerous than the pagans who have shown open enmity towards God.

The church knows those who hate them openly and avoid them. But many times they cannot tell the difference between a good leader and a false one.

If they have bad pastors, deacons, deaconesses, office workers, fathers, mothers, brothers, sisters, false prophets, etc. who appear as angels of light but inward are demons, they are led astray. "Beware of false prophets, which come to you in sheep's clothing, but inwardly they are ravening wolves" (Matthew 7:15).

The false leaders abandon the sheep because they do not own them. They refuse for the freedom of the lambs because they were not the ones who created them. But He who made them cares for them. Even if the whole world would reject His church, He will still love her forever. They are His sweet lambs.

He is their ever loving and tender Shepherd. He says, "I am the good shepherd, and know my sheep, and am known of mine" (John 10:14).

He is a careful and zealous Watcher that can be trusted to save the lost sheep of this world. He knows the troubles they are in and wants to give them blessings instead of sorrows.

He wants to lead them in the way of righteousness instead of sin. He wants to give them eternal life in the place of dangers and death.

He is really very special. But if you see some shepherds not behaving right towards you, please remember that they are just employees.

They may not be ready to die in your place to save you from harm. "But he that is an hireling, and not the shepherd, whose own the sheep are not, seeth the wolf coming, and leaveth the sheep, and fleeth: and the wolf catcheth them, and scattereth the sheep.

The hireling fleeth, because he is an hireling, and careth not for the sheep" (John 10:12, 13).

So do not hurt when the employees are not looking well after you. They came to God and asked for employment. There is yet an employee who has died for the sins of the whole world like their Employer has done for all sinners.

When things are too hot, they will break away from the flock and slip away. They are showing that they are cowards just like everybody else. They are not the Creator and Daddy of the flock who birthed and helped them to grow up.

The Great Shepherd will gather the survivors that bad disciples have driven away from Him. Many people have been forced out of the church. They are in great danger in the wilderness of sin. He instructed Prophet Ezekiel to prophesy against all you bad shepherds that are destroying the church.

Sons and daughters of Adam are lording on the church and on each other in the name of being pastors. "And the word of the LORD came unto me, saying, Son of man, prophesy against the shepherds of Israel, prophesy, and say unto them, Thus saith the Lord GOD unto the shepherds;

Woe be to the shepherds of Israel that do feed themselves! should not the shepherds feed the flocks? Ye eat the fat, and ye clothe you with the wool, ye kill them that are fed: but ye feed not the flock" (Ezekiel 34:1–3).

Some pastors are not shepherding the flock but themselves. They are so eaten up with selfishness.

They only care about the welfares of their own minds, hearts, bodies and spirits. They feast on tithes, offerings, and other gifts of the church without caring about the needs of the flock the Lord has placed in their hands.

They are not looking after the physically and spiritually sick members of their churches. They do not strengthen them with word from the scriptures. Some of them have been placed in responsible positions in which they can mobilize resources for treating their sick church members, educate them and do many other social works for them beside their preaching.

The Creator said that if the pastors do not act up, He will personal lead the mission rescue team in bringing the backslidden Christians from the brink of destruction. After all, He stands to lose if they do not come back to Him. They are His sheep.

When the flock is left unattended, Satan and his stooges will have great demoniac pleasures in destroying them. They will cut off the necks of many and giving fatal wounds to others. Though some of the wounded sheep may survive, they carry the scars for life.

The lost still have the Spirit of God though it is corrupted with sin. They are out there in the wild world of sin. And the Great Spirit of all has gone out to search for them. When they hear that familiar voice from whom they descended, they will walk out of the lion's mouth that is ready to eat them alive, and run away him.

They will follow their Savior. Indeed, there is only one Shepherd in this world. And all the people are but one flock.

Demons and sin may divine them but they are the one spirit that God place in Adam, His firstborn son. "And other sheep I have, which are not of this fold: them also I must bring, and they shall hear my voice; and there shall be one fold, and one shepherd" (John 10:16).

He said that He will search for His flock because He is their Divine Shepherd. He will sit as King in judgment against the bad pastors who did not shepherd them well.

He will fight for the rights of His lost children that unfaithful shepherds had hated and ignored. Everyone needs to be school in Bible knowledge and not only those who are of benefits to the priests.

He said that He would search for them. "For thus saith the Lord GOD; Behold, I, even I, will both search my sheep, and seek them out. As a shepherd seeketh out his flock in the day that he is among his sheep that are scattered; so will I seek out my sheep, and will deliver them out of all places where they have been scattered in the cloudy and dark day.

I will seek that which was lost, and bring again that which was driven away, and will bind up that which was broken, and will strengthen that which was sick: but I will destroy the fat and the strong; I will feed them with judgment" (Ezekiel 34:11, 12, 13).

He will search for them in all the high and low places where they have been driven in their moments of great weakness and temptations. He will bring the lost back into the fold of love and safety. He will look for the outcasts and accept them as people who need His love and protection the most.

He will save them from sin. He will draw the broken, fearful, cowardly, lonely, depressed, worried, etc. in His comforting arms. He will make them strong. They will always have faith in Him and believe in themselves that they can do anything He asks them to do.

He will heal the sick. But He will make slaves of all the pastors who have been fattening themselves on the graces of His church. He will show them that He is the All-Powerful when He sits in judgment against. He will punish to the maxim.

The flock knows that He is their Helper, and they will come out of the world of darkness looking for Him very willingly. They will follow Him alone because it was He who died for them.

He has the full permission of God His Father to be the only Shepherd of the world because He died for their sins. "As the Father knoweth me, even so know I the Father: and I lay down my life for the sheep.

And other sheep I have, which are not of this fold: them also I must bring, and they shall hear my voice; and there shall be one fold, and one shepherd" (John 10:14-16).

Each lamb will know Him very well. They will know His voice and understand His words. They will walk in His footsteps from one eternity to another.

There is only one Shepherd and He is God. He is presiding over one King and that is His church. She is not under the command or rule of angels or human beings but of God alone.

His children will all gather around Him. He will stand as King the Almighty in the midst of His flock. No wolf will come around again to scatter them to the four corners of the earth.

He will save them from the power of demons and sin. "And I will bring them out from the people, and gather them from the countries, and will bring them to their own land, and feed them upon the mountains of Israel by the rivers, and in all the inhabited places of the country.

I will feed them in a good pasture, and upon the high mountains of Israel shall their fold be: there shall they lie in a good fold, and in a fat pasture shall they feed upon the mountains of Israel. I will feed my flock, and I will cause them to lie down, saith the Lord GOD" (Ezekiel 34:13-15).

The rebels are determined to reject God. Their hearts are as strong and lifeless as rocks. But there are soft hearted people among them who can be touched by the Gospel if someone would reach out to them.

Among these ungodly people are the backsliders. Their Messiah said that He has given the opportunity of bringing them back to Him to the pastors. But if they continue to ignore His call, He will bring them Himself.

He will go all over the world to look for them and call them to come back home to Him. He will take them to their heavenly kingdom. But He will not take the pastors who did not reach out to them there.

God is using the employees of the Church only temporarily. He will soon look after you in person.

So you got to be patient with Him. He will come back very soon and full charge of your life in person. Just look up to your Divine Shepherd. He is good.

He will help you. "I am the good shepherd, and know my sheep, and am known of mine. As the Father knoweth me, even so know I the Father: and I lay down my life for the sheep" (John 10:14, 15).

But the Shepherd assures His flock that He is the Excellent Creator and Sweetheart. He will make everything alright at the end of time. He knows everyone who came out of His Spirit.

They are His wealth that He Himself worked hard to create from the soil and His Spirit. The Spirit He took out of Himself and put in them knows Him. When He calls for that other part of Himself, He hears Him and follows Him.

In fact, the time has now come for the Church to have only one Shepherd. These many shepherds in the Church are no longer needed. God is that one Shepherd of His Church. He will tender His sheep with all His infinite love, compassion and tender care.

He will reward them with a kingdom and crowns for trusting their lives in His care. "And when the chief Shepherd shall appear, ye shall receive a crown of glory that fadeth not away" (1 Peter 5:4).

X. The Messiah will take personal charge of the church

The Spirit of God the Father knows the Spirit of the Son. In the same way the Spirit of the Son knows the spirit He put into each one of you. "I have said, Ye are gods; and all of you are children of the most High" (Psalms 82:6).

Everyone on this earth was build out of the Spirit of the Almighty. He says, "Before I formed thee in the belly I knew thee; and before thou camest forth out of the womb I sanctified thee, and I ordained thee a prophet unto the nations" (Jeremiah 1:5).

He knew you before you were born when you were still within Himself. He ordained you to be a god, prophet, king (queen), and lord before you were born because you are a part of His Spirit.

It is very unfortunate that sin has infected God's other Self that He had put in men and women. But He is redeeming people by washing them with divine blood that can cure their spirits of sin and death. They will be pure, holy, and eternal again.

The Messiah has secured freedom for all from the lion's mouth on the Cross of Calvary. And God the Father is crazy about Him because of it.

He loves the Messiah more than He loves Himself for reaching out for the spirits that are suffering and dying down here on earth. He is the Beloved Son because He sacrificed Himself for His brothers and sisters so that they may live eternally, peacefully, and joyously just like Him.

Demons are yet to have the power that can snatch the blood-washed people from the hands of their Savior. "Therefore doth my Father love me, because I lay down my life, that I might take it again. No man taketh it from me, but I lay it down of myself. I have power to lay it down, and I have power to take it again. This commandment have I received of my Father" (John 10:17, 18).

The oil of everlasting life is flowing from the Spirit of the Messiah and into His children. The Messiah is the everlasting Spirit. He put down His life temporary in order to save His beloved spirit-people. He can live eternal and then cut His life for a short time and be completely dead as a Human Being because He can do it.

He is the All-Powerful One. He is the Creator and King of life. He also has that much power over death because He conquered it.

He is the Chief in creating things, and He is the Chief in bringing life from the dead. He will be the Chief in resurrecting you from the dead and recreating you all over again.

God His Father has authorized Him to recreate this world all over again. He will do it because He can do it.

He is that powerful. And if you believe in Him, He will remake your spirit again and unite you permanently with the Spirits of the Trinity.

Everyone who does not have faith in the Triune Godhead is a disobedient spirit. He or she has removed himself or herself from the flock.

Satan's spirit is in control of their thoughts, words and emotions. They are anti-Christs just like Satan.

The Messiah pointed out, "But ye believe not, because ye are not of my sheep, as I said unto you" (John 10:26).

He or she is exposing himself or herself to the dangers of the elements and demons. Such a person will not survive the fires of hell but will be like a dry straw to the tongues of the hungry flames.

But decent spirits will follow the Supernatural Spirit that gave them life. They will adopt the divine way of God as their own cultures and traditions, too. "My sheep hear my voice, and I know them, and they follow me" (John 10:27).

The Messiah will give His flock life that is excellent, perfect, and eternal. He will protect their lives forever. No demons, sin or evil people will cut their throats again.

They are protected species. "And I give unto them eternal life; and they shall never perish, neither shall any man pluck them out of my hand. My Father, which gave them me, is greater than all; and no man is able to pluck them out of my Father's hand" (John 10:28, 29).

God the Father has put His fingers around them and clutches them in the palm of His hand. No devil or any other evil person can climb up to the hands of the All-Powerful One to loosen His fingers around them so that they can pour down rain to their death.

Moreover, the Son has also placed their hands over the flock. God the Father is happy with His Trinity fellow Member that He, too, loves His children very much. The Messiah says, "I and my Father are one" (John 10:30).

He is one with the Father and the Holy Spirit in loving, creating, and saving the people of the world. And no devil, man or woman can unloose the hands of the Trinity to get to His children to hurt them.

God the Father says to all of you that you are His beautiful and precious flock. He loves very deeply, intensely, abundantly and completely. From now on, He is going to fight for the cattle that have been down trodden by cruel and unkind pastures and church elders.

He will judge between the rams and he goats. "And as for you, O my flock, thus saith the Lord GOD; Behold, I judge between cattle and cattle, between the rams and the he goats" (Ezekiel 34:17). He will help the weak, sick, and broken people in the church who are being pushed out or have already been pushed out by the rough males.

The Herder wants to look after His own cattle. He is tired of some of these hirelings who have never cared for His livestock but just wants to enjoy the positions, salaries, businesses, social life, etc.

He will take personal charge of His farm any time now. "Therefore will I save my flock, and they shall no more be a prey; and I will judge between cattle and cattle.

And I will set up one shepherd over them, and he shall feed them, even my servant David; he shall feed them, and he shall be their shepherd. And I the LORD will be their God, and my servant David a prince among them; I the LORD have spoken it" (Ezekiel 34:22–24).

God the Father will stand up to watch over His little flock as their God, King, and Lord. He has already appointed His Son to take personal charge of this earth on His behalf.

He made Him to be incarnated into the human family through the family of King David. He will remove the earthly family of King David from ruling his flock. Their mismanagements and idolatries have caused the dispersions of Israel and, later, the Christians among the wild beasts of the world.

Judeo-Christianity is no longer being administered by a descendant of King David who was also to be the high priest. David's family played the harlot with demons, and they have been severely punished for it. After the Romans murdered the Messiah, they went on very systematic to kill all His male relatives.

The only one that died from natural causes was John the beloved disciple of the Messiah. They made sure that the Jews will never mobilize around a descendant of King David to fight for the reinstatement of the Kingdom of Twelve Tribes of Israel. The lineage of King David has been removed from power permanently.

The Eternal Messiah and King is assuring you over and over again He will destroy the power of sin, death, and demons over you. They will never trouble you again.

The fruits of the Tree of Life will empower you to dominate and defeat them completely. Demons cannot tempt you.

Sin and death cannot exist in your presence again. All the former enemies that ravaged the earth will be afraid of you. They will never come near you again.

XI.   The Shepherd will give you lush pastures to eat and cool water to drink

You will sit down very comfortably while you are enjoying provisions of your Good Shepherd. He will place water beside to drink. You will not travel long distances to fetch water drink. He will place it beside you.

You can literally eat and drink in peace as if you are eating and drinking while you are asleep. "He maketh me to lie down in green pastures: he leadeth me beside the still waters" (Psalms 23:2).

You will always have rest for your soul when the Divine Shepherd leads you. He will carry you in His arms as He leads you through life. He will supply you with the water of peace and not surging seas of troubles.

When they surge towards, He will order them to move away from you. "There is a river, the streams whereof shall make glad the city of God, the holy place of the tabernacles of the most High" (Psalms 46:4).

You will together with the Almighty in His palace where a river carrying the water of life flows through ceaselessly. The water will give much joy and peace when you eat it.

Both the food and water of heaven are holy because the life of God flows in them. He will provide you with safety, peace, and comfort.

God has prepared a good year for you because He is with you all the time. He has come down to the earth to provide for your physical, mental, spiritual, etc. needs.

He has removed fatness of eternal life and joy from His Spirit and placed them in your soul. "Thou crownest the year with thy goodness; and thy paths drop fatness. They drop upon the pastures of the wilderness: and the little hills rejoice on every side.

The pastures are clothed with flocks; the valleys also are covered over with corn; they shout for joy, they also sing" (Psalms 65:11–13).

He will provide for you even in the wild and barren desert. He will give you something to eat and drink in the most uninhabitable place on earth like deserts and winter lands.

He has prepared provisions for all peoples whether they live on the mountains, hills, plains, valleys, or seas. He supplies fortunes and all kinds of blessings for His children.

He has covered the earth with plants, animals, birds, fishes, water, air, gems, oil, etc. for His children.

He has made everyone on earth a millionaire.

The only thing that keeps them from being rich and comfortable is human greed. Few people own billions of dollars. But things will change when God takes over the economy of the earth.

XII. Follow the good example of Christ your Shepherd

You have been given a very high calling by God the Father Himself. He is calling you to be in everything like His Son, Jesus Christ. His Son learned and experienced deep suffering and sorrow first hand even though He was pure, holy, and sinless.

He did not need to go through all those suffering, heartaches and death because He did not deserve them. But He suffered and died, anyway, because His love for you was more than words could express. He demonstrated it practically by sharing in mortalities, heaviness, and weaknesses of your flesh, its afflictions, and death.

God the Father is saying that He has given the life of His Son on the earth as your example in how to think, talk, and live. Follow Him step by step all the way from here to heaven. He never sinned all His entire life on earth. No filthy words ever came out of His mouth.

When the people insulted Him, He did not answer them in like manner. When they tried to force Him to fight, He refused. He never tried to use His omnipotent powers to discipline them. He did not show to them that He was stronger than steel.

He always walked away from confrontations. "For even hereunto were ye called: because Christ also suffered for us, leaving us an example, that ye should follow his steps:

Who did no sin, neither was guile found in his mouth: Who, when he was reviled, reviled not again; when he suffered, he threatened not; but committed himself to him that judgeth righteously" (1 Peter 2:21–23).

He left us an excellent example in how to live holy lives. When the high priests, Sanhedrin, Judas Iscariot, etc. betrayed Him into the hands of the Roman pagans, He did not bring out the rod of discipline and whacked them.

They were clearly in the wrong. But He did not use force to straighten out. He threw Himself into the merciful hands of God the Father who knows how to defend the innocent and uphold their case.

He loved the people of this world so much that He took all their sins upon Himself. His whole Body was saturated with their sins.

The sins of the people dodged His footsteps from birth and into the grave. They persecuted Him. They sold Him into be murdered for a mere thirty pieces of silver. They denied His divinity. They ran Him through a fake court system.

They tortured and nailed Him on the Cross. They threw His dead Body into a hole.

For all appearances, sin thought that it had gotten rid of Him forever. He rose again from the dead as an immortal God after spending only three days and three nights in the bosom. All His sufferings and death were carried out for your freedom from sin. It has no power over you.

All the tortures sin inflicted on Him in order to force Him into eternal death will not be applied to you. The crucifixion was to send Him into hell and never come out of there. But He rose from the dead.

The new life He received was not for Himself but for you. He is now healing your body from infections of damages caused by sin.

No amount of sin in this world will force you to go to hell unless you choose to go there. You only need to confess them and they will be washed away with His precious blood. "If we confess our sins, he is faithful and just to forgive us our sins, and to cleanse us from all unrighteousness" (1 John 1:9).

He has already paid your eternal death in hell. You died with Him together on the Cross of Calvary in order that you may rise up again with Him from the bosom of hell.

God has called the young and the old, men and women, to shepherd His Church.

wpclipart, young shepherd boy, in public domain

Now, your lives are hidden in His life. You are all holy and righteous now.

But you must confess your sins so that you may begin to grow and mature in righteousness. "Who his own self bare our sins in his own body on the tree, that we, being dead to sins, should live unto righteousness: by whose stripes ye were healed. For ye were as sheep going astray; but are now returned unto the Shepherd and Bishop of your souls" (1 Peter 2:24, 25).

You were once His beautiful and holy sheep that Satan stole from Him. But now the blood of Christ is infusing all your body and spirit and remaking you into a precious lamb.

XIII. The Shepherd will make you holy and righteous

The Good Shepherd loves your soul very much. He will wash away all your sins with His precious blood. He will recreate you all over again. He will pick you in His arms, carry and place you into His own way of life. He will tie you to Himself with the tender chains of love so that you can always walk together throughout all eternal life.

He will care for you because He is called Beautiful Love. "He restoreth my soul: he leadeth me in the paths of righteousness for his name's sake" (Psalms 23:3).

God will always guide you in the right path. "Righteousness shall go before him; and shall set us in the way of his steps" (Psalms 85:13).

It is the path that is covered with His footsteps. He has trod the path of righteousness throughout all everlasting years.

His way is the right way. It is straight and well lit by His brightly burning Spirit. You will never stumble and fall into sin because it is not the way of darkness. It is perfect and awesome.

He says, "I lead in the way of righteousness, in the midst of the paths of judgment" (Proverbs 8:20).

The judgment mentioned here is not about condemnation is the execution of right living. When you think like Him, you will always be humble, wise, and intelligent. Those are the marks that can achieve great successes for you throughout all eternities.

The gracious God is good to you. He is protecting your kingdom very zealously until when you come to heaven and take it over. It is your own country to rule and reign over her forever. And now, there is nothing to fear. He is always with you no matter what.

He will save you and take you to heaven to be forever safe. "Surely goodness and mercy shall follow me all the days of my life: and I will dwell in the house of the LORD for ever" (Psalms 23:6).

Fortunes are piled upon each other that go higher up than the heavens. They are all yours. Multiplied grace are heaped high up for you by the One who died for you.

He has made it your traditional to live with grace and by grace only today and forever. Your life is forever sheltered in house of God throughout all everlasting years to come.

Every path the Lord leads you on is covered with grace upon endless grace. It is the way of truth that ennobles and saves. This truth is God Himself. "All the paths of the LORD are mercy and truth unto such as keep his covenant and his testimonies" (Psalms 25:10). He has put a covenant of loyalty on Himself to protect you with His own Almighty life. Evil will never get you again.

There is only one thing you need to ask from God. Invite Him to live in your heart just as He has advised you, and He will give you an eternal holy feast. "Behold, I stand at the door, and knock: if any man hear my voice, and open the door, I will come in to him, and will sup with him, and he with me" (Revelation 3:20).

If you open your heart to Him, He will come in with all the blessings of love, joy, peace, wealth, power, eternal life, etc.

You will feast on His expenses in His house forever. "One thing have I desired of the LORD, that will I seek after; that I may dwell in the house of the LORD all the days of my life, to behold the beauty of the LORD, and to enquire in his temple" (Psalms 27:4).

If you ask for His life and that you want to live together with Him from eternity to eternity, He will happy to give you His heart. He will relocate you from this earth to heaven. And you will always live with Him in His temple forever. He will allow you to see

His beautiful face that is rarely seen by small creatures like angels and people.

You will glorious His whole Spirit that burns with beautiful fire. You will spread out yourself like a mattress or the skin of the Passover lamb that was put out to dry before His throne to thank Him for all the good things He has done for you.

He is a sure refuge in the time when the floods of troubles carry you away. He will lift you out of the raging sea and anchor you securely in Himself. He is the Rock of Ages.

No enemy can find, fight or conquer. He will always love you as if you are His own Almighty and Everlasting Spirit. "For in the time of trouble he shall hide me in his pavilion: in the secret of his tabernacle shall he hide me; he shall set me up upon a rock" (Psalms 27:5).

You will be glad you made the Lord your everlasting refuge. You will hold your high above all the things that had formerly terrorized you. They will never again display their cruelty to you.

They will be thrown down in the deep valley below while you yourself will be riding high up above the clouds on top of the Rock of Ages. "And now shall mine head be lifted up above mine enemies round about me: therefore will I offer in his tabernacle sacrifices of joy; I will sing, yea, I will sing praises unto the LORD" (Psalms 27:6).

You will forever offer your best praises to Him who saw you in your desperate need and gave you everlasting help.

XIV. The Second Coming of the Shepherd

The Good Shepherd will return to collect His sheep

Divine powers, peace, joy, love, and life made the Messiah to stand up on His own two feet after He was dead for three days and three nights. He was completely healed from the ravages of death. He is the Great Shepherd that is leading the entourage of heaven and all the universes in an everlasting march to great joy, peace, and happiness.

He is supplied you generously and abundantly with the blood of the Lord of lords, even of the Messiah of all, to wash away all your sins. In fact, it is the blood that sealed the covenant of eternal love and friendship between you and God the Father.

Your heavenly Father will fill you up completely in all the works of excellences that you will do as if you are creating a new world. His will is that you accept Him as your Messiah in order to enjoy His brainwork and power.

He is your life to live and to enjoy to the full. He is already working in your soul and among all the peoples of the earth to recreate you once again until you are glorious, desirable, lovely, and pleasant in the sight of His Son, Jesus Christ.

He will bring His creation in full completion in

your body. "Now the God of peace, that brought again from the dead our Lord Jesus, that great shepherd of the sheep, through the blood of the everlasting covenant, Make you perfect in every good work to do his will, working in you that which is wellpleasing in his sight, through Jesus Christ; to whom be glory for ever and ever. Amen" (Hebrews 13:20, 21).

This God and Father of all have received the highest acclamations in heaven and all the universes for all the wonderful works He is doing for them. He is immortally awesome and perfect. He is the King of eternity of all eternities.

All you, faithful believers, are being brought back by Messiah your Savior into the hands of the Great Shepherd, God the Father Himself. "And when the chief Shepherd shall appear, ye shall receive a crown of glory that fadeth not away" (1 Peter 5:4).

The King Shepherd will crown you as a junior shepherd king or queen to show you that you are very special to Him. No demon, sin or death will swallow your crown and kingdom again.

He will watch over all of you in Person from one eternity to another with love, tenderness, and joy. You will see, talk, and touch Him as He shepherds you day by day. He will move among you like a shepherd walking among his or her sheep.

Every day, He will drive all of you to good green pastures to graze and then take you to the river to drink Water of eternal life. He will bring you back into the golden palace every evening to rest and sleep in a safe and clean place.

XV.   The Shepherd has created pasturelands in heaven for His flock

The Messiah is the divine King David of heaven and earth just as God the Father has promised to His church. "And I will make with them a covenant of peace, and will cause the evil beasts to cease out of the land: and they shall dwell safely in the wilderness, and sleep in the woods. And they shall no more be a prey to the heathen, neither shall the beast of the land devour them; but they shall dwell safely, and none shall make them afraid" (Ezekiel 34:25, 28).

God has made peace with sinners by offering His Child as the Covenant of Peace. He shed His blood to cover up their sins so that they can be acceptable before the eyes of a holy and righteous God. He will destroy the beasts of the wilderness.

They will no longer eat His sheep. He will bring peace in every corner of the earth. Everywhere they go, there will find no temptations or trials because the demons have been cast out of this world.

The Almighty God the Creator has appeared as the Lord and Helper of the people of this world. As their Savior, He will bring them to the fold and give them a new earth to inherent. He promised, "And I will set up shepherds over them which shall feed them: and they shall fear no more, nor be dismayed, neither shall they be lacking, saith the LORD" (Jeremiah 23:4).

He will wash away their sins. He will help them to produce lots of fruits of righteousness. His words are right and true.

They will build character in His children. "The sayings of the wise are like the sharp sticks that shepherds use to guide sheep, and collected proverbs are as lasting as firmly driven nails. They have been given by God, the one Shepherd of us all" (Ecclesiastes 12:11).

His children will cover the earth and lick every green herb of the field like cattle. The Messiah will be completely honored and exalted through them.

There will be no wicked pastors around anymore to torture them again. God Himself will be their Shepherd. "Behold, the days come, saith the LORD, that I will raise unto David a righteous Branch, and a King shall reign and prosper, and shall execute judgment and justice in the earth.

In his days Judah shall be saved, and Israel shall dwell safely: and this is his name whereby he shall be called, THE LORD OUR RIGHTEOUSNESS" (Jeremiah 23:5, 6).

He is the Messiah and Son of King David. He will save you before you pass away. This is because He saves living people and not the dead who have no breath or memories to show love to Him.

He will stand over His flock as the holy and righteous God, King, and Lord forever. He will rule them justly, righteously, loving, and eternally.

No demon, sin or death will ever again exist among His beautiful flock. He will plant His word in the hearts of His people and they will live by it and not by the orders from unfaithful priests and demons.

The world is His farmland. He will recreate her again and make her to produce much fruits of righteous and eternal people.

He will preside over His farmland as King and Judge to protect and provide for her needs. "Behold, the Lord GOD will come with strong hand, and his arm shall rule for him: behold, his reward is with him, and his work before him" (Isaiah 40:10).

His garden is your soul. He will plant it with fruits and righteousness and make you a very fruitful and luscious Garden of Eden again. He will make you march before Him as His greatest achievement in all the universes.

He will provide for the needs of His flock. Just like the way He had created them, which He did by His own inherent powers, He will also save them. He will gather them in His loving arms to love and comfort them forever. "He shall feed his flock like a shepherd: he shall gather the lambs with his arm, and carry them in his bosom, and shall gently lead those that are with young" (Isaiah 40:11).

He who planted you on the earth will gather you in His arms again. His arms will be full of your children. You will embrace all of you in His arms and you feel the tender and awesome love He has for you.

He will receive all those who young children and bring them into His embrace together with their young ones. He will lead them from eternity to eternity with love and joy.

God said that He has welcomed you into His bosom of love at the right time. And He did it before you were born.

Even before He laid the foundation of the earth, He had already brought you very close to Himself. He watched over your salvation from the everlasting past. He took care of you because He is your eternal Helper.

Now, you only need to ask to appropriate the help that has been reserved for you right from the eternal past. He had protected all of you as the human race from being wiped out by your sins and the demons. "Thus saith the LORD, In an acceptable time have I heard thee, and in a day of salvation have I helped thee: and I will preserve thee, and give thee for a covenant of the people, to establish the earth, to cause to inherit the desolate heritages;

That thou mayest say to the prisoners, Go forth; to them that are in darkness, Shew yourselves. They shall feed in the ways, and their pastures shall be in all high places" (Isaiah 49:8, 9).

He is commanding all the prisoners of sin and death to be set free. He is telling Satan that His children are no longer going to be street urchins who live by jungle laws.

The time of liberation has come. Get out of your sins. They have no power over you. Leave the world of the darkness of sin behind now and show yourself to the people and all heavens that you are holy and righteous.

All the saved of the earth will walk in God their Father like following their shepherd. He has taken personal care of them. He will feed them in the eternal pastures of perfect joy, love, peace, etc.

God the Father gave you His only Adopted Son to assure you that you are His eternal children. He is the Covenant of peace and love between you and Him. He sealed the covenant with the blood of His Son. The relationship between Him and His earthly children is stronger than steel.

All of you have become His intelligent, wise, powerful, awesome, and eternal children. He has appointed His own Son, the Messiah, as your God, King, and Lord.

He is the One ruling and reigning over you on this earth. You are no longer under government of Satan. He will fill the whole earth with His Presence.

His knowledge will be in every mind and wisdom in every heart. "For the earth shall be filled with the knowledge of the glory of the LORD, as the waters cover the sea" (Habakkuk 2:14).

His Presence will bring out a new heaven and earth out of this dying world. Everywhere will be righteous men and women who will inherit the earth and live there forever.

They will never experience hunger or starvation again. They will not know what thirst is. The sun will not belt them with heat like soldiers beating on their enemies with their belts.

The heat of this world will be a thing of the past. "They shall not hunger nor thirst; neither shall the heat nor sun smite them: for he that hath mercy on them shall lead them, even by the springs of water shall he guide them" (Isaiah 49:10).

The One who had mercy on them and took them out of this world of sin will personally shepherd them. He who bought them from sin and death with His precious blood will feed them with food of eternal life and give them water of eternal life to drink. He will walk with them through the lush pastures and along the banks of the river of life.

Men and women who have faith in the salvation of God will live in eternal peace. They will rest and go to sleep anywhere on this earth in peace. They can take a nap on the mountains, hills, valleys, deep in the forests, beaches, islands, gardens, etc. and no one will try to rape, steal, murder, etc.

Evil has been forever eliminated from the earth. They will always enjoy the Amen of the Lord. He is the Answer to all their prayers for love, protection, peace, joy, and eternity.

He will give His life to His children so that they can also be loving, peaceful, happy, joy and everlasting. He is the Truth by which all His children will live and prosper in all the mental, physical, social and spiritual capacities He has endowed them with.

He will remove all obstacles such as demons and the evil they have brought on His children from the world. "And God shall wipe away all tears from their eyes; and there shall be no more death, neither sorrow, nor crying, neither shall there be any more pain: for the former things are passed away" (Revelation 21:4).

He will give every available opportunity to His children to enable them to have maximum growth and exuberance in all aspects of life.

He will usher in the rule of righteous, justice and fairness to all. "And in mercy shall the throne be established: and he shall sit upon it in truth in the tabernacle of David, judging, and seeking judgment, and hasting righteousness" (Isaiah 16:5).

The throne of King Davis has been set up in heaven on which sits the God of gods, King of kings, Lord of lords, Jesus Christ the Almighty. He is loving and merciful to sinners.

He had made Himself one of them in order to get them out of hell. He is the King of life and, therefore, the King of love, peace and joy. He promises: "And I will make with them a covenant of peace, and will cause the evil beasts to cease out of the land: and they shall dwell safely in the wilderness, and sleep in the woods.

And I will make them and the places round about my hill a blessing; and I will cause the shower to come down in his season; there shall be showers of blessing.

And the tree of the field shall yield her fruit, and the earth shall yield her increase, and they shall be safe in their land, and shall know that I am the LORD, when I have broken the bands of their yoke, and delivered them out of the hand of those that served themselves of them" (Ezekiel 34:25–27).

He has cut a covenant of blood with His children. He was cut down on their behalf. His blood was shed to cleanse them from their sins. There are now His eternal children.

No devil or anyone will take them away from Him again. They are the eternal owners of heaven and earth. No demons will sneak in and upset their thoughts and/or government again.

The Lord will make sure that another Satan will not come around His children again after this one has been put to death in hell. "Affliction shall not rise up the second time" (Nahum 1:9). No evil will squeeze the life out of them again as it is doing now.

God has come to live among His people. "He promises, "And I will make them and the places round about my hill a blessing; and I will cause the shower to come down in his season; there shall be showers of blessing" (Ezekiel 34:26).

He will make all the universes around this earth develop relationship of love, respect, honor, joy, etc. with them. The inhabitants of those worlds and universes will pay regular visits to this world and embrace these people with love and joy.

Blessings will pour heaven like rainwater. Everything on this earth will be a blessing of joy, peace, and love.

May the Great Shepherd spread out His table of plentiful help before the people He loves. May He command that people who are sold into the slavery of sin and demons like Joseph be set free.

Make the people of the world your gold just as you had promoted Joseph from slavery to a prince by the Pharaoh of Egypt. May You crown them with Your salvation! May He make them kings and queens to serve Him in His court!

May He shepherd them from one eternity to another with love and joy. "Give ear, O Shepherd of Israel, thou that leadest Joseph like a flock; thou that dwellest between the cherubims, shine forth" (Psalms 80:1).

He who is the King of the angels will arise like the sun. He will save you. He has already ordered all His heavenly slaves to help you get to Him.

The Lord has killed the big fattened bull for the holy feast. He is roasting it for your eternal feast.

The bull is largest heavenly love, joy, comfort, peace, eternity, etc. and laid them all out on the table for you to eat and enjoy yourself as much as you want. Let the feast begin in the full view of all your troubles, sorrows, tragedies, death, and demons.

Enjoy the largeness of His heart even when you are be driven by demoniac forces and you are terribly hard pressed between the rock and hard place. "Thou preparest a table before me in the presence of mine enemies: thou anointest my head with oil; my cup runneth over" (Psalms 23:5).

The Lord has anointed you with His life-giving and sweet-smelling blood. He is massaging your worried and tired head with the sweet-smelling oil of love.

He emptied all His love on you on the Cross of Calvary. "The LORD is the portion of mine inheritance and of my cup: thou maintainest my lot" (Luke 16:5).

He is has willed all His kingdom and all the things that it has such as the holy angels as your slaves, the gold and other jewels of the new City, and all the universes to you. He has put the cup of joy in your mouth and is begging you to drink it.

The Shepherd will make everyone equal in riches and wealth. They will have shelter, clothing, food, clean fresh water, fresh air, land, etc. "Therefore are they before the throne of God, and serve him day and night in his temple: and he that sitteth on the throne shall dwell among them" (Revelation 7:15).

The saints will gather around the honorable throne of the Bridegroom because of the beauty of His holiness and grace. They will always present love and joy before His throne because He is a wonderful provider. They will never stop loving and praising Him come day or night and throughout all eternities.

He who sits on the throne of mighty, grace, and all goodness will always be as sweet as honey to all of them. He will be their power and strength.

He will make them to stand strong. He will always fill them with His eternal and gracious life.

As for you, nothing but rest and comfort will follow around the avenues of all eternities. "They shall hunger no more, neither thirst anymore; neither shall the sun light on them, nor any heat" (Revelation 7:16).

You will never hunger and thirst after you tasted of the Passover feast at the Lord's Supper table. Even the sun, moon, and stars will live in peace with you if they are to survive in the Presence of the Lord.

They were created for your sake and not you to be their slave. They will provide the right amount of light, warmth, energy, etc. to you at all times and throughout all eternities.

The Lamb of God is the supplier of very satisfying love of heaven and earth. He will provide for your needs that to show you that are you loved.

For the Lamb which is in the midst of the throne shall feed them, and shall lead them unto living fountains of waters: and God shall wipe away all tears from their eyes" (Revelation 7:17).

He has taken the throne of honor of the Bridegroom in order to provide for His dearly loved and beautiful and bride. He shepherd her tenderly and loving for all everlasting years at His disposal.

He will make sure that His bride eats the food of eternal life and drinks the water of eternal life so that He can always have her beside Him. He does not want her to suffer, cry and die again.

He has planted the Tree of Life in heaven which used to exist in the Garden of Eden. This tree has offshoots that have covered the whole of heaven.

The fruits have eternal life in them. "And the tree of the field shall yield her fruit, and the earth shall yield her increase, and they shall be safe in their land, and shall know that I am the LORD, when I have broken the bands of their yoke, and delivered them out of the hand of those that served themselves of them.

And I will raise up for them a plant of renown, and they shall be no more consumed with hunger in the land, neither bear the shame of the heathen any more" (Ezekiel 34:27, 29).

Your faith will usher into the Presence of the Almighty to enjoy His provisions immensely and forever without end. He will shower you with overflowing riches to make your life really comfortable and joyful.

You will not eat dirt but you will eat fruits from the Tree of Life which angels also eat. It has helped them to live for over 6,000 years in perfect health.

The bodies and spirits of the saints will be blessed with power, strength, energy, intelligence and wisdom. They will roam the Golden City of Jerusalem, farms and outlying universes without fear or care in the world.

Everywhere there will be peace and security. No demons, bad pastors, etc. will lurk around to tempt them or destroy their spiritualties. "And they shall no more be a prey to the heathen, neither shall the beast of the land devour them; but they shall dwell safely, and none shall make them afraid.

And I will raise up for them a plant of renown, and they shall be no more consumed with hunger in the land, neither bear the shame of the heathen any more" (Ezekiel 34:28, 29).

The new earth will be very fruitful and support the lives of the citizens of heaven adequately. The Tree of Life will yield enough fruits for all the saints and angels to eat and be satisfied. There are also other fruit trees that will provide for them more than enough nourishment.

There grain, nuts, vegetables, etc. farms for the children of heaven to enjoy. They will have more food, water and land more than they need. The air, water and soil will be blessed to produce the perfect ecosystem for the children of the Almighty God.

Heaven and earth will be covered with different kinds of "showers of blessing" too many to count. He will cover them with His Sweet Presence. They will live in peace and joy forever and ever. They are the special and beloved people that the Lord had loved right from the everlasting pasting.

He loves so much that He sacrificed Himself as a Lamb in the place in order that they may live and enjoy His love and the blessings that His infinite powers can create. "Thus shall they know that I the LORD their God am with them, and that they, even the house of Israel, are my people, saith the Lord GOD. And ye my flock, the flock of my pasture, are men, and I am your God, saith the Lord GOD" (Ezekiel 34:30, 31).

The Messiah died to give you everlasting life. "To appoint unto them that mourn in Zion, to give unto them beauty for ashes, the oil of joy for mourning, the garment of praise for the spirit of heaviness; that they might be called trees of righteousness, the planting of the LORD, that he might be glorified" (Isaiah 61:3).

He will remove the age-old mourning for having fallen into sin and the guilt and shame that come with it, their fear of death, etc. from them. They will cry no more because they are sick, hurting or dying. He will give them joy in the place of carrying a sorrowful and mourning heart.

They will never suffer broken-heartedness or shed tears again. Joy will well up from their wombs like an ever flowing river of oil. They will have the joy of having secured and blessed life that is guarded by the Lord Himself.

The saints are the evergreen trees or "Oaks of Righteousness."

They are created for righteous character and nature. They will be adorned inside and out with the glorious and brightly shinning grace and beauty of Jesus Christ. They will shine like golden crowns on the heads of kings or queens. They are the Lord's beautiful sweet-smelling roses or lilies of the valley.

He is highly exalted and respected for saving sinners like you. "When he shall come to be glorified in his saints, and to be admired in all them that believe (because our testimony among you was believed) in that day" (2 Thessalonians 1:9, 10).

The holy ones will worship Him with honest and devoted hearts. He will be so attractive and loveable to them that they will desire nothing else besides Him.

They will love Him first and foremost above their own selves and above any other thing in heaven and on the earth. His salvation has secured for them eternal life that is beyond their wildest dreams or imaginations, and they will be forever grateful and appreciative. He is their eternal God and Messiah.

He will create for them beautiful and fruitful new pastures the likes of which cannot be found on this old earth. He will plant fruit trees, corn, vegetables, nuts, etc. in the pastures and meadows of heaven.

The pastures are interspersed with rivers that flow with the water of life. He will feed them with the food and water of eternal life on the holy hill where the Trinity resides.

Every bit of herb and water belongs to them. They will roam all over heaven and the universes to feed as much as they wanted.

They will grow fat with good health and joy. He will also recreate this earth to be a habitable place for His beloved children.

The new earth will be extremely fertile and fruitful. She will never fail again to yield good fruits for the inhabitants of the earth.

She will be the answer for all your prayers that she should be a safe place to live in. She will provide for all your needs very abundantly from eternity to eternity.

You will trust in her to yield her increase every month very faithfully and eternally well. She will not disappoint you again.

There will be no more earthquakes, tsunamis, drought, heat, dreadful winters, swamps, infections, diseases, harmful parasites, deadly or troublesome viruses, etc.

When you see Him in person taking care of you and all the people of this earth, you will know beyond any possible doubt that He has always meant well for all of you.

He always had you in His heart. "Thus shall they know that I the LORD their God am with them, and that they, even the house of Israel, are my people, saith the Lord GOD.

And ye my flock, the flock of my pasture, are men, and I am your God, saith the Lord GOD" (Ezekiel 34:30, 31).

He calls you His lambs or lambs as an endearment names. He loves you more than you can ever think or image. He is your holy and joyful Passover feast day that will take place every day.

You will eat good things and drink fresh sweet-smelling juice that He calls wine. He has died as your

Passover Lamb so that you may eat, drink, sing, dance and celebrate life every day. Indeed, He is your celebration to enjoy life to the full.

They will live eternally among the Triune Godhead because they are the children that He Himself had given births to. And it is good for both Him and His children to live together like a family that they always ought to have been.

The beautiful and precious flock will rest in an eternal peace like sheep lying down around the feet of God their Father.

The Messiah's résumé to be able to save you

38844830R00251

Printed in Poland
by Amazon Fulfillment
Poland Sp. z o.o., Wrocław